e-Governance for Development

TECHNOLOGY, WORK AND GLOBALIZATION

The Technology, Work and Globalization series was developed to provide policy makers, workers, managers, academics and students with a deeper understanding of the complex interlinks and influences between technological developments, including information and communication technologies, work organizations and patterns of globalization. The mission of the series is to disseminate rich knowledge based on deep research about relevant issues surrounding the globalization of work that is spawned by technology.

Also in the series:

GLOBAL SOURCING OF BUSINESS AND IT SERVICES
Leslie P. Willcocks and Mary C. Lacity

ICT AND INNOVATION IN THE PUBLIC SECTOR
Francesco Contini and Giovan Francesco Lanzara

EXPLORING VIRTUALITY WITHIN AND BEYOND ORGANIZATIONS
Niki Panteli and Mike Chaisson

KNOWLEDGE PROCESSES IN GLOBALLY DISTRIBUTED CONTEXTS
Julia Kotlarsky, Ilan Oshri and Paul C. van Fenema

GLOBAL CHALLENGES FOR IDENTITY POLICIES
Edgar Whitley and Ian Hosein

OFFSHORE OUTSOURCING OF IT WORK
Mary C. Lacity and Joseph W. Rottman

OUTSOURCING GLOBAL SERVICES
Ilan Oshri, Julia Kotlarsy and Leslie P. Willcocks

BRICOLAGE, CARE AND INFORMATION
Chrisanthi Avgerou, Giovan Francesco Lanzara and Leslie P. Willcocks

e-GOVERNANCE FOR DEVELOPMENT: A Focus on Rural India
Shirin Madon

e-Governance for Development

A Focus on Rural India

Shirin Madon

Senior Lecturer in Information Systems,
London School of Economics and Political Science

palgrave
macmillan

First published 2009 by
PALGRAVE MACMILLAN

Palgrave Macmillan in the UK is an imprint of Macmillan Publishers Limited,
registered in England, company number 785998, of Houndmills, Basingstoke,
Hampshire RG21 6XS.

Palgrave Macmillan in the US is a division of St Martin's Press LLC,
175 Fifth Avenue, New York, NY 10010.

Palgrave Macmillan is the global academic imprint of the above companies
and has companies and representatives throughout the world.

Palgrave® and Macmillan® are registered trademarks in the United States,
the United Kingdom, Europe and other countries.

ISBN: 978–0–230–20157–6 hardback

This book is printed on paper suitable for recycling and made from fully
managed and sustained forest sources. Logging, pulping and manufacturing
processes are expected to conform to the environmental regulations of the
country of origin.

A catalogue record for this book is available from the British Library.

A catalog record for this book is available from the Library of Congress.

10 9 8 7 6 5 4 3 2 1
18 17 16 15 14 13 12 11 10 09

Printed and bound in Great Britain by
CPI Antony Rowe, Chippenham and Eastbourne

Contents

Illustrations

Tables

Figures

Preface

The idea for this book developed long before the coining of the term 'e-governance for development'. Indeed, it all started about twenty years ago when I first started my research on the role of ICT for development planning and administration in India. At that time, I was confronted by many important issues regarding the process of managing development programmes and providing welfare. In particular, I noted at that time how the management of development programmes involved a complex process of interaction between the implementing agency and the community involving numerous administrative, social, legal (regulatory) and political issues. These issues are as relevant now as they were then. However, many of the issues have been consistently sidelined over the years while a growing policy focus among the international development community and country governments towards new technological and managerial solutions to problems of development dominated discussion and policy formulation. My more recent field visits to India made me decide that the time was right for a book which unpacked the notion of e-governance from a developmental perspective given the lack of scholarly material in this area.

As I started planning my approach for the book, I was increasingly drawn to literature from development studies. In particular, I gained inspiration for this book through the work of those scholars who have taken a sociological approach to development and governance as this provides me with a 'lens' through which to discuss many of the issues I continue to confront during my ongoing empirical work in rural India. This theoretical lens also provides an antidote to the vast amount of literature that has appeared over the past few years regarding India's emergence as a major player in the global marketplace. No doubt, the country has progressed in terms of achieving high rates of economic growth and is often discussed as a future 'superpower' in this regard. Most of this growth is propelled by global software outsourcing activity in major Indian cities while at least one quarter of the Indian population – the rural poor – remains untouched by this progress. This poses a challenge for overall development in the country – a challenge that has been acknowledged as a priority in the July 2009 Indian budget announcement according to which rural India will be the focus of the current government's five-year term in office.

This book addresses critical issues related to development and governance which are fundamental when implementing e-governance projects in rural India. While a lot of scholarly effort has accumulated regarding how to study the cost and service improvement impact of e-governance projects on citizens and implementing agencies, my approach has been different. I have purposefully decided to adopt an approach that is more grounded in the conditions faced by different rural poor groups. In this way, my study approach emulates the way in which both early and more contemporary sociology of development scholars favour 'depth' of analysis over time. Indeed, there are times when colleagues ask me whether I am 'still' carrying out research in rural India. To that, my reply has been that even a lifetime of research may not be enough to understand how societies develop and the role played by ICT in that process.

There are many people who have helped me to complete this book. First and foremost, I am deeply grateful to Frank Land for reading several draft versions of the book and for providing me with valuable comments and support over the past few months. Over the years, I have appreciated the many useful exchanges I have had with colleagues from the Information Systems & Innovation Group regarding my research, particularly Chrisanthi Avgerou, Susan Scott, Kiran Gopakumar and Matthew Smith. The continued assistance and cooperation of government officials in India are gratefully acknowledged. In particular, officials from the Surat District administration, the Kerala IT Mission and Malappuram District Akshaya Office, and Gumballi PHC and the Karuna Trust. I must also thank the Nuffield Foundation and the British Council who have provided me with funds to travel to India over the past few years.

Finally, I owe thanks to my dear family for always supporting and encouraging me in my research, particularly to Edwin and my daughter Priya who regularly accompanied me on field trips during their summer vacation.

Foreword

I first met Shirin Madon about twenty years ago when she was working on her PhD on the role of computer-based information systems (IS) in rural development administration in India. I was impressed with the thoroughness and dedication of her work, at a time when in-depth field studies of this sort were not common, and certainly not in contexts such as rural India. She has continued this dedicated focus on the role of information and communication technologies in the development of India ever since that time and has produced a series of thoughtful and interesting publications based on careful and detailed field studies. Three of them are reported on in this book, under the label of e-governance projects: MIS for rural self-employment programmes in the state of Gujarat, telecentres for rural outreach in Kerala and health information systems in rural Karnataka.

However, this book is not just about in-depth case studies, but reflects a more ambitious project to link the study of e-governance to broader literatures on governance and, crucially, development. A key argument of the book is that technology-based projects aimed at development goals in specific contexts should not be studied in isolation but in conjunction with a deep investigation of the historical processes of development and governance that have evolved over time in that context. There is an increasing recognition among those who study information and communication technology for development (ICT4D) that the development part has been underemphasised and under-theorised in much of the work to date. Madon's book is a timely and significant contribution to correcting that imbalance.

In order to write this Foreword, I read the whole text, and I found many learning points. Every reader will have their own take on this, but here are just a few of the ideas and messages which I found valuable. At a time when much is made of public-private partnerships and the role of non-governmental organisations (NGOs) in the development arena, the book reminded me of the crucial importance of the role of the state in order to ensure that broader social objectives are foregrounded, not just economic goals. A related point that comes out strongly from the book is the vital role of the frontline fieldworker, such as the local health worker, in ensuring that broad programmes are implemented in locally relevant ways on the ground. From a research perspective, Madon's work makes it clear that there are no short-cuts to understanding what is happening in rural India, but rather that we need the kind of painstaking studies which she has carried out over such an extended period. Finally, on the role of computers, they should not be seen as primarily useful for monitoring and performance evaluation by those at the top, but also as offering opportunities for personal development and capacity-building for workers operating at the front line of rural development.

Who should read this book? It should be a standard text for those interested in ICT4D in the context of India, including policy-makers, managers, local activists and researchers. However, I believe that the book has a wider potential audience than this. While the detailed empirical material is drawn solely from rural India, many of the concepts, arguments and messages of the book are relevant to ICT4D in other countries of the world. In addition, while the book addresses technology-based approaches, its wider contextual focus means that the material of the book will be of relevance to those interested in the broader topics of governance and development. It is heartening to see a book which takes on a topic of high social import, namely how to help the poor of the world through the use of technology, and which does such a good job in articulating key issues, approaches and future challenges. I hope others gain as much as I did in reading and reflecting on this impressive piece of work.

Geoff Walsham
Judge Business School
University of Cambridge

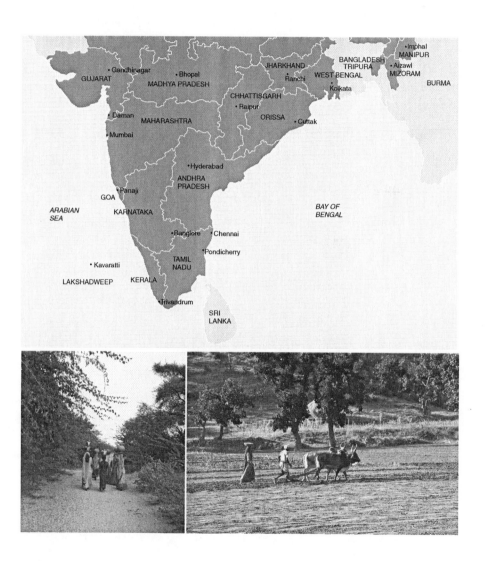

1
Introduction

Information and communication technologies (ICTs) constitute an increasingly important element in the economic planning strategy of the vast majority of developing countries (OECD, 2003; UNDP, 2004). One application that has received special attention in recent years has been the use of ICTs in the pursuit of good governance, usually under the banner of e-governance. In principle, the deployment of ICTs to improve public sector governance is not new. ICTs have for quite some time now played an important role in public sector reform initiatives mainly to improve the efficiency of bureaucracies and to enhance the quality of information for public sector decision-making. What is new is the use of the prefix 'e' and the implications of that addition. Facilitated by the advent of the internet, only recently have these technologies become affordable for mass deployment in the public sector offering the opportunity to increase efficiency of public administration and improve the interface between government and citizens.

Under the e-governance banner, a large number of development interventions, endorsed and supported by the international development community, focus on the role of ICTs for enhancing the efficiency, accessibility and democratic accountability of public administration and collective decision-making (Backus, 2001). In 2003, at the first World Summit of Information Systems (WSIS) conference held in Geneva, it was agreed that all public centres and government should have an online system of administration by 2015.[1] Since then, the support provided for e-governance projects by agencies such as the UNDP and the World Bank has been growing. The United Nations Development programme (UNDP), for example, was recently noted to have implemented 195 e-governance projects that provide information and services to citizens in 110 countries (Azzarello, 2005). According to the World Bank, 'eGovernance can serve a variety of purposes including better delivery of government services to citizens, improved interactions with business and industry, citizen empowerment through access to information, and more efficient government management'.[2] In a similar vein, the central objective as stated in the UNDP's strategic framework for e-governance is 'to empower particularly the poor, women and youth, to actively participate in governance processes and thus enhance democracy'.[3] These are ambitious claims indeed. No less than to transform and enrich the democratic process.

e-Governance initiatives have proliferated in many parts of the developing world. Applications designed to improve the efficiency and effectiveness of public administration are sometimes referred to as e-administration projects (Heeks, 2003; Ndou, 2004). These involve digitisation of data records of individual government departments or implementing sector-specific management information systems to improve the monitoring and reporting functions of large economic development programmes. Applications designed to enhance access to government information and delivery of services to citizens are referred to as e-services projects. These projects aim to improve transparency in government dealings with the public and promote accountability to citizens through the establishment of IT-enabled centres for providing entitlement certificates and facilitating the payment of bills and other dues to government without the need for intermediaries. In rural parts of the developing world, this type of e-governance application finds expression in the telecentre movement which aims to provide a rural outreach facility for citizens to more actively participate in improving their living conditions by engaging in commercial activity and by obtaining government information and services.

However, evidence so far shows that the linkage between better technology and better governance and ultimately better development is not automatic. According to Heeks (2003), approximately 35% of e-governance projects are either never implemented or are abandoned soon after implementation while 50% of projects do not reach their stated objectives. A small percentage of cases have been reported in which e-governance projects have brought some tangible benefits to citizens and government agencies (Bhatnagar, 2004; World Bank, 2007). In some cases, direct gains of e-services applications to citizens have accrued in terms of cost- and time-savings as various government information and services can be obtained from one central IT-enabled service point rather than the citizen having to visit individual government departments. In other cases, e-governance projects have brought benefits to government agencies in terms of more efficient reporting procedures releasing staff for more 'value-added' tasks. However, success in such cases has typically been measured in terms of short-term financial gains rather than in terms of longer-term impact on improving processes of local governance and promoting development. These processes remain largely opaque to e-governance policy-makers and implementers with reform packages continuing to impose standard 'good governance' prescriptions without any explicit analysis of the contextual situation within which such systems are implemented (UNDP, 2004). Drawing on evidence from Jordan, Ciborra (2005) shows that such intervention ultimately leads to more systems unevenly distributed within administrative departments and agencies, and resources allocated unevenly in the population.

The evidence suggests that improving systems of governance is a social not a technological activity. But this is hardly recognised in the current 'e-governance for development' manifesto. Current policy is driven by two theories. First, a theory about development and governance according to which good governance is one of the key requirements for the achievement of human development as inscribed in the UN Millennium Development Declaration's emphasis on the importance of good governance for upholding the principles of democracy (UN, 2000). One of the similarities between the policy mandate of different agencies is that governance is a wider term indicating that government institutions are not the only ones involved in operations regarding citizen welfare. Second, a theory about ICT and the promotion of good governance. Policy literature suggests many ways in which e-governance can support good governance, for example, by improving the efficiency and effectiveness of governments, improving the interface between government administration and citizens, improving transparency and accountability, enabling citizens' access to public information, enhancing citizens' participation in the public policy process, and improving inclusion and participation of stakeholders in good governance processes.

Both these theories have been adopted unproblematically in policy circles and in much of the academic literature on e-governance for development. The objective of this book is to redress this balance by critically reviewing the linkage between development and governance. So far, this type of critique has been missing from much of the literature on this topic. This is not altogether surprising: development is acknowledged to be a situated, context-specific process entangled with indigenous politics and historically formed institutions. But in practice, development is a highly practical activity with pressing economic, social and political reasons for solutions. In many cases, policy-makers find themselves under pressure to use up funds that have been allocated for carrying out 'development' activities over a period of time. Under such conditions, solutions are typically conceived in techno-managerial terms. Most analyses of e-governance projects in developing countries, for example, have been instrumentally focused and tied to project management concerns.

The focus of this book is India which has become over the years perhaps one of the best-known place in the world for information technology. However, in terms of use of information technology, the country is still very backward. In metropolitan areas, for example in the superspeciality hospitals of Bangalore or Delhi or in software companies, high-quality, well-used systems prevail. But in the villages and rural areas, usage is low. This is despite the emergence of e-governance applications aimed at increasing government efficiency and improving the interface between government and citizens. This book is not intended to cover the whole range of e-governance applications. It specifically focuses on applications that support the national planning effort in key social sectors such as rural development, health and agriculture. These particular types of e-governance applications have an overtly developmental orientation referred to by Avgerou (2008) as 'transformational' as they have the potential to transform existing socio-economic and political processes. In this book, the focus is on improving understanding of these processes by tracing (1) the macro-level political and socio-economic factors which influence e-governance policies, and (2) the micro-level social systems such as existing ways of administration and planning and existing social networks which interface between e-governance implementation and improvements in the lives of ordinary people.

This book is divided into three parts. The review of literature in the first part of the book raises many critical issues that move beyond the conventional discourse on e-governance for development towards an alternative 'political economy' approach for understanding this topic. First and foremost, as the study topic of this book is e-governance for development, it seems crucial to commence the inquiry with an understanding of what is meant by development. Chapter 2 traces dominant ideologies in development thinking from the postwar period onwards identifying shifts in policy emphasis between economic and social priorities. The chapter includes a discussion of the ideas behind modernisation and behind subsequent conceptions of development including basic needs, participatory development and Marxist-influenced approaches. The advent of neoliberalism describes how attention has shifted away from a broader social reform agenda towards a more managerialist agenda in development which gives priority role to markets, civil society activism and improved capacity-building.

Chapter 3 unpacks the 'good governance' policy manifesto that has been promoted in developing countries by international agencies to support their economic and political liberalisation programmes. While the bureaucratic element of this policy focuses on administrative simplification and better management capacity, the political element focuses on strengthening systems of democratisation. However, what has been overlooked is the fact that the achievement of both these elements crucially depends on understanding and nurturing existing social, administrative and political systems.

Chapter 4 traces the evolution of the e-governance for Development discourse, describes its key application areas and reviews recent research on the topic. It draws on the critical literature review of development and governance to conceptualise e-governance for development. The study framework proposed is at two levels. Of interest at the macro level are the complex forces which affect public policy-making on development such as urban or sectoral bias and on the governance strategies put in place to achieve these policy priorities. At the micro level, the value of an e-governance project will ultimately depend on how community members are able to actualise the benefits of improved information and services within a particular setting. Interfacing between these two levels are the formal and informal local governance structures comprising administrative, political and social systems.

Part II of the book presents case studies of e-governance applications in India. Chapter 5 provides an introduction to this section describing the author's research approach and the overall research methodology adopted for the case studies. Chapter 6 gives an overview of India's policy trajectory with regards to development priorities, governance reform initiatives and e-governance direction. There is a strong technology-driven vision of development within the country which has influenced the rapid take-up of e-governance in every state of the country. However, caution is raised on two fronts. First, whether this investment is justified in the face of growing inequalities within the country and other basic development priorities. Second, whether the current corporate-facing strategy for implementing these projects will promote developmental gains for rural poor communities.

The next three chapters present case studies of e-governance application in three states in India and across three sectors. Overall development priorities in each state are identified and juxtaposed with the attempts to introduce e-governance applications for the promotion of one key development sector. Chapter 7 describes the case of e-governance for back-end administrative reform in Gujarat's rural development sector. This chapter draws on research carried out over almost two decades documenting changes in the strategies adopted for poverty alleviation and in the adoption of new governance structures put in place for managing various development programmes. Both of these have influenced the implementation of e-governance applications for reporting and local analysis. Chapter 8 describes the case of e-governance for front-end citizen-government interactions through multi-purpose community telecentres. The telecentre project has been implemented by the Kerala government with the specific aim of promoting socio-economic development among the rural population. The telecentres provide a range of commercial and government services to the public. Of particular interest is the way in which these centres have become hubs for the local farming community to meet and discuss issues relevant to their livelihoods. Chapter 9 describes the case of Health Information Systems for improving public health systems for the rural poor community in Karnataka. It begins by tracing the influence of the global health agenda on Karnataka's health priorities. At the micro level, it describes the case of an NGO-run primary health centre looking at the way in which the health system interfaces with processes of local community development.

Part III of this book presents overall reflection of the cases highlighting some of the important findings from the case studies. While this book is entitled e-governance for Development, the reader will find a greater emphasis both in the theoretical and case material on governance and development, rather than on the 'e'. This is not by accident. It is a deliberate attempt by the author to refocus attention on the social context that shapes any kind of innovation. In the literature on the social study of IT, this may not be such a new finding but it is worth re-emphasising particularly with regards to e governance projects in developing countries. It is often the case that governments in developing countries are under political pressure to launch these projects without understanding the important role played by local governance structures in addressing the development needs of the community.

Glossary

ICTs – Information and Communication Technologies
IT – Information Technology
OECD – Organisation for Economic Cooperation and Development
UNDP – United Nations Development Programme
WSIS – World Summit for Information Systems

References

Avgerou, C. (2008) Information Systems in Developing Countries: A critical research review, *Journal of Information Technology,* 23, pp. 133–146.

Azzarello, V. (2005) Report on Mapping UNDP's E-governance Projects, Democratic Governance Group and Bureau for Development Policy, UNDP, August 2005.

Backus, M. (2001) E-governance in Developing Countries, *IICD Research Brief,* 1, March 2001.

Bhatnagar, S.C. (2004) *E-Government – from Vision to Implementation: A practical guide with case studies,* Sage Publications, New Delhi.

Ciborra, C. (2005) Interpreting E-Government and Development: Efficiency, transparency or governance at a distance? *Information Technology & People,* 18, 3, pp. 260–279.

Heeks, R. (2003) Most eGovernment-for-Development Projects Fail: How can risks be reduced? *iGovernment Working Paper Series,* IDPM, University of Manchester, UK.

Ndou, V. (2004) E-Government for Developing Countries: Opportunities and challenges, *EJISDC,* 18, 1, pp. 1–24.

OECD. (2003) Information and Communication Technology (ICT) in Poverty Reduction Strategy Papers (PRSPs).

UN. (2000) UN General Assembly Resolution A/RES/55/2 Millennium Declaration, 18 September 2000.

UNDP. (2004) *Essentials,* The UNDP Evaluation Office, 15, April 2004.

World Bank. (2007) Impact Assessment Study of Computerized Service Delivery Projects from India and Chile, IT @ WB Staff Working Paper No. 2.Available at http://www-wds.worldbank.org/external/default/WDSContentServer/WDSP/IB/2008/04/08/000333038_20080408052408/Rendered/PDF/421470WPOBox327349B01Public1/pdf

Part I

Conceptualising e-Governance for Development

2
What Do We Mean by Development?

This chapter aims to provide a critical literature review of some of the dominant ideologies which have driven development through the decades. It starts with a journey from the modernist concept of progress based on industrialisation and bureaucratic organisation in which the states provided the means by which development would be achieved. In the 1960s and 1970s, various alternative ideologies found expression such as basic needs and participatory development. Marxist scholars presented an alternative ideology in terms of systems of dependency and domination between developed and developing countries and the consequences of these systems on local social structures. Arguments against the role of the state gained increasing credence during the 1970s when economic stagnation, high unemployment and other economic crises affected the world economy. Under neo-liberalism, a new set of relationships has emerged between the state, the market and civil society for the implementation of development projects. The focus has been on strengthening institutional and organisational capacity through improved management and information systems.

Ideas about the meaning behind the term 'development' date back to the period of Enlightenment in the eighteenth century in northern Europe. Colonisers had constructed themselves as agents of progress while once highly advanced civilisations in Latin America, Africa and Asia were thought to be backward and in need of modernisation (Dwivedi *et al.*, 2007). The origins of development theory and discourse are found explicitly in the experiences of post-Second World War European reconstruction under the Marshall Plan. At this time, the term 'development' was first used by US President Harry Truman in 1949 as part of the rationale for postwar reconstruction in 'underdeveloped' parts of the world. With these efforts, a new field of development economics was founded based on Keynesian ideas of planned social change, industrial production and redistributive social policy on which the Marshall Plan had been based. Development economics was driven by a 'modernisation' ideology that countries were underdeveloped because of a lack of economic growth, and policies were called for based on growth theories to stimulate industrialisation, urbanisation, economic growth and improved governance through international financial assistance and technology transfer (Rostow, 1960). According to modernisation theory, traditional low-income societies would pass through a series of pre-ordained stages of development resulting in a modern state and economy based on the western model. The assumption made was that this growth would eventually trickle down and benefit all segments of society. This ideology of development which had prevailed in the last phase of colonial rule and early years of independence was applied to Africa, Asia and Latin America with few modifications.

Economists in the modernisation era acknowledged the need for a change in development objectives from the exclusive pursuit of economic growth to a more advanced notion of growth with equity through state planning (Myrdal, 1958). The modernisation era laid a heavy emphasis on comprehensive national development plans under which specific programmes and project activities were developed with clear objectives and detailed strategic planning by the government. The development planning effort was heavily influenced by its emphasis on technology as well as information. In terms of technology, there was heavy investment made in transferring industrial and agricultural technology from developed countries. In India, for example, mechanisation of rural development and the 1960s Green Revolution significantly increased the yield of wheat and rice crops due to a combination of plant breeders, fertilizers, pesticides and tractors. In terms of information, there was emphasis on mass media as the 'great multiplier' with the idea being that knowledge disseminated through mass communication would eventually lead to an economic and social upliftment of poor people in developing countries raising their aspirations and modernising their lifestyles (Lerner, 1958; Schramm, 1964). Parameters began to appear in league tables to measure the attainment of development in terms of availability of daily newspapers, radios, cinema seats and TV receivers per 100 people.

However, technology transfer and mass media of the 1950s and 1960s had proved at best ineffective in promoting equitable development and at worst served to widen inequalities (Webster, 1984). While the Green Revolution resulted in significant increases in agricultural production in the 1940s to 1960s, it also widened infrastructure and resource inequalities between large and small farmers. Information that was transmitted from broadcast media, for example, on sophisticated cropping techniques used in advanced developed countries, often proved irrelevant for rural poor communities in the developing world. Despite the achievement of high rates of growth in many developing countries up until the 1970s, empirical evidence pointed to the abject failure of growth theories to alleviate poverty. For the first time, poverty came to be discussed as a serious issue in development policy literature, for example, in Dudley Seers and Leonard Joy's 1971 volume entitled 'Development in a Divided World'.

Various powerful discourses surfaced during this decade which focused on supplementing economic growth with provisions to redress the inequitable distribution of resources. The UN assumed international leadership in these efforts creating a new organisation, The United Nations Research Institute for Social Development (UNRISD) in Geneva to undertake the task of developing social indicators (Baster, 1972; UN, 1971). In the 1970s, the World Bank also supported these initiatives arguing that economic growth with redistribution was needed to overcome income and asset inequality (Chenery *et al.*, 1974). The International Labour Organization also contributed to this debate and sought to directly supply impoverished communities with essential goods and services such as food, housing, healthcare and basic education which led to the prioritisation of programmes by governments in developing countries (ILO, 2004; Streeten *et al.*, 1981). This effort to address the basic needs of poor communities resulted in a move away from the singular project approach to designing integrated programmes to address a whole range of needs such as livelihoods, income, health and education (Conyers, 1982; Hardiman and Midgley, 1989). To assist in the implementation of such programmes, governments in developing countries began to engage in administrative reform policies to decentralise authority to local government officers and political representatives as a way of enhancing the coordination and management of development programmes and making them more relevant to the local community (Caiden, 1991). The Basic Needs approach was implemented in an environment of alternative politics that included the rise of ecological and feminist activist groups and Schumacher's Intermediate Technology movement (Schumacher, 1973). This movement became popular in the 1970s mainly through students and activists in the US and Europe and subscribed to the view that large-scale, capital-intensive technology was not 'appropriate' for developing countries, and it instead advocated usage of low-cost, home-grown, small-scale, easy-to-maintain and labour-intensive 'intermediate' technologies.[1]

Over time, criticisms of conventional government-run community development programmes intensified as international donors such as the United Nations Children's Fund (UNICEF) and the World Health Organization (WHO) argued that these programmes were bureaucratic, inefficient, wasteful and often corrupt (Marsden and Oakley, 1982; Mayo, 1975). More resources began to be allocated to non-profit organisations that had begun to promote what became known as community participation – an approach that stressed the importance of an activist style of intervention that relied less on the provision of services than on the active involvement of the poor in development projects (Midgley *et al.*, 1986). The concept of participation was inspired by several trends that were occurring in the social sciences. First, by radical populist ideas in development studies through the work of Chambers (Chambers, 1983; Howes and Chambers, 1979; Narayan *et al.*, 2000). Second, by a growing interest in management and information systems to study the impact of technology on business efficiency and productivity replacing the earlier focus on technology alone with a socio-technical approach to IT implementation (Land and Hirschheim, 1983; Mumford, 1983). The concept of participation has remained central to development discourse since the 1980s with a range of techniques developed for usage during project implementation to consider multiple and minority voices from the community.

Wider critical ideas emanating from Marxism and Maoism also emerged to challenge the hegemony of the 'orthodox' view. The single most radical alternative to modernist development to surface in the 1960s and 1970s was the Marxist-influenced Dependency argument. Popularised by the work of A.G. Frank and other scholars during the 1970s (many from the United Nations Economic Commission of Latin America, ECLA), the focus of analysis in this approach was on explaining the process of underdevelopment in terms of the way peripheral economies were integrated into the capitalist system on unequal terms, primarily as providers of cheap raw materials for export to rich industrialised countries. This intellectual activity was intimately linked not only to political events of the times such as Marxist concerns with anti-imperialism (the Vietnamese war of national liberation against US imperialism) but also with transitions to socialism (the Great Proletarian Revolution in China). The increasingly evident difficulty of capitalist development in poor countries coupled with scepticism about the USSR and communism across the world resulted in the claims of Maoism as an alternative model (Corrigan *et al.*, 1978). Mass politics and its forms of inclusive and dynamic participation as theorised by Mao Zedong and manifested in China generated a form of development centred on third world nationalist trends and on satisfying basic needs through creative collective practices. Examples of this form can be found in Nehru's India in the 1950s, Nkrumah's Ghana, Toure's Guinea, revolutionary Cuba, Allende's Chile in the early 1970s and liberated Mozambique and Nicaragua. In Chile, at the time, President Allende's interest in planning as a rational, scientific process saw the importation of ideas from cybernetics[2] leading to the development of a five-level control model for the Chilean economy. Eventually, however, efforts to produce such a stable information system for the economy failed as the model was unable to predict political events outside its control.

The focus of Marxist intellectual work, evident in 'sociology of development studies', was on analysing how interventions designed to bring about economic growth, such as increasing agricultural productivity through agrarian reform and stimulating urban petty commodity production, affected living conditions and welfare of poor communities in the developing world (Bernstein, 1973; Booth, 1985; Harriss, 1979, 1982; Lipton, 1977). Emphasis in these studies was on development as 'process' rather than 'outcome' with a focus on understanding relations between various groups of people involved in implementing projects. Lipton's study is focused on the dialectics between urban and rural growth in developing countries presenting evidence of the disparities between urban and rural parts of the developing world in terms of income and capital investment. He puts forward the argument that urban bias found in the power structures of most developing countries and in the dominant development ideologies has contributed to a set of policies that hamper long-term growth. Harriss presents a more complex analysis of the shifting dialectics between various categories of peasantry in the agrarian economy drawing on fieldwork in northern Tamil Nadu in 1973–4. He describes how the persistence of conditions of dependence of the poor on the middle and rich peasantry is likely to exist due to the need for the poor to earn money through labour, to borrow money in times of need and due to caste identity which locks the poor into exploitative relations. Harriss's analysis identifies the emergence of a middle peasantry that is fairly independent of rich farmers but cautions that this may not be a stable grouping because of changing conditions. For example, middle peasant groupings are liable to move into dependence upon rich farmers or capitalists partly in response to changes in the size and composition of their families in relation to their resources, and partly due to reliance on rich farmers for technology, loans and for obtaining other vital agricultural inputs.

Anti-statist arguments became increasingly more plausible during the 1970s due to the collapse of global communism. In the same decade, economic stagnation, persistent inflation, high unemployment and other economic difficulties[3] plagued the world economy. This turn of events convinced many that state control and excessively generous social provisions were to blame. The collapse of Bretton Woods financial institutions and the gradual dismantling of Keynesian welfare states ushered in an economic environment that was hostile to government regulation and that favoured market solutions in the belief that classical economic theories were universally applicable and culturally neutral. This alternative political philosophy , greatly influenced by the ideas of US economist Milton Friedman, challenged the basic Keynesian model and promoted an alternative macro-economic policy called monetarism. The political ascendancy of neoliberal theory in western economic theory and public policy from the late 1970s had a big impact on third world economic development. The keystone of these policies, which became known as the Washington Consensus (a consensus among organisations such as the IMF and the World Bank), was wholesale deregulation through macro-economic reforms. The free market and private sector-generated growth were believed to raise productivity thereby raising the living standards of the poor rather than the earlier doctrine of state planning which, it was argued, had led to unproductive rent seeking and misallocation of scarce resources in developing countries (Lal, 1983; Lusk, 1992; De Soto, 1989; Stoesz, 2000). Prahalad's popular book 'Bottom of the Pyramid' has subscribed to this view. The author argues that poverty alleviation is essentially a business development task to be shared among private sector firms that would work collaboratively with civil society organisations and local government to tap the consumer base of the poor (Prahalad, 2005). The suggestion made is that free trade would benefit not only producers in developed countries but also producers (including peasant farmers) and consumers in developing countries as these economic agents would respond rationally to price signals and other incentives. This perspective soon formed the basis of the World Bank's strategy on poverty alleviation in terms of integrating rural producers and informal urban petty commodity workers into markets with cut-backs in social investment, privatisation of social programmes and abandonment of social planning as an integral part of policy-making.

Neoliberalism remained the dominant approach in international development circles well into the 1990s fuelled not only by the collapse of global communism but also by the apparent weaknesses of Asian-model economies. International lending institutions and western financiers now enjoyed increasing power and indulged in greater intervention with an uncritical acceptance of Washington consensus orthodoxy. While neoliberal theory inherited a lot from earlier modernisation prescriptions, a significant deviation was in the reduced role of the state. Many developing countries were faced with huge debts as a result of over-borrowing, as well as escalating global interest rates following the adoption of monetarist policies in the developed countries. Under such circumstances, structural adjustment programmes were introduced for developing countries as a condition for credit (Chossudovsky, 1997; Danahar, 1994; Jain, 1989; Stiglitz, 2002). With particular reference to Sub-Saharan Africa, the World Bank produced a major policy document outlining the necessary economic reforms which then became the principal guide for structural adjustment in Africa and in other developing-country regions (World Bank, 1981).

From this time onwards, neoliberalism began to assume a greater political dimension. As evidence had proved that non-democratic communist states were unable to produce sustained economic growth, it was accepted that democratic politics was essential for a thriving free market economy and vice versa. Western governments were therefore eager to accompany the promotion of economic liberalisation with political liberalisation in the form of democratisation encouraged in this direction by increasing evidence of pro-democracy movements in Latin America, the Philippines, South Korea, Bangladesh, Nepal, Eastern Europe and later in Africa in the 1980s (Huntingdon, 1991). The work of Amartya Sen was influential in promoting the political dimension of development. Building on the ideas of earlier writers, such as Schumacher (1973) who had critiqued dominant economic models of development, Sen saw development as 'freedom' in terms of enabling an individual to pursue what he or she values in life. This freedom, according to Sen (1999, 2001), could include a mix of economic and non-economic aspects such as the freedom to engage in economic transactions, freedom to have political liberties, freedom to lead a healthy life and freedom to be educated. Drawing on his major work on famines in India and China during the 1950s and 1960s, Sen argued that access to media and broadcast information was a basic constituent not only of democratic development but also to economic security (Sen, 1983).

A central insight from Sen's capabilities approach was that public policy should be directed towards the pursuit of both economic and social priorities (Mehrotra and Delamonica, 2007). Sen's work was a strong influence in terms of expanding development dimensions to include new indicators that focused on social development and freedom of expression. These ideas have found support in the growing popularity of rights-based approaches to development in which poverty reduction and livelihood security are strongly associated with strengthening local systems of governance to protect the interests of the poor in society through rich civil society activism (Johnson and Forsyth, 2002; ODI, 1999). Sen's theory of human development also emphasised the importance of interaction between different dimensions of poverty such as short life expectancy, high infant mortality, hunger and malnutrition, disease, unemployment and underemployment, inadequate housing, unsanitary conditions, lack of education, exposure to abuse and violence, lack of voice and vulnerability (Alkire, 2002; Sen, 1983). Sen's work resulted in the publication in 1990 of the first UNDP Human Development Report entitled 'The Concept and Measurement of Human Development' and subsequently to the establishment of the UNDP Human Development Index. Generated interest among scholars to focus not only on consumption and income but also on the assets and capabilities of the poor when examining the extent of poverty (Narayan *et al.*, 2000). Sen's work also led to analyses of the interaction between different indices of development – for example, the livelihoods framework developed by DFID (Carney, 1999; Chambers and Conway, 1992; Duncombe, 2007).

However, in practice, balancing both economic and social development priorities has become difficult with the growing trend towards globalisation. National economies have become increasingly linked through international markets leading to cross-border flows of goods, capital and labour facilitated by innovations in information technology[4] and management know-how. The metaphor of 'the network society' associated with the work of Castells (2004) has been used to describe a society whose social structure is made up of networks powered by microelectronics-based information and communication technologies. A strong theoretical association between ICTs, competitiveness in the global market and economic development has been established through the examples of increasingly significant trade in intangible services such as software exports in many developing countries (Avgerou, 2003; Birdsall, 2002). Many development economists have argued that the steady decline in world-wide income inequality since the mid-1970s has largely been due to economic globalisation of large and once extremely poor countries like China and India (Collier, 2007; Dollar and Kray, 2002; Firebaugh and Goesling, 2004; Barro and Sala-i-Martin, 2003; World Bank, 2002).

The underlying logic behind this ideology has extended not only to the production of ICTs but also to its consumption. Networks were perceived as open structures able to integrate new nodes thereby overcoming the problems associated with exclusion from dominant global networks and ICT usage has been associated with improved managerial performance (Chapman *et al.*, 2003; Noir and Walsham, 2007). Consequently, since the 1990s, there was increasing interest among international development agencies to use ICTs (particular internet connectivity) to bridge the 'digital divide' between the developed and developing countries in key economic and social sectors (Akpan, 2003; Heeks, 2008; Wade, 2002). DFID's 2000 White Paper 'Eliminating Poverty: Making globalisation work for the poor' contained a chapter on bridging the digital divide (DFID, 2002) as did the policy briefs issued by the UNDP at that time (UN, 2001). At a regional level too, initiatives were launched to establish ICT infrastructure, for example, the Southern African Development Community (SADC) established its ICT Policy and Regulatory Support Programme in 2002 aimed at liberalising the region's ICT sector. More recently, the World Summits on Information Systems (WSIS) held in Geneva in 2003 and Tunis in 2005 have continued to put ICT in the limelight.

In contrast to the huge optimism expressed about ICT and globalisation, there is also huge concern about the adverse effects of globalisation on poverty and income distribution in developing countries – a debate that mirrors earlier controversy over the appropriateness of structural adjustment programmes as a development strategy for low-income countries (Cornia, 2004; Culpeper, 2002; Wade, 2004a). Wade has questioned the liberal argument's claim that with increased globalisation, income inequality has been decreasing. Evidence from several studies on the globalisation-poverty relationship suggests that income inequality and poverty have been rising during the past two to three decades (Deaton, 2002; Hughes, 2007; Nissanke and Thorbecke, 2007; Ravallion, 2004, 2007; Unwin, 2007). An important conclusion from this body of work is that the extent to which the poor will benefit from growth depends on the way growth is managed across different sectors of the economy. As Ravallion (2004) argues, a strategy for poverty reduction through investment in growth of the primary agricultural sector has a far greater impact on poverty in developing countries than growth in either the secondary or tertiary sectors.

There is also a need to balance the arguments of those advocating economic growth as the optimal means of reducing poverty with a realistic assessment of the prevailing institutional factors that exist which are needed to support an equitable distribution of the benefits of growth (Jenkins, 2007; Miraftab, 2004; Shamsul Haque, 2000; Unwin, 2007). Despite evidence of growing employment in labour-intensive exports of manufactures and agriculture in Kenya, Bangladesh and Vietnam, Jenkins argues that the requirement of global value chains has meant that these jobs often demand long hours of work and poor working conditions making workers vulnerable in terms of both security of employment and income. Similarly, Bardan (2007) argues that opening up product markets without addressing weak and distorted factor markets or poor infrastructure services in developing countries may not help the poor. For example, the self-employed tend to work on small farms or as artisans and petty entrepreneurs in what amounts to the rural informal sector. These workers face constraints in accessing credit, marketing and insurance, and infrastructure. Analysis of institutional factors in development studies has shown that underdevelopment arose not simply due to a failure of fundamental economic parameters but due to deep-rooted institutional and social factors such as legal structures and tradition which govern the behaviour of economic actors (Ray and Mookherjee, 2000; Rodrik, 2004).

From the IT and Development literature, various theoretical perspectives have been drawn on to critique the simplistic correlation between ICTs and development. For example, institutional theory has been used to critique the 'tool and effect' linkage made between technology and development emphasising how any development intervention involves a path-dependent process governed by a specific social and historical context (Avgerou, 2003; Toye, 1995). This type of analysis has been used to explain why ICT investment in developing countries, in the absence of institutional support, leads to economic divergence rather than convergence between developed and developing countries and within countries (Heeks and Kenny, 2002). More recently, Madon *et al.* (2009) draw on their work in South Africa, Brazil and India to identify crucial processes that affect the institutionalisation of digital inclusion projects. These processes include how the community attributes meaning to the ICT project and gets involved in its implementation, the changing role of government over the project's evolution, and the process of generating content and applications that are relevant to the local community. Perspectives from development theory have also been found useful to understand how ICT can improve the living conditions of communities. For example, the importance of social capital in ICT projects is the theme of a study conducted in rural Peru by Andrade and Urquhart (2009). In particular, the study found that commitment and dedication of community leaders to the villagers was a key factor in sustaining the ICT intervention. Zheng (2009) draws on some of the key concepts from Sen's capabilities approach to provoke reflection on the contribution of ICTs for poverty, inequality and development.

Evidence suggests, then, that integration with the global economy is not a substitute for an anti-poverty strategy within developing countries. Even in countries that have been successful in developing labour-intensive exports, the overall impact of globalisation on poverty has been relatively small (Craig and Porter, 2006; Graham, 2007). The majority of the poor are not engaged in global production but access an increasing flow of information about the living standards of others both within and beyond country borders causing growing frustration with relative income differences (Graham, 2007). However, developing countries find themselves increasingly torn between participating in global economic activity and local domestic development. They are being denied the policy tools to intervene actively for providing basic needs with national assets increasingly sold out on a large scale to international and national private capital (Chossudovsky, 1991; Dwivedi *et al.*, 2007). In this climate, it is highly improbable that developing countries will have the political autonomy to nurture social policies without losing their international competitiveness and scaring away domestic and foreign investors.

This perspective on development has led to a recent resurgence of dependency arguments among 'post-development' scholars who have reworked the radical critiques of the earlier Marxist writers (Cowen and Shenton, 1995; Escobar, 1995). Escobar's influential book 'Encountering Development' argues that the term 'development' is an imposition of modernity. Values of progress as reflected in the experiences of the West are taken to represent knowledge and serve as a vehicle of power to sharpen the distinction between the first and third world making the former responsible for the salvation of the latter. Other writers (Milanovic, 1999; Wade, 2004b) have argued that globalisation benefits the rich countries as well as rich people within both rich and poor countries demonstrating its bad effects on the bulk of the population in poor countries, especially the most vulnerable. They caution that without regulatory and redistributive efforts, globalisation and market liberalisation are unlikely to have a positive impact in reducing poverty. Along similar lines, post-colonial development theorists argue that the current globalisation trends are a form of renewed imperialism through the creation of social, economic, cultural and political dependency of developing countries on the developed world (Sharp and Briggs, 2006). Following the style of early sociology of development writers, with their focus on development as process, studies have documented the way in which development projects have diverted power and resources to outside experts and well-paid functionaries rather than reducing rural poverty (Booth, 1993; Bernstein, 2005; Cooke and Kothari, 2001; Corbridge, 2002; Dwivedi *et al.*, 2007; Harriss, 2002; Kiely, 1995; Lewis and Mosse, 2006; Mosse, 2005). Some writers have linked these ideas to the concept of culture seen as a set of contested relations between individuals within a group and between groups. These relations, shaped by the wider context within which they occur, are taken to be in a constant state of flux (Friedman, 2004; Kuper, 1999; Rao and Walton, 2004; Westrup *et al.*, 2003).

Arguments about the adverse impact of globalisation on developing countries have extended to ICT production and consumption. Similarities have been identified between the modernisation paradigm and current ICT for development initiatives (Ojo, 2004). In both cases, the policy agenda is set and implemented by the world's most powerful nations. It is argued that these technologies perpetuate a new form of dependency of developing countries on the technological expertise and know-how of large MNCs, on bodies set up to regulate standard-setting for internet governance, and on the social values, institutional forms and culture embedded within the technology (Castells, 2000; Parayil, 2005; Wade, 2002; Wilson, 2004; Wilson and Heeks, 2001). In separate studies of the World Bank Development Gateway, Jha *et al.* (2004) and Marres (2004) argue that the website contains information primarily from northern sources with a strong bias towards technology topics rather than social and political topics. Thompson (2004) uses discourse analysis of a speech made by World Bank's James Wolfensohn in 2000 to show how ICT can reinforce or institutionalise uneven networks of capital, production, trade and communication both within developing countries and between regions of the world. Indeed, technological development has been blamed for becoming a distraction from the long-term progress of a society as many developing countries have either already undermined or are in danger of undermining their investment in general human development areas (Heeks, 2008; Thompson, 2008). A recent example is the OLPC (One Laptop Per Child) initiative set up in 2007 by a US non-profit organisation to oversee the creation of an affordable, educational device for use in schools in developing countries.[5] Much controversy surrounds the project as the opportunity cost of investing in technology as opposed to other pressing educational needs is huge. Moreover, there is little evidence to suggest that ICT interventions even in developed country schools have resulted in reduced inequality (Graeff, 2007).

From the 1990s, developed countries saw public policy shifting to centre stage in order to address a variety of concerns ranging from poverty and unemployment to ethnic conflict and gender oppression discussed at the World Summit on Social Development convened in 1995 by the UN in

Copenhagen to address the social costs of neoliberalism (UN, 1996). This trend influenced the policy of international development agencies and theories were espoused by eminent economists such as Sachs (2005) for augmenting the core Washington Consensus to include public funding for key social sectors such as primary education, health, sanitation and the environment. The 2004 WDR Making Services Work for Poor People argued that economic growth alone would not lift the poor out of poverty. Rather, such a strategy needed to be targeted through basic social services such as health and education to compensate for the market failures and social justice issues arising from market-led growth. Development organisations began to get involved in a wide variety of social development activities such as raising standards of living and increasing local participation in development – particularly among women and other vulnerable groups. These social goals became articulated in the Millennium Development Goals (MDGs) declared by the UN in 2005 for which ambitious targets have been set for 2015 (UN Millennium Project, 2006). These targets seek to reduce poverty through interventions in education, health, gender inequality and environmental sustainability by creating new governance relationships in which the private sector and NGOs are given a prominent role. This ideology was echoed in the declaration of similar goals by the Commission for Africa (2005) for enhancing economic growth and eliminating poverty in Africa. Within this discourse, a great deal of attention has been placed on the potential of ICTs to bring about a transformation in the living standards of communities in the developing world (Avgerou, 2008; Heeks, 2005).

Despite prioritising social development, the MDGs have been criticised. As Bond (2006) argues, the aspirational targets that these goals set out to achieve are far less important than the actual social struggles underway across the world among communities for obtaining a basic quality of life. Others have criticised the way in which the MDGs conceptualise the 'social' in overall development. Rather than focusing policy on broader social reforms, the development agenda concentrates on launching micro-level social policies which act as a safety net for vulnerable groups (Elson, 2005; Tendler, 2005; Unwin, 2007). These policies aim to promote community development by boostering 'social capital' – an increasingly popular concept in international development circles. But the narrowing of social policy in terms of social capital has distracted attention away from broader objectives of equitable distribution of income and from the need to strengthen the institutions needed to support such policy (Elson, 2005). Influenced by Third Way politics as it became known,[6] a new method of policy-making came to be promoted driven no longer by government alone but by a new set of relationships (indeed partnerships) between the state, the market and the individual. One of the most significant trends in social policy in developing countries in the

1990s has been the growth of privatisation in health, education and water services – the three basic services which involve most of the MDGs (Mehrotra and Delamonica, 2005). Development agencies have begun to focus on integrating their programmes through consensus-building between public and private agencies including intergovernmental, multilateral and bilateral agencies, NGOs and private sector philanthropists (Gilbert, 2002; World Bank, 1991, 2001).

The development ideology described above is currently encapsulated in what has become the centrepiece of World Bank policy from 1997 onwards under the banner Comprehensive Development Framework (CDF). This framework encompasses a set of mechanisms to guide development and poverty reduction towards institutional and organisational capacity-building in order to attain the MDGs. Indeed, capacity development has been a pervasive concept in international development since the late 1980s. Much of this literature starts from the idea that capacity is about improving management in organisations and using this approach, various reforms have been implemented. These include (1) forging partnerships and consensus-building between governments, donors, the private sector, civil society and other development stakeholders, (2) strengthening governance mechanisms in development, for example in terms of efficiency, transparency and accountability of development processes, (3) strengthening participatory processes and establishing social capital within communities using techniques like participatory rural appraisal, and (4) establishing effective monitoring mechanisms to emphasise the achievement of concrete results using techniques such as logical framework analysis.[7] Following the World Bank's initiative, other development agencies have also adopted the capacity-building strategy. For example, the ADB's Poverty Reduction Strategy, the UNDP's Sustainable Human Development and the similarly themed policy frameworks of bilateral agencies such as USAID, CIDA and AusAID are all variations of the current international development orthodoxy. While the new managerialist approach in development with its focus on capacity-building has been accepted almost unproblematically in development circles, there has been some recent reflection of its usage (Baser and Morgan, 2008; Cooke, 2001; Eade, 1997; Ebrahim, 2007; James and Wrigley, 2007). In their study report, Baser and Morgan argue that capacity-building should involve not just the formal aspects of organisational and institutional change such as structure, skill development and the configuration of tangible assets, but also informal aspects such as altering mindsets, behaviour and trust (Baser and Morgan, 2008). This wider perspective on capacity-building in organisations suggests that the entire development process should be a more context-sensitive and long-term undertaking – one that requires that local implementing agencies have the continuous flexibility to adapt, experiment and learn (Mosse, 1998; Rodrik, 2007).

The focus on capacity-building together with the strong association already established between ICT and economic competitiveness has resulted in a new discourse which has recently surfaced in the ICT4D literature. This discourse has been prompted by the emergence of a new generation of ICT based on two main platforms. First, mobile phones that routinely use applications such as SMS over the telephone network and increasingly provide access to the internet. An example of usage of this technology for development is the Vodafone M-Pesa project which enables remittances to be transferred without cost (Donner, 2006; Opoku-Mensah and Salih, 2007). The large and rapidly increasing number of mobile phone users in developing countries has been presented as providing revolutionary opportunities for promoting social and economic development by opening new markets and providing social services and networks[8] (Heeks, 2008). Second, the internet, the World Wide Web and new web-based social tools[9] coined as Web 2.0. These tools provide the opportunity for alternative approaches to interaction and collaboration of individuals, groups and organisations collapsing traditional barriers of formal organised activity in two ways. Shirky (2008) argues that this technology provides opportunity for disaster management such as in the 2004 Tsunami as well as to organise large-scale political rallies. Moreover it is argued that these tools provide the opportunity for peer-to-peer production moving away from proprietary, closed and restricted power structures towards making processes more open (Benker and Nissenbaum, 2006; Thompson, 2008). There has been much speculation that these new technologies present an opportunity to promote a new type of development, termed Development 2.0, not only challenging old structures of entrepreneurialism but also fundamentally seeking to alter the nature of interaction between citizens and the government by relying less on formal governmental and donor support and more on releasing the communty's own capacity for innovation (Thompson, 2008).

It may be too soon to judge the success of many of these new ideas being discussed in development circles. However, if history is any guide, these latest buzzwords may be yet one more instance of innovations in western domestic policies being translated and applied in international development policy regardless of their relevance (Easterley, 2006; Harriss, 2005; Midgley, 2003). As Easterley argues, the enthusiasm of developed nations to intervene in the policy-making strategies of developing countries remains as strong as ever.

To summarise, while there have been attempts to balance the objectives of economic growth with social development over the decades, the latter remains a largely eclectic and pragmatic set of activities lacking well-defined theoretical perspectives. Earlier forms of social development in the newly independent nations were driven by the idea that the state was the most effective agency for promoting social development. But criticisms of such an approach to social development found expression in the radical populist and Marxist-influenced ideas which relied less on the provision of services by the state and more on the active participation of the poor in their development. The collapse of communism and of the Bretton Woods financial institutions provided ammunition for these anti-state ideas. In recent years, a far more important role has been accorded to markets with a greater emphasis on the role of non-government organisations in promoting capacity-building and community engagement among citizen groups. The diffusion of neoliberalism has had a major influence on social development. Government agencies responsible for social development have been increasingly sidelined resulting in a fragmented and uneven approach to development.

Development perspective adopted in this book

Three key issues surface from this review of the development literature and form an essential platform for a critical approach to the study of e-governance for development:

First, understanding development in terms of a balance between economic and social objectives is an essential starting point for a study of e-governance for development. Many of the projects launched under this policy directive are driven by both economic and social motivations. Sometimes these overlap, while at other times, the economic motivation tends to take over. Experience suggests that economic and social development objectives reinforce each other. On the one hand, social development occurs faster and in a more sustainable way in situations of economic progress, but on the other hand, economic progress itself is facilitated by social development. Eventually, the way in which policies are articulated for their attainment is completely context and time dependent.

Second, the new 'managerialism' in development policy has detracted attention away from a broader social reform agenda through government intervention with serious implications for developing countries. The issue at the forefront of development policy concerns how the current economic downturn will affect developing countries. Lower growth in developed countries means there is less demand for exports from developing countries. This will adversely affect countries that are experiencing rapid growth based on exports, for example, India as well as many African countries that are reliant on one or two primary products for export (Sachs, 2008). The financial crisis will also lead to a reduction in capital inflows through investment as investors shift from riskier emergent markets to more stable locations, and to reduced aid funding (Rojas-Suarez, 2008). While it is hard to predict the impact on individual countries, reduced finances will mean that developing countries have less money available for social development interventions resulting in slower growth and rising inequality. According to the World Bank, the combined effect of the credit crunch will be a 2% reduction in the growth rates of developing countries according to which 80 million more people will live in extreme poverty emphasising the important role of the state in promoting equity (DFID, 2008; Schifferes, 2008).

Third, social analysis has occupied a peripheral position within development discourse in terms of both theoretical and methodological development. In terms of theoretical development, different normative perspectives continue to influence social development thinking today. Some attempts have been made to develop a common conceptual framework recognising the contribution of state direction, entrepreneurship, capacity-building and community engagement in social development (Miah and Tracy, 2001; Midgley, 1995). However, more work in the area of theory-building needs to be supported by an improved approach to 'method' in development studies and more generally in the social sciences (Friedman, 2004; Corbridge, 2007). There is increasing dissatisfaction that the methods of analysis used in the different social science disciplines continue to be largely modeled on the natural sciences, for example, proving or disproving the rightness of a social system based on its existence. Rather than prescribing whether these systems are inherently good or bad, an alternative approach is to understand how change occurs in society.

This book will be guided by the sociology of development approach which provides an opportunity for critical reflection on the linkage between e-governance projects and the betterment of local communities in developing countries. The recent revival of interest in this approach offers a promising way of transcending established theories of development and to focus analysis on understanding historical and social struggles that take place over time between actors who are constantly deploying strategies to resist and negotiate their position within their local environment. The next chapter critically reviews the literature on governance reform as a conduit for promoting development.

Glossary

Basic Needs – a philosophy of development first propagated by the International Labour Organization in 1971 according to which priority should be given to uplifting the poorest of the poor through an integrated package of basic services

Bretton Woods – A system of monetary management which established the rules for commercial and financial relations among the world's major industrial states in the mid-twentieth century

CDF – Comprehensive Development Framework
DFID – Department for International Development
ICT4D – Information and Communication Technology for Development
Social Capital – a concept developed in sociology and used in other human sciences to refer to the value of connections between individuals and groups in society
ILO – International Labour Organization
IMF – International Monetary Fund
Intermediate technology – This refers to relatively cheap, easy to maintain and use tools and technologies that can be used in developing countries to increase productivity
Marshall Plan – A plan devised by US Secretary of State George Marshall for rebuilding and creating a stronger foundation for Western European countries after the Second World War
MDGs – The UN Millennium Development Goals launched in 2000
UN – United Nations
UNDP – United Nations Development Programme
UNICEF – United Nations Children's Fund
Washington Consensus – This was a consensus between Washington DC-based institutions such as the IMF, World Bank and the US Treasury Department according to which a set of ten economic policies prescriptions should form the standard reform package for developing countries that are undergoing crises
UNRISD – United Nations Research Institute for Social Development
WHO – World Health Organization
World Bank Development Gateway – This is a multi-million dollar internet-based development knowledge initiative launched in 1999 by the World Bank

References

Akpan, P.I. (2003) Basic Needs to Globalization: Are ICTs the missing link? *Information Technology for Development,* 10, pp. 261–274.
Alkire, S. (2002) *Valuing Freedoms: Sen's capability approach and poverty reduction,* Oxford University Press, Oxford.
Andrade, A.E. and Urquhart, C. (2009) The Value of Extended Networks: Social capital and an ICT intervention in rural Peru, *Information Technology for Development,* 15, 2, pp. 108–133.
Avgerou, C. (2003) The Link between ICT and Economic Growth in the Discourse of Development. In *Organization Information Systems in the Context of Globalization,* edited by M. Korpela, R. Montealegre and A. Poulymenakou, Kluwer Academic Publishers, The Netherlands.
Avgerou, C. (2008) Information Systems in Developing Countries: A critical research review, *Journal of Information Technology,* 23, pp. 133–146.
Bardhan, P. (2007) Globalization and Rural Poverty. In *The Impact of Globalization on the World's Poor: Transmission mechanisms,* edited by M. Nissanke and E. Thorbecke, Palgrave Macmillan, Hants, pp. 145–163.
Barro, R. and Sala-i-Martin, X. (2003) *Economic Growth,* MIT Press, Cambridge, MA.
Baser, H. and Morgan, P. (2008) Capacity, Change and Performance. Study Report of the European Centre for Development Policy Management.
Baster, N. (1972) *Measuring Development,* Frank Cass, London.
Beer, S. (1981) *The Brain of the Firm,* Wiley, New York.

Benker, Y. and Nissenbaum, H. (2006) Commons-based Peer Production and Virtue, *The Journal of Political Philosophy,* 14, 4, pp. 394–419.

Bernstein, H. (2005) Development Studies and the Marxists. In *A Radical History of Development Studies: Individuals, Institutions and Ideologies,* edited by Uma Kothari, pp. 111–138, Zed Books, London.

Bernstein, H. (ed.) (1973) *Underdevelopment and Development: The Third World today,* Penguin, Harmondsworth.

Birdsall, N. (2002) Asymmetric Globalisation: Global markets require good global politics. Center for Global Development, USA.

Bond, P. (2006) Global Governance Campaigning and MDGs: From top-down to bottom-up anti-poverty work, *Third World Quarterly,* 27, 2, pp. 339–354.

Booth, D. (1985) Marxism and Development Sociology: Interpreting the impasse, *World Development,* 13, 7, pp. 761–787.

Booth, D. (1993) Development Research: From impasse to a new agenda. In *Beyond the Impasse: New Directions in Development Theory,* edited by Frans J. Schuurman, pp. 49–77, Zed Books, London.

Caiden, G.E. (1991) *Administrative Reform Comes of Age,* Walter de Gruyter, Berlin and New York.

Carney, D. (1999) Sustainable Livelihood Approaches Compared, Department for International Development, London.

Castells, M. (2000) *The End of Millennium,* Blackwell, Oxford.

Castells, M. (2004) Informationalism, Networks and the Network Society: A theoretical blueprint. In *The Network Society: A cross-cultural perspective,* edited by M. Castells, Edward Elgar, Cheltenham, UK.

Chambers, R. (1983) *Rural Development: Putting The Last First,* Longman, London.

Chambers, R. and Conway, G.R. (1992) Sustainable Rural Livelihoods: Practical concepts for the 21st century, *IDS Discussion Paper 296,* Institute of Development Studies, Brighton.

Chapman, R., Slaymaker, T. and Young, J. (2003) Livelihoods approach to Information and Communication in Support of Rural Poverty Elimination and Food Security, ODI-DFID-FAO, London.

Chenery, H., Ahluwalia, M., Bell, C., Duloy, J.H. and Jolly, R. (1974) *Redistribution with Growth,* Oxford University Press, Oxford.

Chossudovsky, M. (1991) Global Poverty and New World Economic Order, *Economic and Political Weekly,* 2 November 1991, pp. 2, 527–537.

Chossudovsky, M. (1997) *The Globalization of Poverty: Impacts of IMF and World Bank Reforms,* Zed Books, New York.

Collier, P. (2007) *The Bottom Billion: Why the poorest countries are failing and what can be done about it,* Oxford University Press, Oxford.

Commission for Africa (2005) *Our Common Interest. Report of the Commission for Africa,* Commission for Africa, London.

Conyers, D. (1982) *An Introduction to Social Planning in the Third World,* John Wiley & Sons, Chichester, UK.

Cooke, B. (2001) From Colonial Administration to Development Management, IDPM Discussion Paper Series, Working Paper No. 63, University of Manchester.

Cooke, B. and Kothari, U. (eds) (2001) *Participation – the New Tyranny?* Zed Books, London.

Corbridge, S. (2002) Development as Freedom: The spaces of Amartya Sen, *Progress in Development Studies,* 2, 3, pp. 183–217.

Corbridge, S. (2007) The (Im)possibility of Development Studies, *Economy and Society*, 36, 2, pp. 179–211.

Cornia, G.A. (2004) *Inequality, Growth and Poverty in an Era of Globalisation and Liberalisation*, Oxford University Press, Oxford.

Corrigan, P., Ramsay, H., Sayer, D. (1978) *Socialist Construction and Marxist Theory*, Macmillan, London.

Cowen, M. and Shenton, R. (1995) The Invention of Development. In *Power of Development*, edited by J. Crush, Routledge, London.

Craig, D. and Porter, D. (2006) *Development Beyond Neoliberalism? Governance, poverty reduction and political economy*, Routledge, Oxon.

Culpeper, R. (2002) Approaches to Globalization and Inequality within the International System. Paper presented for UNRISD Project on Improving Knowledge on Social Development in International Organizations, September.

Danahar, K. (ed.) (1994) *Fifty Years Is Enough: The case against the World Bank and the International Monetary Fund*, South End Press, Boston, MA.

Deaton, A. (2002) Is World Poverty Falling? *Finance & Development*, 39, 2, pp. 1–6.

DFID. (2002) The Significance of Information and Communication Technologies for Reducing Poverty. Department for International Development.

DFID. (2008) Speech made by Rt. Hon. Douglas Alexander, Secretary of State for International Development, Department of International Development at an LSE Public Event 'The Impact of the Global Economic Downturn on the World's Poorest Countries and the Launch of the International Growth Centre', 10 December, London School of Economics and Political Science.

Dollar, D. and Kraay, A. (2002) Growth Is Good for the Poor, *Journal of Economic Growth*, Springer, 7, 3, pp. 195–225.

Donner, J. (2006) The Use of Mobile Phones by Microentrepreneurs in Kigali, Rwanda: Changes to social and business networks, *Information Technologies and International Development*, 3, 2, pp. 3–19.

Duncombe, R. (2007) Using the Livelihoods Framework to Analyze ICT Applications for Poverty Reduction through Microenterprise, *Information Technologies and International Development*, 3, 3, pp. 81–100.

Dwivedi, O.P., Khator, R. and Nef, J. (2007) *Managing Development in a Global Context*, Palgrave Macmillan, Hants.

Eade, D. (1997) *Capacity-Building: An approach to people-centred development*, Oxfam, Oxford.

Easterley, W. (2006) *The White Man's Burden*, Oxford University Press, Oxford .

Ebrahim, A. (2007) Rethinking Capacity Building, Capacity.org, 31, 16. Available at www.capacity.org

Elson, D. (2005) Social Policy and Macroeconomic Performance: Integrating 'the Economic' and 'the Social'. In *Social Policy in a Development Context*, edited by Thandika Mkandawire, pp. 63–80, Palgrave Macmillan, Hants.

Escobar, A. (1995) *Encountering Development: The making and unmaking of the Third World*, Princeton University Press, Princeton, NJ.

Firebaugh, G. and Goesling, B. (2004) Accounting for the Recent Decline in the Global Income Inequality, *American Journal of Sociology*, 110, 2, pp. 283–312.

Friedman, J. (2004) Introduction: What Can Social Science Do? *Critical Review*, Nos. 2–3, pp. 143–322.

Gilbert, N. (2002) *Transformation of the Welfare State: The silent surrender of public responsibility*, Oxford University Press, New York.

Graeff, E. (2007) Current Possibilities of Creating More Equality: One laptop per child and the oversimplification of the global digital divide, MPhil essay. Available at www.u8development.com/default/components/com_fireboard/uploaded/files/Graeff__Substantive_1__2007_12_04.doc

Graham, C. (2007) Globalization, Poverty, Inequality and Insecurity: Some insights from the economics of happiness. In *The Impact of Globalization on the World's Poor: Transmission mechanisms*, edited by M. Nissanke and E. Thorbecke, Palgrave Macmillan, Hants, pp. 235–271.

Hardiman, M. and Midgley, J. (1989) *The Social Dimension of Development: Social policy and planning in the Third World*, Gower, Aldershot.

Harriss, J. (1979) Why Poor People Stay Poor in Rural South India, *Social Scientist*, 1, 1, pp. 20–47.

Harriss, J. (1982) *Capitalism and Peasant Farming: Agrarian structure and ideology in northern Tamil Nadu*, Oxford University Press, Mumbai.

Harriss, J. (2002) *Depoliticizing Development. The World Bank and Social Capital*, Anthem Press, London.

Harriss, J. (2005) Great Promise, Hubris and Recovery: A participant's history of development studies. In *A Radical History of Development Studies: Individuals, Institutions and Ideologies*, edited by Uma Kothari, pp. 17–47, Zed Books, London.

Heeks, R. (2005) ICTs and MDGs: On the wrong track? February 2005. Available at www.i4donline.net

Heeks, R. (2008) ICT4D 2.0: The next phase of applying ICT for international development, *Computer*, pp. 78–85.

Heeks, R. and Kenny, C. (2002) ICTs and Development: Convergence or Divergence for Developing Countries? In *Proceedings of the 7th International Conference of IFIP WG9.4 ICTs and Development: New Opportunities, Perspectives and Challenges*, Bangalore, India.

Howes, M. and Chambers, R. (1979) Indigenous Technical Knowledge: Analysis, implication and issues, *IDS Bulletin*, 10, 2, Institute of Development Studies, Sussex.

Hughes, B. (2007) Assessing Strategies for Reducing Poverty, *International Studies Review*, 9, pp. 690–710.

Huntingdon, S.P. (1991) *The Third Wave: Democratisation in the late twentieth century*, University of Oklahoma Press, Oklahoma.

ILO. (2004) Report of the World Commission on the Social Dimension of Globalisation, International Labour Organisation, Geneva.

Jain, R.B. (1989) *Bureaucratic Politics in the Third World*, Gritanjali Publishing House, New Delhi.

James, R. and Wrigley, R. (2007) Investigating the Mystery of Capacity Building: Learning from the Praxis Programme, Conference Paper, INTRAC.

Jenkins, R. (2007) Globalization, Production and Poverty. In *The Impact of Globalization on the World's Poor: Transmission mechanisms*, edited by M. Nissanke and E. Thorbecke, Palgrave Macmillan, Hants, pp. 163–187.

Jha, A., Seymour, V. and Sims, S. (2004) Evaluation of the Development Gateway – Final Report. Prepared for Bretton Woods Project. Development Studies Institute, LSE.

Johnson, C. and Forsyth, T. (2002) In the Eyes of the State: Negotiating a 'rights-based approach' to forest conservation in Thailand, *World Development*, 30, 9, pp. 1591–1605.

Kiely, R. (1995) *Sociology & Development: The impasse and beyond*, Routledge, London.

Kuper, A. (1999) *Culture: The Anthropologists' Account*, Harvard University Press, London.

Lal, D. (1983) The Misconceptions of 'Development Economics', *Finance and Development*, June, pp. 10–13.

Land, F. and Hirschheim, R.A. (1983) Participative Systems Design: Its rationale and techniques, *Journal of Applied Systems Analysis*, 10, pp. 91–107.

Lerner, D. (1958) *The Passing of Traditional Society: Modernizing the Middle East*, Free Press, Glencoe, IL.

Lewis, D. and Mosse, D. (2006) Encountering Order and Disjuncture: Contemporary anthropological perspectives on the organization of development, *Oxford Development Studies*, 34, 1, pp. 1–13.

Lipton, M. (1977) *Why Poor People Stay Poor. A study of urban bias in world development*, Temple Smith, London.

Lusk, M. (1992) Social Development and the State in Latin America: A new approach, *Social Development Issues*, 14, 1, pp. 10–21.

Madon, S., Reinhard, N., Roode, D. and Walsham, G. (2009) Digital Inclusion Projects in Developing Countries: Processes of Institutionalisation, *Information Technology for Development*, 15, 2, pp. 95–108.

Marres, N. (2004) Tracing the Trajectories of Issues, and Their Democratic Deficits, on the Web, *Information Technology & People*, 17, 2, pp. 124–149.

Marsden, D. and Oakley, P. (1982) Radical Community Development in the Third World. In *Community Work and the State*, edited by G. Craig, N. Derricourt and M. Loney, Routledge and Kegan Paul, London, pp. 153–163.

Mayo, M. (1975) Community Development: A radical altenrative? In *Radical Social Work*, edited by R. Bailey and M. Brake, Edward Arnold, London.

Mehrotra, S. and Delamonica, E. (2005) The Private Sector and Privatization in Social Services, *Global Social Policy*, 5, 2, pp. 141–174.

Mehrotra, S. and Delamonica, E. (2007) *Eliminating Human Poverty: Macroeconomic and social policies for equitable growth*, Zed Books, London.

Miah, M.R. and Tracy, M.B. (2001) The Institutional Approach to Social Development, *Social Development Issues*, 23, 1, pp. 58–64.

Midgley, J. (1995) *Social Development: The development perspective in social welfare*, Sage Publications, Thousand Oaks, CA.

Midgley, J. (2003) Social Development: The intellectual heritage, *Journal of International Development*, 15, pp. 831–844.

Midgley, J., Hall, A., Hardiman, M. and Narine, D. (1986) *Community Participation, Social Development and the State*, Methuen, New York.

Milanovic, B. (1999) True World Income Distribution, 1988–1993: First calculation based on household surveys alone, World Bank, Washington DC.

Miraftab, F. (2004) Public-Private Partnership: The trojan horse of neoliberal development, *Journal of Planning Education and Research*, 24, pp. 89–101.

Mosse, D. (1998) Process-oriented Approaches to Development Practice and Social Research. In *Development as Process: Concepts and methods for working with complexity*, edited by David Mosse, John Farrington and Alan Rew, Routledge, London.

Mosse, D. (2005) *Cultivating Development: An ethnography of aid policy and practice*, Pluto Press, London.

Mumford, E. (1983) *Designing Human Systems*, Manchester Business School, Manchester.

Myrdal, G. (1958) *Value in Social Theory*, Routledge, London.

Narayan, D., Patel, R., Schafft, K., Rademacher, A. and Koch-Schulte, S. (2000) *Voices of the Poor: Can anyone hear us?* Oxford University Press for the World Bank, Oxford.

Nissanke, M. and Thorbecke, E. (eds) (2007) *The Impact of Globalization on the World's Poor: Transmission mechanisms*, Palgrave Macmillan, Hants.

Noir, C. and Walsham, G. (2007) The Great Legitimizer: ICT as myth and ceremony in the Indian healthcare sector, *Information Technology and People,* 20, 4, pp. 313–334.

ODI. (1999) What Can We Do With A Rights-Based Approach To Development? *ODI Briefing Paper* 1999 (3), Overseas Development Institute, London.

Ojo, T. (2004) Old Paradigm and Information & Communication Technologies for Development Agenda in Africa: Modernisation as Context, *Journal of Information Technology Impact,* 4, 3, pp. 139–150.

Opoku-Mensah, A. and Salih, M. (eds) (2007) *African E-Markets: Information and economic development in Africa,* International Books, Utrecht.

Parayil, G. (2005) The Digital Divide and Increasing Returns: Contradictions of informational capitalism, *The Information Society,* 21, 1, pp. 41–51.

Prahalad, C.K. (2005) *The Fortune at the Bottom of the Pyramid: Eradicating poverty through profits,* Wharton School Publishing, NJ.

Rao, V. and Walton, M. (2004) Culture and Public Action: Relationality, Equality of Agency and Development. In *Culture and Public Action,* edited by V. Rao and M. Walton, Stanford University Press, Stanford, CA.

Ravallion, M. (2004) Pro-poor Growth: A primer, World Bank Policy Research Working Paper 3242, World Bank, Washington DC.

Ravallion, M. (2007) Looking Beyond Averages in the Trade and Poverty Debate. In *The Impact of Globalization on the World's Poor: Transmission mechanisms,* edited by M. Nissanke and E. Thorbecke, Palgrave Macmillan, Hants, pp. 118–145.

Ray, D. and Mookherjee, D. (2000) What's New in Development Economics? In *A Reader in Development Economics,* edited by D. Ray and D. Mookherjee, Blackwell, London.

Rodrik, D. (2004) Rethinking Growth Policies in the Developing World, Luca d'Agliano Lecture in Development Economics, October 2004.

Rodrik, D. (2007) A New Paradigm in Development Economics? Dani Rodrik's weblog – Unconventional thoughts on economic development and globalization. Available at http://rodrik.typepad.com/dani_rodriks_weblog/2008/02/a-new-paradigm.html

Rojas-Suarez, L. (2008) U.S. Financial Crisis Will Mean Slower Growth, Rising Inequality in Developing World, Center for Global Development, Posted on 22 September 2008. Available at http://blogs.cgdev.org/globaldevelopment/2008/09/us_financial_crisis_will_mean.php

Rostow, W.W. (1960) *The Stages of Economic Growth: A non-communist manifesto,* Cambridge University Press, Cambridge.

Sachs, J. (2005) *The End of Poverty: How can we make it happen in our lifetime,* Penguin Books, London.

Sachs, J. (2008) Seven Questions: Jeffrey Sachs, Foreign Policy Portal. Available at http://www.foreignpolicy.com/story/cms.php?story_id=4517

Schifferes, S. (2008) Slowdown 'To Hit Poor Countries'. BBC News Economics Reporter, Story from the BBC News 04/09/2008. Available at http://news.bbc.co.uk.go/pr/fr/-/1/hi/business/7595626.stm

Schramm, W. (1964) *Mass Media and National Development,* Stanford University Press, Stanford, CA.

Schumacher, E.F. (1973) *Small Is Beautiful: A study of economics as if people mattered,* Sphere Books Ltd. Reading, MA.

Seers, D. and Joy, L. (1971) (eds.) *Development in a Divided World,* Penguin, Harmondsworth.

Sen, A. (1983) Poverty and Famines: An essay on entitlement and deprivation. In *The Amartya Sen and Jean Dreze Omnibus,* Oxford University Press, New Delhi.

Sen, A. (1999) *Development as Freedom,* Knopf, New York.

Sen, A. (2001) What Is Development About? In *Frontiers of Development Economics: The future in perspective,* edited by Gerald M. Meier and Joseph E. Stiglitz, The International Bank for Reconstruction and Development, Washington DC, pp. 506–513.

Shamsul Haque, M. (2000) Significance of Accountability under the New Approach to Public Governance, *International Review of Administrative Science,* 66, pp. 599–617.

Sharp, J. and Briggs, J. (2006) Postcolonialism and Development: New dialogues? *The Geographical Journal,* 172, 1, pp. 6–9.

Shirky, C. (2008) *Here Comes Everybody: The power of organizing without organizations,* The Penguin Press, New York.

De Soto, H. (1989) *The Other Path: The invisible revolution in the third world,* Harper and Row, New York.

Stiglitz, J.E. (2002) *Globalization and Its Discontents,* Norton, New York.

Stoesz, D. (2000) *Poverty of Imagination: Bootstraps capitalism, sequel to welfare reform,* University of Wisconsin Press, Madison, WI.

Streeten, P., Burki, S.J., Ul Haq, M., Hicks, N. and Stewart, F. (1981) *First Things First: Meeting basic needs in developing countries,* Oxford University Press, New York.

Tendler, J. (2005) Why Social Policy Is Confined to a Residual Category of Safety Nets and What to Do about it. In *Social Policy in a Development Context,* edited by Thandika Mkandawire, pp. 119–143, Palgrave Macmillan, Hants.

Thompson, M. (2004) Discourse, 'Development' and the 'Digital Divide': ICT and the World Bank, *Review of African Political Economy,* 31, 99, pp. 103–123.

Thompson, M. (2008) ICT and Development Studies: Towards development 2.0, *Journal of International Development,* 20, pp. 821–835.

Toye, J. (1995) The New Institutional Economics and its Implications for Development Theory. In *The New Institutional Economics and Third World Development,* edited by J. Harriss, J. Hunter and C.M. Lewis, Routledge, London, pp. 48–70.

UN. (1971) Social Policy and Planning in National Development, *International Social Development Review,* 3, pp. 4–15.

UN. (1996) Report of the World Summit for Social Development, Copenhagen 6–12 March 1995, United Nations, New York.

UN. (2001) Making New Technologies Work for Human Development, United Nations Development Programme, Oxford University Press, Oxford.

UN Millennium Project (2006) Millennium Project. Available at www.unmillenni umproject.org

Unwin, T. (2007) No End to Poverty, *Journal of Development Studies,* 43, 5, pp. 929–953.

Wade, R. (2002) Bridging the Digital Divide: New route to development or new forms of dependency, *Global Governance,* 8, pp. 443–466.

Wade, R. (2004a) Is Globalization Reducing Poverty and Inequality? *World Development,* 32, 4, pp. 567–589.

Wade, R. (2004b) *Governing the Market,* Princeton University Press, Oxford.

Webster, A. (1984) *Introduction to the Sociology of Development,* Macmillan, Hants.

Westrup, C., Al Jaghoub, S., El Sayed, H. and Liu, W. (2003) Taking Culture Seriously: ICTs, culture and development. In *The Digital Challenge: Information technology in the development context,* edited by S. Krishna and S. Madon, Ashgate, Aldershot, Hants.

Wilson, E.J. (2004) *The Information Revolution and Developing Countries,* MIT Press, Cambridge, MA.

Wilson, G. and Heeks, R. (2001) Technology, Poverty and Development. In *Poverty and Development – Into the 21st Century,* edited by Tim Allen and Alan Thomas, Oxford University Press, Oxford.

World Bank (1981) Accelerated Development in Sub-Saharan Africa, Washington DC.
World Bank (1991) World Development Report, 1991: The challenge of development, World Bank, Washington DC.
World Bank (2001) World Development Report 2000/2001: Attacking poverty, World Bank, Washington DC.
World Bank (2002) Global Economic Prospects and the Developing Countries 2002: Making trade work for the world's poor, World Bank, Washington DC.
Zheng, Y. (2009) Different Spaces for e-Development: What can we learn from the capability approach? *Information Technology for Development,* 15, 2, pp. 66–83.

3
Linking Governance and Development

This chapter reviews the way in which the linkage between governance and development has been conceptualised. This linkage is important because it ultimately affects the implementation of development policies. According to current orthodoxy, 'good governance' is one of the key requirements for the achievement of democratic development. This perspective on governance consists of a bureaucratic and a political element. The bureaucratic element refers to simplifying procedures and work flow within the administration through the adoption of management techniques and procedures. The political element refers to promoting democratic development through the inclusion of non-state actors such as the private sector and NGOs. Taking a critical stance, it is argued that the current good governance agenda fails to conceptualise the mutual connectedness between these two elements. Ultimately, this chapter shows that it is the interplay of local administrative, political and social systems that leads to democratic governance.

There is widespread agreement in the policy literature that governance is fundamental to development (DFID, 2006; ODI, 2006). The first public appearance of the concept of good governance was in a 1989 World Bank report on Africa which argued that 'underlying the litany of Africa's development problems is a crisis of governance' (World Bank, 1989). This crisis was used by the Bank to explain why its policies of structural adjustment and economic liberalisation, which it had long been urging African governments to adopt, were not working. The tentative answer was that although the programmes and projects that the Bank had helped to finance were technically sound, the required administrative and government frameworks were not in place because of corruption, secrecy in policy-making, lack of accountability, disregard for the law, lack of concern for the private sector and political exploitation of the public sector. The focus on governance was the World Bank's answer to this dilemma as articulated in its 1992 paper 'Governance and Development', and this response set the scene for a new orthodoxy in development thinking.

One of the most important theoretical points implied by structural adjustment was the positive correlation between civil society action and good governance outcomes. It was advocated that the private sector and civil society organisations could make a more significant contribution to development than the state bureaucracy on its own (Jeffries, 1993). Therefore, it was decided that governance reform would be directed at freeing up state-controlled resources that could be better used and managed by other institutions. The overarching goal was to equip these institutions, and through them, the country as a whole, with the tools and capacity to manage their own development process and to ultimately become self-reliant. Officially, the Bank had a bureaucratic, rather than a political, agenda following on from the 1980s New Public Management (NPM) strategy of administrative simplification based on disaggregation, competition and an entrepreneurial culture (Corbridge *et al.*, 2005; Hyden and Court, 2002). Good governance aimed to further improve the bureaucratic competence and accountability of the public sector through a strategy that emphasised the need for an open and integrated public service (Dunleavy *et al.*, 2005; Manning, 2001).

By the 1990s, this largely administrative governance agenda was extended to a political mandate although under the guise of terms such as 'institutional change' and 'good governance' (Hewitt de Alcantara, 1998; Moore, 2006). This new orthodoxy of the international development community, most notably international financial institutions and bilateral donors, challenged conventional notions of state sovereignty by threatening to withhold aid to countries that limited freedom of expression and association unless they could show commitment to altering their prevailing political set-up. Facilitated by the end of the Cold War, this led to a particular concern for multi-party politics and democratisation in Sub-Saharan Africa and ex-USSR nations. In Latin America and South Asia, while some funding was tied to ideological considerations such as womens' right, attention became focused more on the institutions of democracy and on the need to strengthen civic associations (Hewitt de Alcantara, 1998). Along with policies that were put forward to privatise or at least regulate some parts of the economy, measures were proposed to transfer some of the powers of the central government to local government institutions and NGOs.

Democracy came to be seen as the route to development because it was assumed to provide a more conducive environment for market-led economic development carrying the potential for a more efficient, accountable and hence less corrupt government (Moore, 2006). During the modernisation era, evidence had accumulated to suggest an associated trajectory between economic development and democracy both in developed and developing countries. According to this, democracy was perceived a function of economic development, not a prerequisite of it (Cutright, 1963; Lipset, 1960). But the experience of rapid economic development in non-democratic societies made the relationship between the two unclear. Indeed, it was argued that premature introduction of democracy could actually hamper development in its early stages when there is a greater need for effective state action for capital accumulation to stimulate infrastructure and investment (Bhagwati, 1966; Zakaria, 1994). Some alternative viewpoints surfaced at the time to suggest that the relationship between economic development and democracy was not a simple one (Huntington, 1965) but these were overshadowed by the establishment of a comprehensive economic and political strategy by the main western bilateral aid donors according to which development was to be promoted best by a market-friendly state presiding over a predominantly capitalist economy operating within a liberal democratic political system. In practice, evidence showed how donors tended to be less concerned with other components of good governance and more concerned with the incidence of market-unfriendly policies in recipient countries (Aubut, 2004). This common underlying shape of the concept of good governance as having both an economic and political mandate has come to be articulated by all the major western governments, particularly the British, French, German, US and Nordic governments supported by the main international and regional development institutions (IDS, 1993).

The major criticism lodged against current governance reform activity is that it entirely ignores the fact that such reform is not simply available to order but that it requires a particular type of environment to establish and sustain it (Heeks and Kenny, 2002; Leftwich, 2000; Rodrik, 2008). Indeed, most developing countries found themselves under pressure to create conditions that took decades, even centuries, to achieve in developed countries (Leftwich, 1993, 2000; Grindle, 2004). Yet this criticism has had very little impact on operational practices despite evidence showing that developing countries may well require the establishment of governance arrangements that are different from those prevailing in developed countries – for example, economic institutions that privilege investment rather than innovation to encourage incumbent firms (Acemoglu *et al.*, 2006). The primary role of public service institutions in terms of supporting the country's development priorities was overshadowed by measuring public sector performance in terms of cross-country comparisons and benchmarking of efficiency in service provision.

A central argument of this book is to challenge the 'good governance' prescriptions found in contemporary development policy discourse. These prescriptions have resulted in the measurement of reform interventions in terms of static outcome parameters focused on efficiency and cost-reduction rather than on improving living conditions of communities in the developing world. Most accounts of governance reform remain focused on the effects of new forms of partnerships and relations on administering public sector programmes, rather than on whether these new arrangements actually lead to gains in social welfare (Bang, 2003; Daly, 2003; Rose, 1996; Scott, 1998).

The growing body of critical literature in the fields of public policy, social science and international political economy provides a useful starting point of departure for an alternative conceptualisation of governance. A common theme in this literature is that governance is a process of interaction between state and society. This view of governance draws strength from several social theories that focus on the interplay in society between action (studied by identifying the intentions of actors) and structure (studied by identifying the environment within which action takes place) and finds expression in the work of sociology of governance scholars. Here, governance implies a complex set of institutions and actors from the public, private and voluntary sector with no single actor having the knowledge or resources to tackle problems on their own (Kjaer, 2004; Kooiman, 2003; Rhodes, 1996, 1997). Interactions between these actors are perceived as necessarily complex because each actor or entity has a different historical legacy of interests and as a result, all kinds of tensions and conflicts surface during the process of governance reform. Hyden *et al*. (2004) use this broad approach to study how interactions between players are constituted and managed over time in six different arenas of governance (1) civil society – to shape the way citizens become aware of and raise issues in public (2) political society – to shape the way issues are combined into policy by political institutions (3) government – to shape the way policies are made by government institutions (4) bureaucracy – to shape the way policies are administered and implemented by public authorities (5) economic systems – to shape the way state and market interact to promote development (6) judicial system – to shape the setting for resolution of disputes and conflicts.

A second theme identified in critical governance literature relates to the roll back of the state implicit in policy manifesto following the Washington Consensus. From the perspective of macro-economic policy in developed countries, several crucial strategic roles of the state have been identified for coordinating the plurality of institutional arrangements in economic policy-making (Gray, 1995; Haggard, 1990; Jessop, 1998, 2002; Stoker, 1998). In the context of developing countries, several writers have questioned the relevance of this policy prescription. Stiglitz (2002) draws on examples of countries such as China, Malaysia and Poland whose governments have succeeded in changing towards free market regimes by a careful sequencing of the opening of the economy to the building of necessary institutions and home-grown policies sensitive to the specific needs and concerns of the country. Jayal and Pai (2001) argue similarly that the state remains central in the international sphere to preserve the country's national sovereignty and autonomy in global affairs while at the same time selectively absorbing the benefits of the expanding global market. Wade (1990) presents evidence from East and South East Asian countries which have managed to achieve average annual growth rates of more than 4% between 1965 and 1997 and where governments have had a more prominent interventionist role. In these countries, government has also played a significant role in fostering high-tech industries and technological innovation across industries.

Other writers have critiqued the growth of privatisation in the provision of basic social services as a result of the lack of government resources, low-quality public capacity and pressure to liberalise the economy (Mehrotra and Delamonica, 2005). The position taken by the World Bank (World Bank, 2004) and other international agencies has been to expand the use of market mechanisms such as insurance and the practice of users paying (at least a proportion) for welfare provision. Drawing on historical evidence from both developed and developing countries, Mehrotra and Delamonica (2005) argue that while financial sustainability and consumer choice may improve as a result of privatisation of basic social services, the implications for consumer welfare are ambiguous. A strategic role for the state is also identified in terms of creating synergy among interventions in various social sectors given that these interventions complement each other. In order to uphold ethical and normative aspects of democratic governance, the state has an obligation to promote equitable development amidst the diversity of interests, preferences, values and ideas involved in the development process (de Gay, 2005; Goodsell, 2005; Kallinikos, 2006; Leftwich, 2000; Olsen, 2005). The state bears a responsibility to its citizens to contest the nature and direction of economic development in order to include programmes of economic and social empowerment to bring the marginalised more fully into productive economic activity and to help them integrate into society (de Gay, 2005; Goodsell, 2006; Olsen, 2005). For example, in a developing-country context, this implies a responsibility for the state in liberating the poor, especially the landless rural poor from the continued domination of traditional landed elites which may include introducing land reforms, extending property rights, providing training, creating jobs and mobilising credit. This view is endorsed by other scholars who have studied the influences of state legislation on the increasing inclusion of rural poor women in social and economic activities in Bangladesh and South Korea (Moon, 2002; Paul, 1992).

A third and related critical issue identified in governance literature, particularly in the context of developing countries, relates to the notion of accountability and its meaning (Goetz and Jenkins, 2005; Moore, 1993). The concept is a broad one and often discussed together with transparency. In order to be held accountable, public sector agencies need to make 'transparent' to citizens information about their performance (Kaufmann and Bellver, 2005; Moore, 2006). If government performance with respect to welfare provision is satisfactory, this increases the level of trust and the overall legitimacy of government operations in the eyes of citizens (Hyden *et al.*, 2004; Vigoda and Yuval, 2003).

Transparency in the use of public funds coincides with the widespread endorsement by international agencies to reduce corruption (Lancaster in Moore, 2006). The 1992 World Bank Governance and Development Report emphasised that increased transparency of information would help markets function more efficiently by reducing corrupt practices. International organisations have taken the lead in publishing cross country data on corruption since the mid 1980s emphasising its magnitude and negative impact on economic growth (Lipset and Lenz, 2001). Apart from the need for transparency in operations, mechanisms need to exist to actually hold public sector agencies accountable to the public. This requires the ability of the judicial system to enforce legal and constitutional rights – something that is often lacking in many developing countries. For example, drawing on research carried out by the Development Research Centre on Citizenship, Participation and Accountability, Newell and Wheeler (2006) found that in South Africa, the Constitution gives people the right to water, but the government has been unable to fulfil this right in practice. In discussing accountability biases, Goetz and Jenkins (2005) point to the distinction between de jure and de facto accountability – that is, who one is accountable to according to law or accepted procedures which corresponds to common usage of democratic accountability, and who one is accountable to because of their power to impose sanctions. In many developing countries, governments are de facto more accountable to external donors rather than domestic institutions like parliament since the withdrawal of international grants and loans or the threat of doing so if certain policy actions are not taken constitute a serious sanction.

The issue of democratic accountability raised by critical governance scholars is an important one because it provides a way of deepening our understanding of the interplay between state and society. Evidence suggests that the bureaucracy plays an important role in ensuring that effective accountability mechanisms exist for democratic development, despite the general neo-liberal distrust of public bureaucracies (Moore, 1993; Evans and Rauch 1999; Goodsell, 2005). Merit-based bureaucracy has been shown to foster economic growth in developing countries and promote poverty reduction (Evans and Rauch, 1999; Henderson *et al.*, 2007; Kaufmann *et al.*, 2003). Hyden *et al.* (2004) present evidence from 16 developing countries to reveal a strong correlation between effective accountability mechanisms and an effective bureaucracy. However, to establish an effective bureaucracy requires capacity among administrators not only in terms of staffing levels, technical and managerial skills for budgeting, planning, monitoring and evaluation (UN, 2005) but also in terms of adaptation and learning through experimentation (Chambers, 2005). The strengthening of administrative capacity implies providing not just central government agencies but local authorities with political and financial resources to exercise democratic accountability effectively. A well-working bureaucracy needs an adaptive and responsive local administration which has the freedom to exercise discretion and flexibility to direct funds according to local priorities (Bovens and Zouridis, 2002; Hyden *et al.*, 2004; Murray, 1993; Rondinelli, 1993). Bovens and Zouridis found that relations between the state and citizens worsened when there was a decrease in the level of flexibility available for street-level bureaucrats when trying to solve problems related to the provision of services. In Mozambique, committed local authorities used discretion to double health staff and focused on outreach improving vaccination coverage by 8% (Mehrotra, 2006).

Administrative capacity is deficient in most developing countries due to constant demands made on staff not only in terms of time and effort in preparing routine reports but also in terms of motivational cost (Chambers, 2005; McCourt, 2006). The demoralisation of extension staff so often found in developing countries can be attributed to the heavy burden placed on them due to the flood of instructions and poorly articulated demands for information coming from higher levels of the bureaucracy. This lack of administrative capacity has affected decentralisation efforts over the past few decades. The change in development objectives from the pursuit of economic growth to a strategy of growth with equity in the 1970s prompted many developing countries to make serious efforts towards decentralising their development planning and management functions to the sub-national areas in their countries (APDC, 1987; Mathur, 1983; Rondinelli, 1981, 1993). Decentralisation[1] was seen as a means of improving the way plans are prepared and implemented by providing more accurate and detailed information about local needs and conditions and encouraging coordination between the various agencies involved in planning and implementing programmes (Dasgupta, 1989). Experiences with decentralisation policies during this period were mixed with some success stories, for example in Kenya, Tanzania and Papua New Guinea, but many failures (Conyers and Hills, 1984). A renewed policy thrust towards political decentralisation occurred in the 1990s in many developing countries including India, Indonesia, the Philippines and countries in Latin America. In general, with all these efforts, while local administrative organisations were given broad powers in some countries to perform development planning and management functions, adequate resources to carry them out were often withheld with a debate in the literature as to whether this was due to lack of political will from higher echelons or due to poor management capacity at local level (Conyers, 2007; Shams *et al.*, 1987). Notwithstanding these experiences, the decentralisation agenda continues to circulate widely in most developing countries with approval not just from Bretton Woods institutions but also from the world's leading consulting companies in international development such as Accenture.

A deeper understanding of the nature of democratic governance involves blurring the boundaries between the bureaucratic and political elements of governance. In effect, this translates to blurring the boundaries between state and society. Accountability of local government to citizens does not just concern formal administrative or political sanctions. Decentralisation has also been affected by the local cultural norms and systems that shape day-to-day practice in a locality (Craig and Porter, 2006; Luckham *et al.*, 2000; Manor, 1999; Shoib and Jones, 2003). Craig and Porter's study in Pakistan found that while local government had been assigned some rights to raise revenue, the taxes assigned to them were never likely to match their expenditure requirements. Instead, older and more established cultural factors such as allegiance to senior bureaucrats allowed top-down alignment to dominate. As a result, most of the development budget remained controlled from above through vertical programmes undermining local government's sovereignty.

When there are major inequalities at the village level, as in many Asian and Latin American countries, decentralisation of decision-making powers has reinforced existing power structures and has done little to meet the basic needs of the population. Therefore, in many developing countries such as Bangladesh, Cote d'Ivoire, Ghana, Kenya, Mexico, Nigeria, Uganda and Papua New Guinea, traditional leaders have retained control, opposing power to be given to local government officers (UNDP, 2003; Zuckerman, 1989). In such cases, decentralised governance has been reduced to a largely technical/managerial activity rather than providing the local bureaucracy with sufficient power to nurture local political activity needed for democratic development (Ferguson, 1994; Harriss, 2002).

As the good governance policy mandate gained momentum, efforts aimed at strengthening local administrative capacity were increasingly sidelined in favour of a discourse that revolved around social capital formation and a rich and vibrant civil society (Landell-Mills, 1992). Participation in voluntary local associations would result in a vibrant civil society which would act as a vital check on the activities of the state and lead to improved service delivery (Held, 1987; Narayan, 1999). The term 'social capital', which had hardly received a mention in development discourse earlier, gained prominence during the latter half of the 1990s in the social sciences, particularly in development studies, and came to be considered as 'the missing link' in development (Schuurman, 2003; World Bank, 1998). Two prominent social capital scholars, Bourdieu and Coleman, emphasised different aspects of social capital theory. Bourdieu's interest was in the social relations between different classes, strata and groups in society which affected their access to resources and which perpetuated class differentiation (Bourdieu, 1985). Coleman focused less on relations between classes and more on resources which can be obtained due to participation in voluntary associations (Coleman, 1990). While in both cases social capital was not seen as a characteristic of society as a whole, Coleman's interpretation of the term was taken forward and popularised in development circles by extending the concept as an important development goal for entire societies. Robert Putnam's influential work aimed to demonstrate that the differences both in government performance and in levels of economic development between regions of Italy can best be explained by variations in civic engagement measured by political participation, newspaper readership and participation in voluntary associations. Later on in his work, social capital was more of less associated with voluntary association affiliation and the lack of social capital was identified as responsible for a wide range of problems such as failing public education and security in the US as well as failure of cooperative agricultural arrangements in developing countries (Putnam, 1993, 2000). The concepts of participation, civil society and social capital appeared deceptively attractive implying a deep respect for the needs and aspirations of common people and was heavily promoted by the World Bank in the 1990s. This policy direction showed consistency with the neoliberal agenda of reducing the role of the state, particularly so as to make possible large cuts in public expenditure. At the same time, it offered the Bank a way out from the crisis of legitimacy it was facing at the time by demonstrating a move away from an exclusively economic agenda (Bayliss and Fine, 2007; Bebbington *et al.*, 2004; Fine, 2003, 2007; Schuurman, 2003).

However, the World Bank's enthusiasm for 'social capital' as a way of promoting development soon generated criticism. As Craig and Porter (2006) argue, the power of citizens' voice is routinely overstated to drive the political economy in developing countries. The concept is discussed almost as if it exists in a vacuum. However, the existence of civil society and social capital presupposes an institutional framework which is put in place through the agency of the state aimed at impartiality of treatment and equality of individuals as citizens before the law. It is when people generally believe in the legitimacy and influence of these institutions that civil society flourishes (Bebbington, 2007; Fine, 2001; Putnam, 2000; Schuurman, 2003).[2] While civil society agencies do have important roles to play in delivering services and raising voices, this can have the effect of diluting the accountability of state agencies to citizens in terms of important social regulatory issues such as access to land and labour rights. Harriss' (2001) study of community development in Kerala shows how local inequalities were addressed through both local state involvement (e.g., land reforms) and through the nurturing of political processes. Such wider accountability in key economic sectors requires a medium-term financial and political commitment from the government. Tendler's (1997) study in Northeast Brazil – a state with the poorest record of human development in the country – shows a similar pattern. In this case, central government strengthened local government by giving publicity to the efforts of local government employees rewarding their good performance and denigrating complaints they received from the public.

The notion of social capital also presupposes that this resource on its own can lead to betterment in the lives of community members. Little explanation has been given as to how and why interpersonal trust between members of one group (bonding ties) can be translated into generalised and societal trust across various groups in a community (bridging ties) (Cleaver, 2005; Harriss, 2001). Many scholars brought evidence to show situations where there may be a high degree of trust (bonding ties) but groups could be hostile to each other (lack of bridging ties) (Fine, 2001; Harriss, 2001; Narayan, 1999; Portes, 1998; Pretty, 2003; Putnam, 2000; Schuller *et al.*, 2000). Evidence suggests that even in cases where communities have a lot of mutuality and reciprocity, this resource needs to be operationalised through various intermediaries such as local government agents, politicians, private sector players and other community mediators. The role of the intermediary in connecting citizens with government in the context of developing countries is particularly relevant. Few people in developing countries approach figures of authority as individual citizens aware of their rights. Their links to government are as members of named populations (e.g., tribals, slum dwellers, drought-prone farmers) via the mediating action of a political boss or local government intermediary. In some cases, for example, where ethnic conflicts exist and where access to government representation is difficult, this has created space for the establishment of alternative or competing governance structures such as the mafia or faith groups (Bardhan, 1997). Moore and Putzel (1999) highlight the skills and competences that local politicians can bring to bear on development problems including the ability to represent anti-poverty measures as being in the wider public interest or creating pressure to exercise an exit option from the development project when they believe energies are better spent elsewhere.

The role of the intermediary is also important to convert social capital to resources for the local community. Krishna (2002) coined the term 'active social capital' to refer to the process whereby networking between community members only becomes useful when activated and made productive through the intervention of capable agents as the practical influence of poorly literate, disorganised citizens over local politicians is often weak. These mediators are typically local government agents who build up social relationships with the community (Evans, 1996; Fuller and Harriss, 2001). Alliances with state reformists and the cultural norms and loyalties that build up around them can sometimes offer resources to popular organisations. For example, in Lam's (1994) analysis of Nepal, farmers needed inputs that they could not supply themselves. The state played an important role in organising inputs and providing intangible collective goods in the form of legal recognition of local farmer groups. In discussing the role of the state in promoting social capital formation and civil society activity in East Asian countries in the 1960s and 1970s, Evans (1996) and Weiss (1998) noted how public sector institutions maintained strong coordination with societal actors to tap sources of local intelligence. In other cases, village headmen or other sections of the village 'elite' may be better able to influence service delivery by having privileged access to major public works contracts (Roy, 2008). However, cultural norms dictate that these elites are often obliged to share out their gains with government officials and politicians and that such situations do not help to expand the political space available to poor people. A more recent form of mediator has been identified as the telecentre operator – normally relatively younger, better educated and informed about access to state and market agencies than traditional mediators (Keniston and Kumar, 2003).

Literature suggests, then, that the bureaucratic and political elements of governance are intimately linked through a dialectic between central government, state government, local administration, political bodies, civil society organisations and citizens (Harriss, 2001; Mehrotra, 2006; White, 2006). When creating local authorities, central government needs to ensure sufficient resources and to create institutional structures to ensure the necessary physical and social space to allow the voice of citizenry to emerge and be heard by local authorities (Conyers, 2007; Mohmand and Cheema, 2007; Robinson, 2007; Turner and Hulme, 1997; UNDP, 2003). Similarly, civil society activism needs to be channelled through the mediation of local state and political representatives for social welfare gains to accrue to community members bringing the government back into the picture as an important actor in promoting democratic governance.[3] Such complex relations are nurtured over time within particular contexts and cannot be imposed by development institutions that may attempt to engineer 'artificial networks' within communities (Portes and Landolt, 2000; Pretty, 2003).[4] Understanding of the complex relations that exist between central government, local government and civil society can be enhanced through the recent work of sociology of development scholars (Cooke and Kothari, 2001; Corbridge *et al.*, 2005; Harriss, 2001, 2002; Hyden, 1997; Sivaramakrishnan, 1995; Smith and Kulynych, 2002; World Bank, 2004). In a fascinating book based on fieldwork conducted in eastern India, Corbridge *et al.* describe how people's perception of the 'state' is shaped by a series of encounters at the local level. The authors investigate the income support, empowerment and protective functions of the state in three states of Bihar, Jharkhand and West Bengal. The focus was on the Employment Assurance Scheme, primary education and legal struggles and on how different groups of rural society encountered the state in these arenas. One of the guiding premises of the book is that the state still matters greatly to people in rural India – as corroborated by other scholars (Alsop and Kurey, 2005). For example, a tribal woman in rural India is more likely to turn to a local politician or government official for assistance in obtaining an entitlement such as a ration card or pension, or for employment or to register a death. The bridge between government and the public is built through state and political actors – that is, the loose community of recognised political parties and their operatives, local political brokers and councillors, and lower-level public servants who depend on favours of politicians.

Some scholars have, for analytical purposes, separated democratic govern-ance into two basic dimensions. First, the constitutionally defined realm of formal political, administrative and legal entities which set the institutional framework of a democratic regime. Second, the formal and informal organisa-tions and channels which connect politicians, officials and agencies with civil society (Crisp, 2000; Houtzager *et al.*, 2008). Crisp calls these the exterior and interior worlds of democratic politics. His research in Venezuela shows that the interior arena is particularly important in societies in which socio-economic resources are highly unequal since this is the cultural context within which powerful elites can interact with their political and government counterparts and influence the policy process. Other writers refer to this interior world in terms of the 'deep politics' of society (Bang, 2003; Daly, 2003; Fuller and Harriss, 2001; Mehrotra, 2006; Osella and Osella, 2000, 1996; Roy, 2008). In their study in Kerala, Osella and Osella focus on the annual festival of Onam in Kerala, to show how personalised relations and patronage connect people and the state through a combination of mediated relationships and shared cultural prac-tices. The study focuses on a rural panchayat in south Kerala characterised by a small and declining elite, a rapidly expanding middle class, and a substantial and increasingly impoverished working class, many of whom work as casual labourers. The festival which signifies the Malayali New Year and falls between mid-August and mid-September is celebrated by Hindus and non-Hindus as a time when the unity of the family, kinship ties and patron-client relationships are particularly emphasised with exchanges of gifts between them. The festival is celebrated by government sponsored cultural and sporting events. Onam serves as an occasion to surface many social and economic tensions. It is a time when collective moral values get renewed and the perceived immorality of current day life gets criticised. Recent targets of annual reprimands in the press and in speeches by politicians and state officials during the Onam season are the emerging middle classes representing a corrupt neo-colonial influence on traditional culture and moral values. The narrative by Osella and Osella reminds us that the state is ultimately composed of people who reconstitute their relationships as patrons (for example, rich landowners or politicians) and clients (for example, casual labourers or lower-caste villagers). Mehrotra (2006) terms this type of democratic governance as 'deep democratic decentralisation' arguing, along with others (Brett, 2003; Slater and Watson, 1989), that this occurs only when local government actively enables the articulation of 'voice' by the local community.[5]

To summarise this chapter, the good governance agenda prescribes vari-ous parameters for developing countries as part of international development assistance including efficiency, accountability and democratisation. Efforts have been made to improve bureaucratic performance by streamlining the role of government and introducing new systems of accountability. At the same time, the policy thrust has been towards decentralised planning through participation of citizen groups and civil society bodies. The scope of this chapter has been to show that the bureaucratic and political elements of good governance are mutually reinforcing and defined by the cultural norms in which they are embedded. On the one hand, an effective bureaucracy needs to nurture local political processes to ensure that development interventions remain relevant. On the other hand, civil society activism needs to be channelled through local state and political representatives for citizens' deliberations about their development priorities to lead to tangible outcome. Ordinary people in rural parts of the developing world routinely access services through the mediation of local state and political representatives. However, as Chatterjee (2004) reminds us, these players are precisely the ones whose dissolution is called for under the good governance agenda.

Governance perspective adopted in this book

From the literature review on governance and development, three key issues are identified which are important to keep in mind.

First, the agenda of good governance is a policy directive launched by international development agencies to support their policies of economic and political liberalisation. There are two main elements to this agenda – a bureaucratic and a political element. The bureaucratic element focuses on administrative simplification through decentralisation. In recent years, this has been coupled with the introduction of managerialist influences within development policy through techniques such as capacity-building, integration and increased usage of ICTs. Its political element focuses on strengthening systems of democratisation in developing countries by making government information transparent and by promoting accountability mechanisms to enable citizens to hold government responsible for the provision of public services and welfare.

Second, while the good governance agenda call for a reduction in the role of the state, the critical governance literature argues that the state remains a crucial player in regulating the institutional environment and in upholding democratic values – a viewpoint reinforced by Stiglitz (2008) in his remarks about the consequences of the economic downturn for developing countries. The state plays an important role in the execution of development programmes by setting the criteria against which we hold public officials accountable, sometimes creating a bias towards particular policy prescriptions. For example, if the performance of a government programme is measured by the number of self-help groups formed, this may suggest a policy move to encourage further group formation even though it offers no guarantee that the most vulnerable community members will necessarily be included. At the local level, administrators and politicians play a crucial role in providing legitimacy of public service delivery, nurturing community mobilisation and participation, and securing resources for the achievement of development priorities.

Third, the critical governance literature attempts to conceptualise the linkage between its bureaucratic and political elements. This conceptualisation is represented in terms of interactions between various players. Rather than viewing decentralisation as a unique administrative concept, it is accepted that local capacity to plan and implement programmes depends on the interface between local government and citizens. Similarly, rather than viewing democratisation as a concept related uniquely to community mobilisation, it is accepted that there is a vital role to be played by local government in nurturing this mobilisation. Seen in this way, the achievement of democratic governance structures involves understanding both the formal and informal context and processes of change in the local administrative, political and social systems. These interactions can become the site for political struggle between individuals and groups and the site for intermediation and resolution of conflicts.

The next chapter brings together key issues from the critical review of the development and governance literature to present a framework for the study of e-governance for development.

Glossary

Good governance – a form of governance that embodies certain ideals including participation, transparency, accountability, responsiveness, efficiency, equity and consensus-orientation

New Public Management – a management philosophy used by governments in the 1980s to modernise the public sector

Street-level bureaucrats – refers to a public agency employee who interfaces with the public

References

Acemoglu, D., Aghion, P. and Zilibotti, F. (2006) Distance to Frontier, Selection and Economic Growth, *Journal of the European Economic Association*, 4, March, pp. 37–74.

Alsop, R. and Kurey, B. (2005) *Local Organizations in Decentralized Development: Their functions and performance in India*, World Bank, Washington DC.

APDC. (1987) *Building from Below: Local initiatives for decentralised development in Asia and Pacific*, Asian and Pacific Development Centre, Kuala Lumpur, Malaysia.

Aubut, J. (2004) The Good Governance Agenda: Who wins and who loses – some empirical evidence for 2001. Development Studies Institute Working Paper No. 04–48, London School of Economics and Political Science.

Bang, H.P. (2003) Governance as Political Communication. In *Governance as Social and Political Communication,* edited by Henrik P. Bang, Manchester University Press, Manchester.

Bardhan, P. (1997) Method in the Madness? A political-economy analysis of the ethnic conflicts in less developed countries, *World Development,* 25, 9, pp. 1381–1398.

Bayliss, K. and Fine, B. (eds) (2007) *Privatization and Alternative Public Sector Reform in Sub-Saharan Africa: Delivering on electricity and water,* Palgrave Macmillan, Basingstoke.

Bebbington, A. (2007) Social Capital and Development Studies II: Can Bourdieu travel to policy, *Progress in Development Studies,* 7, pp. 155–162.

Bebbington, A., Guggenhein, E., Olson, E. and Woolcock, M. (2004) Grounding Discourse in Practice: Exploring social capital debates at the World Bank, *Journal of Development Studies,* 40, 5, pp. 33–64.

Bhagwati, J. (1966) *The Economics of Underdeveloped Countries,* Weidenfelt and Nicholson, London, p. 204.

Bourdieu, P. (1985) The Forms of Capital. In *Handbook of Theory and Research for the Sociology of Education,* edited by John Richardson, Greenwood, Westport, CT.

Bovens, M. and Zouridis, S. (2002) From Street-level to System-level Bureaucracies: How information and communication technology is transforming administrative discretion and constitutional control, *Public Administration Review,* 62, 2, pp. 174–184.

Brett, E.A. (2003) Participation and Accountability in Development Management, *The Journal of Development Studies,* 40, 2, pp. 1–29.

Chambers, R. (2005) *Ideas for Development,* Earthscan, London.

Chatterjee, P. (2004) *The Politics of the Governed: Reflections on Popular Politics in Most of the World,* Columbia University Press, New York.

Cleaver, F. (2005) The Inequality of Social Capital and the Reproduction of Chronic Poverty, *World Development,* 33, pp. 893–906.

Coleman, J.S. (1990) *Foundations of Social Theory,* Harvard University Press, Cambridge MA.

Conyers, D. (2007) Decentralisation and Service Delivery: Lessons from Sub-Saharan Africa, *IDS Bulletin,* 38, 1, pp. 18–33.

Conyers, D. and Hills, P. (1984) *An Introduction to Development Planning in the Third World,* John Wiley & Sons, Chichester.

Cooke, B. and Kothari, U. (2001) The Case for Participation as Tyranny. In *Participation: The new tyranny?* edited by B. Cooke and U. Kothari, Zed Books, London.

Corbridge, S., Williams, G., Srivastava, M. and Veron, R. (2005) *Seeing the State: Governance and Governmentality in India,* Cambridge University Press, Cambridge.

Craig, D. and Porter, D. (2006) *Development beyond Neoliberalism: Governance, poverty reduction and political economy,* Routledge, Abingdon, Oxon.

Crisp, B. (2000) *Democratic Institutional Designs: The powers and incentives of Venezuelan politicians and interest groups,* Stanford University Press, Stanford, CA.

Cutright, P. (1963) National Political Development: Measurement and analysis, *American Sociological Review,* 28, pp. 253–264.

Daly, M. (2003) Governance and Social Policy, *Journal of Social Policy,* 32, 1, pp. 113–128.

Dasgupta, S. (1989) Computerised Rural Information System Project (CRISP): Some insights into information systems and development planning. Paper presented at the International Workshop on Information Technology, Kuala Lumpur, September.

De Gay, P. (ed.) (2005) *The Values of Bureaucracy,* Oxford University Press, Oxford.

DFID. (2006) Making Governance Work for the Poor. White Paper published 13 July.

Dunleavy, P., Margetts, H., Bastow, S. and Tinkler, J. (2005) New Public Management Is Dead – Long live digital-era governance, *Journal of Public Administration Research and Theory*, 16, 3, pp. 467–494.

Evans, P. (1996) Government Action, Social Capital and Development: Reviewing the evidence on synergy, *World Development*, 24, 6, pp. 1119–1132.

Evans, P. and Rauch, J. (1999) Bureaucracy and Growth: A cross national analysis of the effects of 'Weberian' state structures on economic growth, *American Sociological Review*, 64, pp. 748–765.

Ferguson, J. (1994) *The Anti-politics Machine: 'Development', Depolitisation and Bureaucratic Power in Lesotho*, University of Minnesota Press, Minneapolis.

Fine, B. (2001) *Social Capital versus Social Theory: Political economy and social sciences at the turn of the millennium*, Routledge, London.

Fine, B. (2003) Social Capital: The World Bank's fungible friend, *Journal of Agrarian Change*, 3, 4, pp. 586–603.

Fine, B. (2007) Social Capital, *Development in Practice*, 17, 4, pp. 566–574.

Fuller, C.J. and Harriss, J. (2001) For an Anthropology of the Modern Indian State. In *The Everyday State & Society in Modern India*, edited by C.J. Fuller and V. Benei, Hurst Publishers, London.

Goetz, A.M. and Jenkins, R. (2005) *Reinventing Accountability*, Palgrave Macmillan, Basingstoke, Hants.

Goodsell, C.T. (2005) The Bureau as Unit of Governance. In *The Values of Bureaucracy*, edited by Paul du Gay, Oxford University Press, Oxford.

Goodsell, C.T. (2006) A New Vision for Public Administration, *Public Administration Review*, 66, 4, pp. 623–635.

Gray, J. (1995) *Enlightenment's Wake*, Routledge, London.

Grindle, M.S. (2004) Good Enough Governance: Poverty reduction and reform in developing countries, *Governance: An International Journal of Policy, Administration and Institutions*, 17, 4, pp. 525–548.

Haggard, S. (1990) *Pathways from the Periphery*, Cornell University Press, Ithaca, NY.

Harriss, J. (2001) Public Action and the Dialectics of Decentralisation: Against the myth of social capital as 'the missing link in development', *Social Scientist*, 29, 11–12, pp. 25–40.

Harriss, J. (2002) *Depoliticizing Development. The World Bank and Social Capital*, Anthem Press, London.

Heeks, R. and Kenny, C. (2002) ICTs and Development: Convergence or Divergence for Developing Countries? *Proceedings of the 7th International Conference of IFIP WG9.4 ICTs and Development: New Opportunities, Perspectives and Challenges*, Bangalore, India.

Held, D. (1987) *Models of Democracy*, Polity Press, Cambridge.

Henderson, J., Hulme, D., Jalilian, H. and Phillips, R. (2007) Bureaucratic Effects: 'Weberian' state agencies and poverty reduction, *Sociology*, 41, 3, pp. 515–532.

Hewitt de Alcantara, C. (1998) Uses and Abuses of the Concept of Governance, *ISSJ*, 155, pp. 105–113.

Hirschman, A.O. (1970) *Exit, Voice, and Loyalty: Responses to decline in firms, organisations, and states*, Harvard University Press, Cambridge MA.

Houtzager, P., Joshi, A. and Lavalle, A.G. (eds) (2008) State Reform and Social Accountability: Brazil, India and Mexico, *IDS Bulletin*, 38, 6.

Huntington, S. (1965) Political Development and Political Decay, *World Politics*, April, pp. 386–430.

Hyden, G. (1997) Civil Society, Social Capital and Development: Dissection of a complex discourse, *Studies in Comparative International Development*, 32, 1, pp. 3–30.

Hyden, G., Court, J. and Mease, K. (2004) *Making Sense of Governance: Empirical evidence from 16 developing countries,* Lynne Reinner Publications, London.

Hyden, J. and Court, J. (2002) Governance and Development: Trying to sort out the basics. United Nations University, World Governance Survey, Discussion Paper 1, August 2002.

IDS. (1993) *Good Government,* 24, 1, p. 7.

Jayal, N.G. and Pai, S. (eds) (2001) *Democratic Governance in India: Challenges of poverty, development and identity,* Sage Publications, New Delhi.

Jeffries, R. (1993) The State, Structural Adjustment and Good Government in Africa, *Journal of Commonwealth and Comparative Politics,* 31, 1, March.

Jessop, B. (1998) The Rise of Governance and the Risks of Failure: The case of economic development, *ISSJ,* 155, pp. 29–45.

Jessop, B. (2002) *The Future of the Capitalist State,* Polity Press, Cambridge.

Kallinikos, J. (2006) The Institution of Bureaucracy: Administration, pluralism, democracy, *Economy and Society,* 35, 4, pp. 611–627.

Kaufmann, A., Kraay, A. and Mastruzzi, M. (2003) Governance Matters III: Governance indicators for 1996–2002, Policy Research Working Paper Series 3106, World Bank, Washington DC.

Kaufmann, D. and Bellver, A. (2005) Transparenting Transparency: Initial empirics and policy applications, World Bank.

Keniston, K. and Kumar, D. (eds) (2003) *The Four Digital Divides,* Sage Publications, New Delhi.

Kjaer, A.M. (2004) *Governance,* Polity Press, Cambridge, UK.

Kooiman, J. (2003) *Governing as Governance,* Sage Publications, London.

Krishna, A. (2002) *Active Social Capital: Tracing the roots of development and democracy,* Columbia University Press, New York.

Lam, W.F. (1994) Institutions, Engineering Infrastructure and Performance in the Governance and Management of Irrigation Systems: The case of Nepal. PhD Dissertation, School of Public and Environmental Affairs and Department of Political Science, Indiana University, Bloomington, IN.

Landell-Mills, P. (1992) Governance, Civil Society and Empowerment in Sub-Saharan Africa: Building the institutional basis for sustainable development, World Bank, Africa Technical Department, Washington DC.

Leftwich, A. (1993) Governance, Democracy and Development in the Third World, *Third World Quarterly,* 14, 3, pp. 605–625.

Leftwich, A. (2000) *States of Development: On the primacy of politics in development,* Cambridge Polity Press, Cambridge.

Lipset, S.M. (1960) *Political Man,* Heinemann, London, p. 403.

Lipset, S.M. and Lenz, S. (2001) Corruption, Culture and Markets. In *Culture Matters: How values shape human progress,* edited by L. Harrison and S. Huntington, Basic Books, New York.

Luckham, R., Geotz, A.M. and Kaldor, M. (2000) Democratic Institutions and Politics in Contexts of Inequality, Poverty and Conflict: A conceptual framework. IDS Working Paper No. 104, Institute of Development Studies, University of Sussex.

Manning, N. (2001) The Legacy of the New Public Management in Developing Countries, *International Review of Administrative Science,* 67, 2, pp. 297–312.

McCourt, W. (2006) The Human Factor in Governance: Findings and prospects for development, *Management in Development Working Paper Series, Paper No. 16,* Institute of Development Policy and Management, University of Manchester.

Manor, J. (1999) *The Political Economy of Democratic Decentralization,* World Bank, Washington DC.

Mathur, K.M. (1983) Administrative Decentralisation in Asia. In *Decentralisation and Development,* edited by G.S. Cheema and D.A. Rondinelli, Sage Publications, Beverly Hills, CA, pp. 59–76.

Mehrotra, S. (2006) Governance and Basic Social Services: Ensuring accountability in service delivery through deep democratic decentralisation, *Journal of International Development,* 18, pp. 263–283.

Mehrotra, S. and Delamonica, E. (2005) The Private Sector and Privatization in Social Services, *Global Social Policy,* 5, 2, pp. 141–174.

Mohmand, S.K. and Cheema, A. (2007) Accountability Failures and the Decentralisation of Service Delivery in Pakistan, *IDS Bulletin,* 38, 1, pp. 45–60.

Moon, S. (2002) Carving out Space: Civil society and the women's movement in South Korea, *The Journal of Asian Studies,* 61, 2, pp. 473–500.

Moore, M. (1993) Declining to Learn from the East? The World Bank on 'Governance and Development', *IDS Bulletin,* 24, 1, Institute of Development Studies, UK.

Moore, M. (2006) Good Government? (Introduction), *IDS Bulletin,* 37, 4, pp. 50–57.

Moore, M. and Putzel, J. (1999) Thinking Strategically about Politics and Poverty, *Working Paper No. 101,* Institute of Development Studies, University of Sussex.

Murray, R. (1993) Towards a Flexible State, *IDS Bulletin – New Forms of Public Administration,* 23, 4, pp. 78–88.

Narayan, D. (1999) Bonds and Bridges: Social capital and poverty. Poverty Group, PREM, World Bank, July 1999. Available at http://poverty2.forumone.com/files/12049_narayan.pdf

Newell, P. and Wheeler, J. (2006) Making Accountability Count, *IDS Policy Briefing,* 33, Institute of Development Studies, University of Sussex.

ODI. (2006) Governance, Development and Aid Effectiveness: A quick guide to complex relationships, *ODI Briefing Paper,* March.

Olsen, J.P. (2005) Maybe It Is Time to Rediscover Bureaucracy, *Journal of Public Administration Research and Theory,* 16, 1, pp. 1–24.

Osella, F. and Osella, C. (1996) Articulation of Physical and Social Bodies in Kerala, *Contribution to Indian Sociology,* 30, 1, pp. 37–68.

Osella, F. and Osella, C. (2000) The Return of King Mahabali: The politics of morality in Kerala. In *The Everyday State & Society in Modern India,* edited by C.J. Fuller and V. Benei, Hurst & Company, London, pp. 137–163.

Paul, B.K. (1992) Female Activity Space in Rural Bangladesh, *Geographical Review,* 82, 1, pp. 1–12.

Portes, A. (1998) Social Capital: Its origins and applications in modern sociology, *Annual Review of Sociology,* 24.

Portes, A. and Landolt, P. (2000) Social Capital: Promise and pitfalls of its role in development, *Journal of Latin American Studies,* 32, pp. 529–547.

Pretty, J. (2003) Social Capital and Connectedness: Issues and implications for agriculture, rural development and natural resource management in ACP countries, CTA Working document.

Putnam, R. (1993) *Making Democracy Work: Civic traditions in modern Italy,* Princeton University Press, Princeton, NJ.

Putnam, R. (2000) *Bowling Alone: The collapse and revival of American Community,* Simon & Schuster, NY.

Rhodes, R. (1996) The New Governance: Governing without government, *Political Studies,* 44, pp. 652–667.

Rhodes, R. (1997) *Understanding Governance: Policy networks, governance and accountability,* Open University Press, Birmingham.

Robinson, M. (2007) Does Decentralisation Improve Equity and Efficiency in Public Service Delivery Provision? *IDS Bulletin*, 38, 1, pp. 7–18.

Rodrik, D. (2008) Second-Best Institutions. John F. Kennedy School of Government, Harvard University, Cambridge, MA.

Rondinelli, D.A. (1981) Government Decentralization in Comparative Perspective: Theory and practice in developing countries, *International Review of Administrative Science*, 2, 47, pp. 133–145.

Rondinelli, D.A. (1993) *Development Projects as Policy Experiments: An adaptive approach to development administration*, Routledge, London.

Rose, N. (1996) Governing 'Advanced' Liberal Democracies. In *Foucault and Political Reason*, edited by A. Barry, T. Osborne and N. Rose, UCL Press, London.

Rothstein, B. (2003) Social Capital, Economic Growth and Quality of Government: The causal mechanism, *New Political Economy*, 8, 1, pp. 49–71.

Roy, I. (2008) Civil Society and Good Governance: (Re-)conceptualising the interface, *World Development*, 36, 4, pp. 677–705.

Schuller, T., Baron, S. and Field, J. (2000) Social Capital: A review and critique. In *Social Capital: Critical perspectives*, edited by S. Baron, J. Field and T. Schuller, Oxford University Press, Oxford.

Schuurman, F.J. (2003) Social Capital: The politico-emancipatory potential of a disputed concept, *Third World Quarterly*, 24, 6, pp. 991–1010.

Scott, J. (1998) *Seeing Like a State: How certain schemes to improve the human condition have failed*, Yale University Press, New Haven, CT.

Shams, K., Siedentopf, H. and Sosmena, G. (1987) Organising Local Initiatives for Decentralised Rural Development: The regional experience. In *Building from Below: Local initiatives for decentralised development in Asia and Pacific*, edited by A. Bhatt, L. Carino, K. Shams, H. Siedentopf and G. Sosmena, Vol. 1, Asian and Pacific Development Centre, Kuala Lumpur, pp. 107–142.

Shoib, G. and Jones, M. (2003) Focusing on the Invisible: The representation of IS in Egypt, *Information Technology & People*, 16, 4, pp. 440–460.

Sivaramakrishnan, K. (1995) Situating the Subalterns: History and anthropology in the subaltern studies project, *Journal of Historical Sociology*, 8, 4, pp. 395–429.

Slater, R. and Watson, J. (1989) Democratic Decentralisation or Political Consolidation: The case of local government reform in Karnataka, *Public Administration and Development*, 19, pp. 147–157.

Smith, S. and Kulynych, J. (2002) It May be Social, but Why Is It Capital? The social construction of social capital and the politics of language, *Politics & Society*, 30, 1, pp. 149–186.

Stiglitz, J. (2002) *Globalization and Its Discontents*, Penguin Books, London.

Stiglitz, J. (2008) You Ask the Questions, the Independent People. Posted on 24 March 2008. Available at www.independent.co.uk/news/people/profiles/joseph-stiglitz-you-ask-the-questions-799885.html

Stoker, G. (1998) Governance as Theory: Five propositions, *ISSJ*, 155, pp. 17–28.

Tendler, J. (1997) *Good Government in the Tropics*, Johns Hopkins University Press, Baltimore, MD.

Turner, M. and Hulme, D. (1997) *Governance, Administration and Development*, Kumarian press, West Hartford, CT.

UN. (2005) Unlocking the Human Potential for Public Sector Performance. World Public Sector Report 2005, Department of Economic and Social Affairs, United Nations, New York.

UNDP. (2003) Deepening Democracy in a Fragmented World. Human Development Report, Oxford University Press, Oxford.

Vigoda, E. and Yuval, F. (2003) Managerial Quality, Administrative Performance and Trust in Governance: Can we point to causality? *Australian Journal of Public Administration,* 62, 3, pp. 12–25.

Wade, R. (1990) *Governing the Market: Economic theory and the role of government in East Asian industrialisation,* Princeton University Press, Princeton, NJ.

Weiss, L. (1998) *The Myth of the Powerless State. Governing the economy in a global era,* Polity Press, Cambridge.

White, G. (2006) Towards a Democratic Developmental State, *IDS Bulletin,* 37, 4, pp. 60–71.

World Bank (1989) Sub-Saharan Africa: From crisis to sustainable growth, Washington DC.

World Bank (1992) Governance and Development, World Bank Publications, Washington DC.

World Bank (1998) The Initiative on Defining, Monitoring and Measuring Social Capital, Social Capital Initiative, Working Paper No. 1, Washington DC.

World Bank (2004) Making Services Work for Poor People, Oxford University Press, Washington DC.

Zakaria, F. (1994) A Conversation with Lee Kuan Yew, *Foreign Affairs,* 73, 2.

Zuckerman, E. (1989) Adjustment Programs and Social Welfare, World Bank Discussion Paper No. 44, Washington DC.

4

e-Governance for Development

This chapter traces the evolution of the e-governance for development discourse, describes key applications and reviews current research on this topic. It then presents a conceptualisation of e-governance for development drawing on key issues raised from earlier discussions of development and governance. The conceptual framework has different levels of analysis. At the macro level, of interest are the development policy priorities which exist within a particular context and the strategies adopted for their achievement. At the micro level, of interest is the ability of individual community members to benefit from improved governance services which includes analysing cultural norms within the community. In between these two levels are local administrative, political and social 'intermediaries' who provide a crucial interface between the formal and informal governance structure to bring about developmental benefits for communities.

e-Governance is perceived by international development agencies as a key policy priority and an important element of the good governance agenda. Decades of evidence from the private sector in developed countries showed that IT investment could lead to economic growth through increased productivity gains, refuting earlier concerns about the productivity paradox[1] (Brynjolfsson and Hitt, 1998; Dedrick and Kraemer, 2003; OECD, 2002). However, more recent evidence shows that these findings do not have universal validity. Dewan and Kraemer (2000) identify a marked difference in terms of the structure of returns from capital investment between developed and developing countries. In the context of developing countries, their study shows that returns to capital IT investment are not significant while returns to non-IT capital investment are significant. Further, the growing significance of the internet in all activities of economic and social life is providing an opportunity for using technology to reduce the role of the state in favour of market-led development. A widening of the label from 'e-government' to 'e-governance' appeared in the literature providing scope for public sector IT projects to incorporate private and non-profit organisations for the delivery of public services by means of outsourcing and partnerships (Riley, 2003).

e-Governance encompasses a portfolio of different types of applications described in the literature in terms of a 'stages of growth' continuum (Bhatnagar, 2009; Heeks, 2001; Ranerup, 1999). The first stage in this continuum known as e-administration is described as the use of ICT to improve the internal efficiency of government through automation of back-office functions and the introduction of management information systems (MIS) to support the planning and monitoring of development programmes. At the second stage, known as e-services, it is generally assumed that many of the back-office functions and databases are already in digital format, and the focus is switched to publishing information for citizens through websites which are used to provide a direct entry point for citizen services. As the technologies matured, the level of interactivity and integration has increased. At the third stage of the continuum, known as e-participation or e-development, it is assumed that implementation of back-office digitisation is already complete and that a computerised interface exists for citizens to interact with government. The focus of e-governance now switches to usage of ICTs to foster wider public participation in policy-making processes through such means as electronic voting, petitioning systems and virtual discussion forums. The idea of e-governance implementation proceeding in stages finds expression in the various 'maturity models' that have been developed to help governments identify their state of advancement with regards to e-governance based on their technical, organisational and managerial competence (Baum and Maio, 2000; Gronlund *et al.*, 2006; Layne and Lee, 2001). One example of a maturity model proposed by Gronlund *et al.* (2006) helps developing countries identify their stage of e-governance maturity with regards to their organisational, institutional and policy environment. More recently, the term 'transformational' governance has been used in the literature to represent a stage of e-governance maturity that displays a culture of sharing data, infrastructure, resources and standards (The Cabinet Office, 2005).

There is now accumulated evidence to suggest that many e-governance projects implemented in both developed and developing countries have not resulted in significant improvements in citizen services and welfare (Benjamin, 2001; Gartner, 2002; Heeks, 2003, 2006; Kanungo, 2003; Sify Business, 2004; Symonds, 2000; UNDESA, 2003). In cases where usage is low, a generic problem has been lack of equity in providing access to e-governance applications. But even when access is provided, many citizens have not considered these applications relevant for their lives. Various approaches have been proposed for improving our understanding of why e-governance projects have not resulted in improved public service delivery. Stakeholder theory has been found useful to identify the different actors involved in planning and implementing a project and their various interests such as different levels of government, private players and civil society organisations (Scholl, 2001). Diffusion of innovations theory has been employed to study how a new application is piloted and eventually becomes institutionalised within a particular organisational context (Lazer, 2003). The majority of literature, however, has tended to adopt a rather narrow managerialist view of public sector reform without acknowledging the variety of formal and informal policy-related, institutional, organisational and social factors which influence how technology is accepted and used (Fountain, 2001; Gasco, 2003; Heeks and Bailur, 2007; Jaeger and Thompson, 2003). A recent contribution to the e-governance literature has been the inclusion of more socially focused theories. Heeks (2006) uses a socio-technical approach to study how e-governance applications address both social and technical priorities within an organisation. Another recent theoretical contribution is provided by Garson (2006) who analyses e-governance from a political-theory point of view engaging in discussions about policy issues such as privacy, the digital divide and freedom of speech and their relevance for understanding the impact of projects.

e-Governance projects are being implemented by international development agencies and national/provincial governments at an accelerated pace in many parts of the developing world. From the mid-1980s, huge investments were made to implement public sector IT projects in many developing countries primarily targeted towards improving the planning and administration of large economic development programmes (Han and Walsham, 1989; Madon, 1993). Earlier, one of the major bottlenecks to the state planning effort had been the lack of micro-level data about the status and priorities of communities and the launching of decentralised information systems was aimed at improving local administrative capacity to manage these programmes. However, these projects resulted in no significant impact on public sector reform for a variety of reasons. First, as a consequence of lack of financial and human resources leading to the existence of inadequate systems of information handling and management (Bhatnagar, 1997; Cain, 1996; Heeks, 2000). Second, because of poor capacity within the local administration for the analysis and use of data. Based on experience of several ministries in Kenya, Peterson (1991) identifies how poor training and motivation have resulted in a lack of demand for analysis by administrators. Third, in terms of the lack of political will to decentralise data and decision-making powers to local agencies (Walsham, 1992). There were also a host of cultural factors that influenced these projects such as the importance paid to status and hierarchy within the administration and the allegiance of public officials to caste and social ties within the community (Heeks, 2002; Madon, 1993).

The focus on improving local administrative capacity through ICT was short lived with lack of clarity about how e-administration projects and the bureaucracy impact each other in reciprocal ways (Jain, 2004; Madon, 2006).

While this type of application was seen as a tool for reforming the planning and administrative apparatus, its effective implementation was often prevented by the inertia within bureaucracy to experiment and learn from the field.

From 2000, there was much optimism expressed by development agencies about how e-governance can advance the agenda of 'good governance' using such rhetoric as bridging the digita divide, promoting democracy, increasing transparency and accountability of government and encouraging greater private sector involvement in civil affairs (O'Okot-Uma, 2000). The World Bank took a leading role in promoting 'eGovernance for development' with the creation in 1995 of the Information for Development Programme (InfoDev).[2] Also, it launched a web site specifically for e-governance with case studies, toolkits, and other utilities.[3] Many other institutions such as the World Bank and the UN have followed suit. For instance, the United Nations has launched an online network in Public Administration and Finance (UNPAN) to promote cooperation among developing countries in terms of sharing of experiences, knowledge and practices in e-governance implementation and policy. In many cases, e-governance projects were implemented in developing countries by development agencies directly or by national governments who had received funding from agencies. While it had been common practice to hire external consultants to transfer business practices such as business process re-engineering, enterprise information infrastructure and customer relations management systems to developing countries, e-governance implementation resulted in consultants for the first time intervening in the explicitly political setting of their government administration. For example, various international agency reports have been published focusing on the need for developing countries to strengthen their state and political institutions by emulating the institutions of advanced market economies (InfoDev, 2005; Stiglitz, 2002; UNDP, 2002; World Bank, 2002, 2004).

e-Governance projects in developing countries are generally categorised as e-administration or e-services projects (Bhatnagar, 2004, 2009; Heeks, 2001; Ndou, 2004; O'Okot-Uma, 2000). In a recent World Bank-sponsored study, 73 ICT projects in the public sector were identified for which evaluation documents were analysed (World Bank, 2007). The majority of these projects, typically categorised in the first two stages of the e-governance maturity model, were e-administration or e-services types of projects. The e-administration projects were concerned with MIS for particular government departments, or for back-office applications in government such as payroll, financial reporting, or planning. However, many of the challenges from earlier public sector IT projects continue to haunt modern e-administration applications. Around one half of e-governance applications identified in the World Bank study fall into the category of e-services applications reflecting the major neoliberal thrust in current public policy towards improved service-orientation within government. Such applications include the computerisation of routine transactions such as bill payments, registration of births, deaths and marriages, land registration, and the provision of entitlement certificates such as income or caste certificates.

E-services projects also include the rapid proliferation of multi-purpose rural community telecentres which have been established in many parts of the developing world by international development agencies and country governments.[4] These centres have the task of promoting development in different sectors such as education, health and agriculture. Telecentres, typically owned by private entrepreneurs, offer communication services, training on IT and non-IT subjects, serve as a hub for local commercial and social activity and provide government information and services to rural communities (Fillip and Foote, 2007; IDRC, 2003; Proenza, 2001; Roman and Colle, 2003). Numerous players including government, local administration, local political bodies, private entrepreneurs, large corporates, civil society organisations and the community are involved in implementing these projects and the manner in which these players interact influences their long-term financial, social and political sustainability (Bailey, 2008; Bhatnagar, 2004; Harris *et al.*, 2003; Hunt, 2001; Kanungo, 2004; Muthukumaraswamy, 2004; Reilly and Gomez, 2001; Roman and Colle, 2002; Soriano, 2007; Stoll *et al.*, 2004; Whyte, 2000). While short-term gains of these projects are typically observed (such as increased earnings for telecentre owners, greater awareness of IT), these projects have so far had minimal impact in terms of ameliorating the living conditions of the community.

This book is focused on the developmental potential of e-governance projects focusing on e-administration and e-services projects as these constitute the majority of current implementations. E-administration projects hold significant developmental implications. By using information technology to improve the functioning of the bureaucracy in its role of planning and administering large economic development programmes, e-administration projects can target huge sections of the population improving their living conditions (Henderson *et al.*, 2007). E-services projects can also impact development by providing citizens with direct access to (1) documents such as land title deeds or caste certificates which can be used to promote equity in the allocation of resources and (2) vital information and services for basic welfare and for improving economic productivity.

So far, however, we know little about the extent to which these types of e-governance projects promote development as research in this area has been conducted in a largely anecdotal and piecemeal fashion (Peters *et al.*, 2004; World Bank, 2007). E-readiness frameworks have tried to measure how ready countries are to reap benefits from e-governance by considering their organisational, technical, institutional and policy environment.[5] These approaches tend to be factor-based and aimed at a macro-level assessment of a country's readiness for e-governance. The influence of factors that are not amenable to quantitative measurement have also been addressed. For example,

Kovacic (2005) considers the important influence of national culture on e-governance readiness models and Sudan (2005) points to important aspects of e-Government such as leadership, organisational capacity, the regulatory environment and the quality of public-private relationships. In the context of rural poor communities in the developing world, there is increasing evidence that the impact of e governance depends not only on macro level contextual factors, but also on identifying local information sources (Blattman and Jensen, 2003) and on the interactions and political struggles which take place at micro level (Evans and Yen, 2005; Heeks, 2002, 2004; Heeks and Stanforth, 2007; Hudson, 1999; InfoDev, 2005; Madon, 2005b; Madon *et al.*, 2007; Peled, 2000; Sreekumar, 2007). For example, Heeks and Stanforth (2007) focus on the way in which different stakeholders in an e-governance project in Sri Lanka stand to gain or lose power. Other scholars have emphasised the importance of political support from local institutions for the successful implementation of e-governance projects in developing countries (Bhatnagar, 2004; Kumar and Best, 2006; Madon, 2005b; Madon *et al.*, 2008). In a recent World Bank study of e-governance in India and Chile, impact was measured in a variety of ways including impact of economic and non-economic costs and benefits to citizens and businesses, and impact on agencies' workflow and procedures (Bhatnagar, 2009; World Bank, 2007).

A basic reference model used for the study of e-governance implementation today which incorporates many of the elements discussed above is the E-Government Project Success Appraisal Model (Figure 4.1) employed by scholars in several countries including the US and India.[6] Guiding the model are strategic outcomes representing broad policy priorities which are seen to drive the direction of government. For example, a key global policy priority is the administrative simplification of core processes by integrating government departments and agencies through the provision of decentralisation, one-stop shops and web portals.

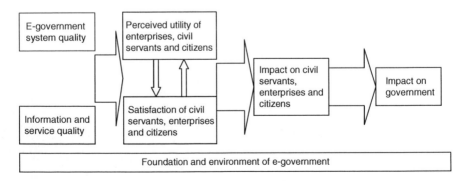

Figure 4.1   e-Government project success appraisal model (taken from Hu *et al.*, 2005)

Building on this basic model, various dimensions of value have been identified and studied in different e-governance projects (Madon and Kiran,
2003; World Bank, 2007). First, value to government in terms of tangible cost
savings/avoidance often by introducing new services to citizens and businesses
such as online tax return filing. Various institutional models of e-government
have been identified to enable coordination in key functions such as strategy
and policy-making, administration and technology (Hanna *et al.*, 2009). In a
recent World Bank-sponsored study of seven e-services projects, the ability of
the government agency to cope with the filing of tax returns was enhanced
through e-governance which brought about a re-engineering and integration
of services (World Bank, 2007). Second, value to users in terms of improved
services, reduced cost and/or time savings to citizens and reduced administrative burden to businesses. In the World Bank study referred to above, citizens
indicated an overwhelming preference for the e-governance application as
opposed to manual operations as their costs of accessing the service had been
reduced both in terms of number of trips and waiting times. Accumulated
knowledge regarding value creation to clients in the private sector has been
used to develop parameters for measuring the benefits of e-governance to citizens (eGEP, 2005; Gupta and Jana, 2003; Janssen *et al.*, 2004; Lau, 2005; Ray
and Venkata Rao, 2004).

The third dimension of value suggested by the model relates to value
to society at large due to improvements in various aspects of governance
activity with consequent ramifications for the attainment of development
priorities. This has been by far the most difficult dimension to measure.
One aspect of value to society is to improve democratic accountability
through greater transparency of information made possible by e-governance
applications (Bhatnagar, 2003, 2009; Panzardi *et al.*, 2002; Sturges, 2004;
Vasudevan, 2006). Taking a more critical approach, studies undertaken in
Jordan (Ciborra, 2005) and China (Ma *et al.*, 2005) show how e-governance
projects have resulted in greater control by the state on citizens rather than
improved democracy.

The correlation between transparency and citizen trust in government was
investigated in several studies (Avgerou *et al.*, 2005; Parent *et al.*, 2004; Shadrach
and Ekeanyanwu, 2003). In their study in Brazil and Chile, Avgerou *et al.* found
that while e-governance had led to the creation of trustworthy institutions by
enabling better interactions with the government, the system had little overall impact on promoting equitable development in the country – indeed, the
system had proved irrelevant for two-thirds of the population who are poor.
The World Bank study referred to above found that developmental impact of
e-governance implementation was low with many citizens arguing that there
were other more pressing development priorities that need to be addressed
(Bhatnagar, 2009; World Bank, 2007).

Some scholars have used a more processual approach to analyse how changing perceptions of service providers and citizens can shape the course of an e-services project (Madon, 2003, Madon, 2005a). From a development angle, Garnham (2000) adopted a Capabilities Approach to explore whether new options for communications such as the mobile telephone (cell phone) and the internet should automatically be added to the capability set of citizens as a matter of entitlement. Sen's Capabilities Approach was also used by Madon (2004) to move the discussion of e-governance evaluation beyond traditional criteria of expenditure, infrastructure, access and skills to assess the value of these applications for fulfilling citizens' aspirations. Along the theme of 'entitlement', Thomas (2009) argues that unlike in advanced industrialised countries where the right to information lies at the heart of liberal democratic values in terms of freedom of expression, the struggle in many developing countries is more about having the right to information for the attainment of basic development priorities such as drought, employment, health, food security. The linkage between information and basic development needs has resulted in the constitution of the Right to Information legislation in many developing countries. In India, for example, this movement which began with the rural peasants and farmers movement (MKSS) in Rajasthan in the early 1990s has now spread rapidly throughout the country resulting in the national Right to Information Act in 2005 and various state level acts (Sivakumar, 2004).

The issue of intermediation discussed in the previous chapter in relation to democratic governance structures resurfaces as important for understanding the societal value of e-governance applications. Heeks (2001) argues that in a developed country context, e-services applications are driven by a disintermediated model of direct digital connection between government and individual citizens. However, accumulated evidence from e-governance projects in India and South Africa shows that there remains an important role for human intermediaries to ensure equitable access to resources for all members of the community and to ensure that community voice is represented in terms of development priorities (Belle and Trusler, 2005; Colle, 2005; Gopakumar, 2006; IIITB, 2005; Nair *et al.*, 2006; Parkinson, 2005; Prakash and De, 2007; Rangaswamy, 2006; Srinivasan, 2006; Tacchi, 2005). This argument finds support in a UNESCO-sponsored study on telecentres in developing countries in which Nair *et al.* (2006) describe how a network of women trained in computer usage served as crucial intermediary agents to connect groups of ten or more rural poor women from among the most marginalised members of the community. Another example of the crucial role of the human intermediary in governance activity is taken from a study of the Bhoomi land records computerisation project in India (Prakash and De, 2007). The study describes how the village accountant was a crucial government official intermediary for helping small farmers obtain assistance from development programmes. This government official would routinely use his discretionary powers and village connections to improve farmers' access to cultivable land, to obtain assistance from state-sponsored schemes and to obtain bank loans. However, with the introduction of the e-governance project, this local administrator who used to act as an important intermediary for small farmers no longer has a role.

e-Governance implementation is also affected by social systems that exist at the community level and the cultural norms they embody. Rarely accessible to e-governance policy-makers and implementers, these systems can only be understood by local intermediaries. The UNESCO telecentre study shows the importance of existing social networks for the creation of new social space. The study report describes deep-rooted cultural norms about female mobility held within individual households and the neighbourhood which affected access by these community members to the Namma Dhwani Media Centre in Karnataka. In this project, prevailing self-help groups helped to form new social networks that interacted with the cable radio station. The advantage of identifying and working with existing civil society networks is clear also in Project Nabanna which commenced in February 2003 in rural West Bengal – a region where poverty is rampant. As most of the poor are landless and live on public land owned by the panchayat[7] with no source of income, they are compelled to seek wage labour or to be part of a self-help income-generating scheme. The UNESCO study describes the strength of existing networks of women in one of the three centres set up in Baduria village. The geographic layout of the area is such that villages are arranged in discrete clusters with little interaction taking place between them. However, within any particular cluster, the study describes how there is intense and highly localised social interaction among the women folk. This is despite the fact that these women have come together relatively recently due to migration rather than based on generations of natal relatives. These strong bonds between women folk within the clusters have been directed towards both economic and social motives, for example to promote income-generating activities and to use the network to simply chat and gossip about domestic issues. Project Nabanna has very much piggy-backed onto this existing social network supporting the argument made in other studies (Dlamini, 2004) for combining new channels of communication through ICTs with traditional (newsletter and face-to-face) means. For example, a regular activity of project Nabanna is to visit rural poor women in public places taking a laptop along to show a video about relevant social issues such as health or other important topics such as the dowry system.

The UNESCO study is mindful of the fact that inherent in many existing social networks are issues of social inclusion/exclusion, particularly against women. This point comes across in the Namma Dhwani Media Centre project. Deep-rooted community constraints on female mobility including power relationships that exist within household and neighbourhood networks have affected the ability of women to participate in the project; for example, the tension that exists between women who live in neighbourhoods because of marriage and those who live there because of residence. The study report documents a similar finding with the Akshaya telecentre project in Kerala. In this case, the project exposes many examples of social exclusion against the poor minority Muslim fishing communities in Kerala. These villagers have traditionally been excluded from public spaces such as libraries, community entertainment centres and adult education centres.

To summarise this chapter, the implementation of e-governance projects is an important element of the current good governance policy agenda. Most projects are classified as e-administration or e-services applications and have overtly developmental objectives. The impact of these projects, however, on improving the living conditions of communities is poorly understood. Most evaluation approaches have taken a managerialist view of measuring success in terms of short-term cost and time benefits rather than focusing attention on measuring gains to society. As the literature review suggests, the study of e-governance requires an approach that addresses both macro-level contextual factors and ongoing processes of change within local social, administrative and political systems.

Towards a framework for the study of e-governance for development

If e-governance projects are being implemented for the purposes of promoting development through improved governance, then surely a framework for the study of e-governance for development must be based on how we conceptualise both development and governance. Despite the proliferation of e-governance projects in developing countries, this type of theorisation is lacking. Abstract parameters of measuring e-governance projects such as the extent of infrastructure in place, network coverage or the number of applications available online continue to dominate policy attention. The key issues identified in this critical review of the literature enable a conceptualisation of the study domain of e-governance for development which is represented in Figure 4.2.

At the highest level of abstraction, e-governance is widely accepted as a core element of international development strategy guided by the current good governance orthodoxy. According to this policy drive, e-governance can promote development by improving the efficiency, accountability, transparency of government operations and by promoting citizen engagement in development activity. These macro forces may bias public policy-making at the national and state levels, for example, towards the promotion of e-governance for urban areas or towards applications in the secondary and tertiary sector at the

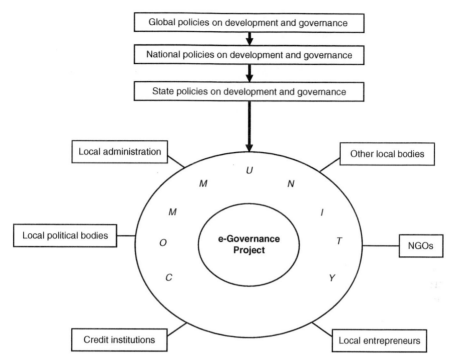

Figure 4.2   Conceptualising e-governance for development

expense of applications designed to promote welfare and social development. A study of e-governance for development needs to identify these biases and challenges within specific contexts and the institutional and policy challenges faced by country government to regulate for more equitable access to resources, for example, through labour laws.

At the local level, the value of an e-governance project depends on the agency of individuals and communities to actualise benefits in their living conditions which in turn depends on the institutions or structures which enable or constrain that benefit to be realised.[8] It is easy to see how such an approach makes intuitive sense. For example, in the case of an e-services project designed to provide an entitlement certificate, the inherent value of the service to the client (citizen, government or business) depends on the ability of the citizen to actually acquire a loan with the entitlement certificate. This, in turn, depends on his or her own actions and on the support received from various authorities such as local banks who may be biased against lending to small farmers or local artisans. Although democratisation or 'citizen empowerment' is supposed to be the cornerstone of e-governance for development initiative, a lot depends not just on the extent of civil society activity but on the interface created between the e-governance system and the community. There are many social barriers that may exclude certain groups from the benefits of e-governance and local government must have the autonomy and motivation to foster dialogue between community members and to shift resources according to local needs. This is typically a difficult undertaking for local administration offices where even public records are not yet fully digitised and where the culture of the administration does not encourage autonomy and experimentation.

The linkage between e-governance and development can only be understood through a context-specific inquiry. We must engage with understanding process of change at both macro and micro level and how this process is affected by the introduction of an e-governance application. The approach in this study draws inspiration from scholars who have adopted a sociological approach to the study of development and governance as reviewed earlier. The overall context for the study is India and within each case-study setting, the aim is to study the social and political struggles that exist within communities – for example, the relative strength of self-help groups, farmers lobbies or health workers in a particular society, their level of internal solidarity, their self-identity and representativeness, their organisational and political resources.

In Part II of this book, let us turn our attention to e-governance in India. Over the past 50 years, India has undergone very many changes in terms of economic and political ideologies. In recent years, e-governance has become a cornerstone of government policy with every state in the country encouraged to put in place the necessary infrastructure to improve living conditions in both urban and rural parts of the country. In terms of the country's development priorities, rural poverty continues to be a serious concern resulting in huge sums of money being directed towards setting up e-governance systems to help rural poor communities improve their living conditions. The empirical work looks at three such projects in India. Geographically, my cases are drawn from three states in India and in each case, the projects are localised to district or community level. Each of our cases focuses on a different 'development' sector highlighting the importance of that sector to overall development of the state.

Glossary

Panchayat – elected council
UNESCO – United Nations Educational, Scientific and Cultural Organization

References

Avgerou, C., Ciborra, C., Cordella, A., Kallinikos, J. and Smith, M. (2005) The Role of Information and Communication Technology in Building Trust in Governance: Towards effectiveness and results. Inter-American Development Bank, Washington, DC.

Bailey, A. (2008) Issues Affecting the Social Sustainability of Telecentres in Developing Contexts: A field study of sixteen telecentres in Jamaica, *EJISDC*, 36, 4, pp. 1–18.

Baum, C. and Maio, A. (2000) Gartner's Four Phases of E-Government Model, Gartner.

Belle, J. and Trusler, J. (2005) An Interpretivist Case Study of a South African Rural Multi-purpose Community Centre, *The Journal of Community Informatics*, 1, 2, pp. 140–157.

Benjamin, P. (2001) Community Development and Democratisation through Information Technology: Building new South Africa. In *Reinventing Government in the Information Age*, edited by Richard Heeks, Routledge, London, pp. 194–210.

Bhatnagar, S.C. (1997) Information Technology-Enabled Public Sector Reforms: Myth or reality? Keynote speaker at International Conference on Public Sector Management for the Next Century, University of Manchester, 30 June–02 July.

Bhatnagar, S.C. (2003) E-government and Access to Information, *The Global Corruption Report 2003*, Transparency International, Berlin.

Bhatnagar, S.C. (2004) *E-Government – from Vision to Implementation: A practical guide with case studies*, Sage Publications, New Delhi.

Bhatnagar, S.C. (2009) *Unlocking E-Government Potential: Concepts, cases and practical insights*, Sage Publications, New Delhi.

Blattman, C. and Jensen, R. (2003) Assessing the Need and Potential of Community Networking for Development in Rural India, *The Information Society*, 19, pp. 349–364.

Brynjolfsson, E. and Hitt, L. (1998) Beyond the Productivity Paradox, *Communications of the ACM*, 41, 8, pp. 49–55.

The Cabinet Office (2005) Transformational Government – Enabled by Technology. The Stationery Office, UK Government, London.

Cain, P. (1996) Making the Transition to the Electronic Age: Managing electronic and paper records as a strategic resource for good government in developing countries, *Information Technology for Development*, 7, pp. 159–167.

Ciborra, C. (2005) Interpreting E-Government and Development: Efficiency, transparency or governance at a distance, *Information Technology & People*, 18, 3, pp. 260–279.

Colle, R.D. (2005) Memo to Telecentre Planners, *EJISDC*, 21, 1, pp. 1–13.

Dedrick, J. and Kraemer, K.L. (2003) Redefining Processes and Organization with IT, CRITO, University of Irvine Working Paper, Irvine, CA.

Delgadillo, K., Gomez, R. and Stokk, K. (2002) *Community Telecentres for Development: Lessons from Community Telecentres in Latin America and the Caribbean*, IDRC, Canada.

DeSanctis, G. and Poole, M.S. (1994) Capturing the Complexity in Advanced Technology Use: Adaptive structuration theory, *Organization Science*, 5, 2, pp. 121–147.

Dewan, S. and Kraemer, K.L. (2000) Information Technology and Productivity: Evidence from country-level data. Centre for Research on Information Technology and Organizations (CRITO), University of Irvine, Irvine, CA.

Dlamini, H. (2004) Banikoara Multimedia Community Centre, Benin: A window to the world, *Information for Development*, 11, 9, pp. 6–11.

eGEP. (2005) eGovernment Economics Project. Prepared for the eGovernment Unit, DG Information Society and Media, European Commission.

Evans, D. and Yen, D. (2005) E-government: An analysis for implementation: Framework for understanding cultural and social impact, *Government Information Quarterly*, 22, pp. 354–373.

Fillip, B. and Foote, D. (2007) *Making the Connection: Scaling telecenters for development*, Information Technology Application Center, Academy for Education Development, Washington DC.

Fountain, J. (2001) *Building the Virtual State: Information Technology and Institutional Change,* Brookings Institute, Washington DC.

Garnham, N. (2000) Amartya Sen's 'Capabilities' Approach to the Evaluation of Welfare and Its Application to Communications. In *Beyond Competition: Broadening the Scope of Telecommunications Policy,* edited by B. Cammaerts and J.C. Burgelmans, VUB University Press, pp. 25–37.

Gartner (2002) GartnerEXP Says a Majority of E-Government Initiatives Fail or Fall Short of Expectations. Available at http://symposium.gartner,com/story.php. id.1367.s.5.html

Garson, D. (2006) *Public Information Technologies and eGovernance: Managing the virtual state,* Jones and Bartlett, Sudbury, MA.

Gasco, M. (2003) New Technologies and Institutional Change in Public Administration, *Social Science Computer Review,* 21, 1, pp. 6–14.

Giddens, A. (1979) *Central Problems in Social Theory,* Macmillan, London.

Giddens, A. (1984) *The Constitution of Society: Outline of the theory of structuration,* Polity Press, Cambridge.

Gopakumar, K. (2006) E-government Services through Telecentres: The role of human intermediary and issues of trust, *Proceedings of the 2006 International Conference on ICT and Development,* Berkeley, CA.

Gronlund, A., Andersson, A. and Hedstrom, K. (2006) Right on Time: Understanding eGovernment in developing countries. In *Social Inclusion: Societal and organizational implications for information systems,* edited by E. Trauth, D. Howcroft, T. Butler, B. Fitzgerald and J. DeGross, Springer, New York.

Gupta, M.P. and Jana, D. (2003) E-government Evaluation: A framework and case study, *Government Information Quarterly,* 20, pp. 365–387.

Han, C.K. and Walsham, G. (1989) Public Policy and Information Systems in Government: A mixed level analysis of computerisation. Research Paper Number 3/89. Management Studies Group, Cambridge University.

Hanna, N.K., Qiang, C.Z., Kimura, K. and Kuek, S.C. (2009) National E-Government Institutions: Functions, models and trends, *Information and Communications for Development, Extending Reach and Increasing Impact,* World Bank, Washington DC.

Harris, R., Kumar, A. and Balaji, V. (2003) Sustainable Telecentres? Two cases from India, *Digital Challenge: Information Technology in the Development Context,* Ashgate, Aldershot, Hants, pp. 124–136. Available at http://www.developmentgateway.org/node/133831/ sdm/docview?docid=442648

Heeks, R. (2000) Government Data: Understanding the barriers to citizen access and use, *Information Systems for Public Sector Management Working Paper No. 10,* Institute of Development Policy & Management, University of Manchester.

Heeks, R. (2001) Understanding eGovernance for Development, IDPM Working Paper Series, No. 11, Institute of Development Policy & Management, University of Manchester. Available at www.man.ac.uk/idpm/idpm_dp.htm#g

Heeks, R. (2002) e-Government in Africa: Promises and practice, *Information Polity,* 7, pp. 97–114.

Heeks, R. (2003) Most eGovernment for Development Projects Fail: How can risks be reduced, *iGovernment – Information, Systems, Technology, and the Public Sector, Working Paper No. 14,* Institute of Development Policy and Management, University of Manchester.

Heeks, R. (2004) eGovernment as a Carrier of Context, *i*Government Working Paper Series, No. 15, Institute of Development Policy and Management, University of Manchester.

Heeks, R. (2006) *Implementing and Managing eGovernment: An international text,* Sage Publications, London.

Heeks, R. and Bailur, S. (2007) Analyzing e-government research: Perspectives, philosophies, theories, methods, and practice, *Government Information Quarterly,* 24, pp. 243–265.

Heeks, R. and Stanforth, C. (2007) Understanding e-Government Project Trajectories from an Actor-Network Perspective, *European Journal of Information Systems,* 16, pp. 165–177.

Henderson, J., Hulme, D., Jalilian, H. and Philips, R. (2007) Bureaucratic Effects: 'Weberian' state structures and poverty reduction, *Sociology,* 41, 3, pp. 515–532.

Hu, Y., Xiao, J., Pang, J. and Xie, K. (2005) A Research on the Appraisal Framework of E-Government Project Success. Proceedings of the 7th International Conference on Electronic Commerce, ICEC, 05.

Hudson, H. (1999) Designing Research for Telecentre Evaluation, *Telecentre Evaluation: A global perspective (Report of an International Meeting on Telecentre Evaluation),* Far Hills Inn, Quebec, IDRC. Available at www.idrc.ca/telecentre/evaluation/nn/01 TOC.html

Hunt, P. (2001) True Stories: Telecentres in Latin America and the Caribbean, *EJISDC,* 4, 5, pp. 1–17.

IDRC. (2003) *Information and Communication Technologies for Development in Africa Vol. 2: The experience with community telecentres,* edited by Florence Etta and Sheila Parvyn-Wamahiu, CODESRIA/IDRC.

IIITB. (2005) Information and Communication Technologies for Development: A comparative analysis of impacts and costs from India. Indian Institute of Information Technology, Bangalore. Report for a project funded by the Department of Information Technology, Government of India and Infosys Technologies, Bangalore. Available at http://www.iiitb.ac.in/ICTforD/ict4d.htm

InfoDev. (2005) E-Ready for What? E-Readiness in Developing Countries: Current status and prospects towards the Millennium Development Goals. Available at www.infodev.org/files/2049_file_InfoDev_E_Rdnss_Rpt_rev11May05.pdf

Jaeger, P.T. and Thompson, K.M. (2003) E-government around the World: Lessons, challenges, and future directions, *Government Information Quarterly,* 20, pp. 389–394.

Jain, A. (2004) Using the Lens of Max Weber's Theory of Bureaucracy to Examine E-Government Research, *Proceedings of the 37th Hawaii International Conference on System Sciences (HICSS'04) 5–8 January 2004.*

Janssen, D., Rotthier, S. and Snijkers, K. (2004) If You Measure It They Will Score: An assessment of international e-government benchmarking. 2nd International Conference on eGovernance: From Policy to Reality, Colombo, Sri Lanka, 29 November–1 December.

Kanungo, S. (2003) Information Village: Bridging the digital divide in rural India. In *The Digital Challenge: Information Technology in the Development Context,* edited by S. Krishna and S. Madon, Ashgate, Hants, pp. 103–124.

Kanungo, S. (2004) On the Emancipatory Role of Rural Information Systems, *Information Technology & People,* 17, 4, pp. 407–422.

Kovacic, Z.J. (2005) The Impact of National Culture on Worldwide eGovernment Readiness, *Informing Science Journal,* 8, pp. 143–158.

Kumar, R. and Best, M.L. (2006) Impact and Sustainability of E-Government Services in Developing Countries: Lessons learned from Tamil Nadu, India, *The Information Society,* 22, pp. 1–12.

Lau, E. (2005) Electronic Government and the Drive for Growth and Equity, OECD.

Layne, K. and Lee, J. (2001) Developing Fully Functional E-government: A four-stage model, *Government Information Quarterly*, 18, pp. 122–136.

Lazer, D. (2003) How to Maintain Innovation.gov in a Networked World? Digital Government Workshop at the Kennedy School of Government, Harvard University. Available at http://www.ksg.harvard.edu/cbg/dgworkshop/lazer.pdf

Ma, L., Chung, J. and Thorson, S. (2005) E-government in China: Bringing economic development through administrative reform, *Government Information Quarterly*, 22, pp. 20–37.

Madon, S. (1993) Introducing Administrative Reform through the Application of Computer-based Information Systems: A case study in India, *Public Administration & Development*, 13, pp. 37–48.

Madon, S. (2003) IT Diffusion for Public Service Delivery: Looking for plausible theoretical approaches. In *Information Systems and the Economics of Innovation*, edited by C. Avgerou and R. La Rovere, Edward Elgar, UK.

Madon, S. (2004) Evaluating the Developmental Impact of E-Governance Initiatives: An exploratory framework, *Electronic Journal of Information Systems in Developing Countries*, 20, 5, pp. 1–13.

Madon, S. (2005a) Evaluating eGovernance Projects in India: A focus on micro-level implementation. In *Handbook of Critical Information Systems Research: Theory and Application*, edited by D. Howcroft and E. Trauth, Edward Elgar, Gloucester.

Madon, S. (2005b) Governance Lessons from the Experience of Telecentres in Kerala, *European Journal of Information Systems*, 14, 4, pp. 401–417.

Madon, S. (2006) IT-Based Government Reform Initiatives in the Indian State of Gujarat, *Journal of International Development*, 18, pp. 877–888.

Madon, S. and Kiran, G.R. (2003) Information Technology for Citizen-Government Interface: A study of FRIENDS project in Kerala. World Bank Global Knowledge Sharing Program (GKSP). Available at www1.worldbank.org/publicsector/bnpp/egov-update.htm

Madon, S., Sahay, S. and Sudan, R. (2007) E-Government Policy and Health Information Systems Implementation in Andhra Pradesh, India: Need for articulation of linkages between the macro and the micro, *The Information Society*, 23, pp. 327–344.

Madon, S., Walsham, G., Reinhard, N. and Roode, D. (2008) Digital Inclusion Projects in Developing Countries: Processes of institutionalisation, *IT for Development*, 15, 2, pp. 95–108.

Mayanja, M. (2003) The African Community Telecentres: In search of sustainability, The World Bank Institute. Placed on the Communication Initiative site on 18 April 2003. Available at http://old.developmentgateway.org/download/165918/In_search_of_sust_telecenters_DG.doc

Muthukumaraswamy, M. (2004) Awakening Rural India through CICs, *Information for Development*, 11, 9, pp. 25–35.

Nair, S., Jennaway, M. and Skuse, A. (2006) Local Information Networks: Social and technological considerations, UNESCO.

Ndou, V. (2004) E-Government for Developing Countries: Opportunities and challenges, *EJISDC*, 18, 1, pp. 1–24.

O'Okot-Uma, R. (2000) Electronic Governance: Reinventing good governance. Proceedings of the Workshop on Electronic Governance, September 2000. Available at http://www1.worldbank/org/publicsector/egov/okot-uma.pdf

OECD. (2002) ICT and Business Performance – Empirical Findings and Policy Implications. OECD.

Orlikowski, W. and Robey, D. (1991) Information Technology and the Structuring of Organizations, *Information Systems Research,* 2, 2, pp. 143–169.

Panzardi, R., Calcopietro, C. and Ivanovic, E.F. (2002) Electronic Government and Governance: Lessons for Argentina. World Bank, New-Economy Sector Study, Washington DC, July.

Parent, M., Vandebeek, C.A. and Gemino, A. (2004) Building Citizen Trust through e-Government, *Proceedings of the 37th Hawaii International Conference on System Sciences (HICSS),* Hawaii, January.

Parkinson, S. (2005) *Telecentres, Access and Development: Experiences and lessons from Uganda and South Africa,* ITDG Publishing, Warwickshire.

Peled, A. (2000) First-Class Technology – Third-Rate Bureaucracy: The case of Israel, *Information Technology for Development,* 9, pp. 45–58.

Peters, R.M., Janssen, M. and Van Engers, T. (2004) Evaluating Government Impact: Existing practices and shortcomings. Proceedings of ICEC'04 – Sixth International Conference on Electronic Commerce, edited by Marjin Jannsen, Henk Sol and Rene Wagenaar.

Peterson, S.B. (1991) From Processing to Analysing: Intensifying the use of micro-computers in development bureaucracies, *Public Administration and Development,* 11, pp. 491–510.

Prakash, A. and De', R. (2007) Importance of Development Context in ICT4D Projects: A study of computerisation of land records, *Information Technology & People,* 20, 3, pp. 262–282.

Proenza, F.J. (2001) Telecenter Sustainability: Myths and opportunities, *The Journal of Development Communication,* 12, 2, pp. 94–109.

Ranerup, A. (1999) Internet-enabled Applications for Local Government Democratisation. In *Reinventing Government in the Information Age,* edited by R. Heeks, Routledge, London.

Rangaswamy, N. (2006) Social Entrepreneurship as Critical Agency: A study of rural internet kiosks, *Proceedings of the 2006 International Conference on ICT and Development,* Berkeley, CA.

Ray, S. and Venkata Rao, V. (2004) Evaluating Government Service: A customers' perspective of e-Government, Paper presented at the 2nd International Conference on E-Government, 29 November–01 December, Colombo, Sri Lanka.

Reilly, K. and Gomez, R. (2001) Comparing Approaches: Telecentre evaluation experience in Asia and Latin America, *EJISDC,* 4, 3, pp. 1–17.

Riley, T. (2003) eGovernance vs. E-Government, *i4d,* November–December.

Roman, R. and Colle, R.D. (2002) Themes and Issues in Telecentre Sustainability, *Development Informatics Working Paper Series, Paper No. 10,* Institute of Development Policy and Management, University of Manchester.

Roman, R. and Colle, R.D. (2003) Content Creation for ICT Development Projects: Integrating normative approaches and community demand, *Information Technology for Development,* 10, pp. 85–94.

Scholl, H.J. (2001) Applying Stakeholder Theory to E-Government: Benefits and limits, *Proceedings of the 1st IFIP Conference on E-Commerce and E-Government,* Zurich, Switzerland.

Shadrach, B. and Ekeanyanwu, L. (2003) Improving the Transparency, Quality and Effectiveness of Pro-Poor Public Services using the ICTs: An attempt by Transparency International. Paper presented at the 11th International Anti-Corruption Conference, Seoul, 25–28 May.

Sify Business (2004) Most eGovernance Projects Fail, 5 November. Available at http://sify.com/finance/fullstory.php?id=13605188

Sivakumar, S.K. (2004) A Battle for Information, *Frontline*, 18–31 December, 21, 26.

Sood, A.D. (2003) Information Nodes in the Rural Landscape, *I4D*, 1, 1, pp. 14–22.

Soriano, C.R. (2007) Exploring the ICT and Rural Poverty Reduction Link: Community telecenters and rural livelihoods in Wu'an, China, *EJISDC*, 32, 1, pp. 1–15.

Sreekumar, T.T. (2007) Decrypting eGovernance: Narratives, power play and participation in the Gyandoot Intranet, *EJISDC*, 32, 4, pp. 1–24.

Srinivasan, R. (2006) Where Information Society and Community Voice Intersect, *The Information Society*, 22, pp. 355–365.

Stiglitz, J. (2002) *Globalization and Its Discontents,* Penguin Books, London.

Stoll, K., Menou, M., Camacho, K. and Khellady, Y. (2004) Learning About ICT's Role in Development: A framework towards a participatory, transparent and continuous process, IDRC, Ottawa, Canada.

Sturges, P. (2004) Corruption, Transparency and a Role for ICT? *International Journal of Information Ethics,* 2, November.

Sudan, R. (2005) The Basic Building Blocks of e-Government. In *E-Development: From excitement to effectiveness,* edited by Robert Schware. Prepared for the World Summit on the Information Society, Tunis, November 2005, World Bank Group.

Symonds, M. (2000) Government and the Internet, survey, *Economist,* 355, 24 June.

Tacchi, J. (2005) Finding a Voice: The potential of creative ICT literacy and voice in community multimedia centres in South Asia, Information Society Research Group, Working Paper No. 3, LSE.

Thomas, P. (2009) Bhoomi, Gyan Ganga, E-Governance and the Right to Information: ICTs and development in India, *Telematics and Informatics,* 26, 1, pp. 20–31.

UNDESA. (2003) E-Government as a Free Lunch? *Development Administration,* 106, pp. 6–8.

UNDP. (2002) Deepening Democracy in a Fragmented World. Human Development Report, Oxford University Press, Oxford.

Vasudevan, R. (2006) Changed Governance or Computerized Governance? Computerized property transfer processes in Tamil Nadu (India). *Proceedings of the 2006 International Conference on ICT and Development,* Berkeley, CA.

Walsham, G. (1992) Decentralisation of Information Systems in Developing Countries: Power to the people. In *Social Implications of Computers in Developing Countries,* edited by S.C. Bhatnagar and M. Odedra, Tata McGraw-Hill, New Delhi.

Whyte, A. (2000) Assessing Community Telecentres: Guidelines for Researchers, International Development Research Centre, Ottawa, Canada.

World Bank (2002) Global Economic Prospects and the Developing Countries 2002: Making trade work for the world's poor, World Bank, Washington DC.

World Bank (2004) Making Services Work for Poor People. World Development Report, World Bank, Oxford University Press.

World Bank (2007) Impact Assessment Study of Computerized Service Delivery Projects from India and Chile, IT @ WB Staff Working Paper No. 2. Available at http://www-wds.worldbank.org/external/default/WDSContentServer/WDSP/IB/2008/04/08/000333038_20080408052408/Rendered/PDF/421470WPOBox327349B01Public1/pdf

Part II
Case Studies

5
Researching e-Governance for Development

In this chapter, I discuss my approach to researching e-governance for development. My inquiry over the years has been shaped by policy shifts that have occurred regarding the relationship between administration, governance and development. Guided by a constructivist epistemology, my research adopts a critical stance to 'taken-for-granted' theories about governance reform and aims to interpret the views of the various producers and consumers of e-governance projects. My research design adopts a longitudinal perspective and presents three case studies of e-governance in India. Each case is from a different state and is targeted at a different sector. I conclude this chapter by describing some of the methodological issues and challenges that have arisen.

Researching e-governance for development comes as a natural progression for me given my earlier interest in IT in the governmental sector in India. From the late 1980s into the early 1990s, as part of my doctoral studies I had been involved with examining patterns of factors that influenced the implementation of information systems for rural development planning and management. At the time, the academic community of development studies had no interest in IT, and information systems scholars were arguing that developing countries needed to emulate the IT-enabled success stories from the West. My case study provided insights into the difficulties and challenges encountered in implementing technological change in the context of development administration. The findings from my study showed that acceptance and usage of ICTs derived from local administrators having the flexibility to direct the technology towards their own requirements (Madon, 1992). The findings from my longitudinal study and the work of many other scholars at the time produced knowledge that became increasingly valuable as the role of IT in development became widely recognised.

Over the past decade, I have extended my field of inquiry beyond IT in the government sector to broader issues of governance and development drawing support from the critical literature in this area. The real world issue I am investigating refers to understanding the e-governance phenomenon from a social study point of view. This means studying the social events which have shaped the phenomenon and the impact of this on processes of governance and development. My research to date has adopted a constructivist perspective because the kind of knowledge or understanding I expect to gain is about day to day processes citizens are engaged in such as earning a living and seeking welfare services. I give more importance to theory-building in my research, rather than testing an already established model of e-governance for development.

My earlier research on decentralised information systems for development planning was guided by the methodological rationale of contextualist analysis which focused on the interaction between different layers of context (i.e., regional, national and local) and processes of change brought about by the introduction of IT for administrative reform. More recently, the research tradition I identify myself with is reflexive methodology which is an approach that has appealed to a broad range of researchers in the social sciences. There are two basic characteristics of this approach – reflexivity and interpretation. Reflexivity stimulates critical reflection on taken-for-granted theories based on important issues which have surfaced regarding e-governance for development. My literature review has drawn on various middle-range theories that have helped me adopt such a critical stance. These theories derive from critical thought in the fields of development studies and political science. It has also been useful to draw insights from literature specific to the various sectors for which the e-governance projects have been implemented. For example, for my research on health information systems, I have found theories from the health systems literature useful to draw on. As part of the theory-building exercise, I have focused on current social processes and their consequences for communities using my fieldwork to generate knowledge to support or reshape my theoretical ideas.

My research follows a case study approach. At the highest level, the case chosen for investigation is a historical process – that of e-governance implementation in India. All over India, there are many similar e-governance initiatives being implemented in different states – each defined by their own history and context. The research identifies embedded units of analysis characterised by state and by sector. My focus is on the states of Gujarat, Kerala and Karnataka. These three states were chosen partly due to opportunistic reasons and partly because of the types of projects I sought to study. My research in Gujarat goes back to the early 1990s when I was a doctoral student and research over the years has given me an opportunity to study the many changes that have occurred in the rural development sector. I started research on e-governance in Kerala in 2000 intrigued by the state's unique socio-political legacy and what this might mean for e-governance activity. After following e-services implementation in urban parts of the state, I started to focus on the impact of telecentre implementation on rural farming communities in north Kerala. My choice of Karnataka as a study site is more recent and arises out of my involvement in a British Council academic exchange programme on IT for improving public health systems in rural Karnataka. The project commenced in 2007 in collaboration with the Indian Institute of Management in Bangalore and Imperial College, London.

I have adopted a longitudinal research design which has enabled me to track changes particularly since social settings have inertia and change sometimes takes months, even years to be observed. Over time, various causal connections have been observed. For example, how usage of ICTs is influenced by local relevance of application. Similarly, how front-end e-services type applications rely on back-end e-administration systems to function. Even though it has not been possible to prove causality, the ability to understand how conditions change over time has been valuable and will be useful for future studies.

My research adopts an ethnographic approach to gain an interpretation of the multiple perspectives provided by the participants. This approach has been recommended by methodology experts as being particularly suited for critical study of this type (Fife, 2005). Ethnographic research involves both macro level and micro level of information gathering and analysis.

Macro-level data gathering

Historical data sources

Secondary and primary forms of historical research have enabled me to develop a contextual understanding of development and governance in India and in the three states. Without a solid understanding of some of the major historical patterns of governance reform state-wise and nationally, it would be extremely difficult to arrive at an adequate understanding of the role of e-governance for development. While secondary historical sources were utilised for this background contextual information, I saw advantages in using some primary historical sources, particularly within individual states. In many cases, I found that the self-serving nature of much historical documentation resulted in much of the secondary source material summarising large-scale changes sometimes glossing over important individual differences that can be found in the actions of real historical actors. For example, primary source historical material of individual telecentre entrepreneurs' case histories gave me access to competing voices that existed during a specific time period. Also, discussions with retired senior administrators provided me with alternative perspective to official government documentation. A case in point is the undocumented negative attitude shown by many senior bureaucrats towards the shift in anti-poverty programmes from household schemes to group-oriented credit mobilisation schemes.

Current data sources

Many contemporary sources have provided me with an understanding of the macro-context that embeds e-governance projects in India. First, basic statistical data published by various ministries such as the Ministry of Information and Communication Technology, Ministry of Health, Ministry of Agriculture and Rural Development have been consulted to understand current ideologies and how they translate into the implementation of schemes. Second, apart from government reports, basic political economy literature on India and on the states provided me with an insight into contemporary governance and e-governance policy. Most of this material is published in India and available from good academic bookshops. During every trip, a few days are built into my field research devoted to searching for relevant material.

Despite the bias in research against publications from mass media sources, I found newspaper articles and media briefs of use in my research. Such information provided me with a local understanding which could not be obtained elsewhere. For example, newspapers gave me an insight into wider public attitudes towards certain issues which could not be obtained from more official data. The intent of gathering information from such mass media sources has been to gain a broader understanding of what is considered to be newsworthy and therefore of public concern in the community and to gain a background that would allow one to place the more parochial concerns of the local area of a research site against the wider social issues relevant to the country as a whole. An example taken from the UK context to illustrate this point refers to the recent publicity in the press received by the National Programme for Information Technology (NPfIT) in which serious concerns have been expressed over the scope, planning, budgeting and practical value of the programme.[1] Taking an example from the Indian context, a large number of articles have appeared in the press in recent times expressing fear over the 'take-over' of telecentres in India by large IT and communication companies.

These documentary sources were complemented with discussions held with central and state government staff and with academics at various institutions such as the Indian Institutes of Management in Ahmedabad and Bangalore, the Centre for Development Studies in Trivandrum, Kerala.

Micro-level data gathering

Basic field methods of interviewing and participant observation were used throughout the research with a view to establishing a rapport with the people being studied and developing a feeling about what it is like to be a member of the community. According to methodologists, the more time we stay in a community, the better we can internalise the basic beliefs, fears, hopes and expectations of the community under study (Spradley, 1979, 1980). My initial research in Gujarat involved staying at the study site for several months. Since 2000, the duration of my fieldwork has been approximately 4–6 weeks per year. The process involved trial and error, particularly in terms of learning how to behave according to the social and cultural patterns of behaviour that prevail. The key to this process is good observational skills. For example, initially I had not realised that there is a hierarchy to be observed when interacting with the bureaucracy that sometimes precludes holding informal conversations with junior level staff such as drivers or peons.

In terms of interview style, my aim was not to limit the responses of people I study through structured interviews or closed questions. For the most part, semi-structured interviews allowed some control or steering but without the need to use close-ended questions. Often such interviews would be in an informal setting such as a rickshaw or someone's house and bordered on a conversational interview format in which questions were asked in random order as part of an overall discussion. These questions centred around the themes of my prior reading of secondary literature. In one case, close-ended structured interviews proved to be valuable in terms of gathering information about the community's health-seeking behaviour in rural Karnataka. However, there were situations in which semi-structured interviews did not work well. For example, when talking to self-help groups in Gujarat, my respondents were too shy to reply or speak other than a 'yes' or 'no' response in a 1-1 situation. What worked better in such cases were group interviews in which I sat down with a small group of rural poor ladies and asked them several questions related to their situation. I found that this way, one lady's answer would often trigger off other ladies to contribute to the discussion.

Analysis

The point of analysis is to link human behaviour in specific environments to larger patterns of socio-economic, political and cultural importance. While at the outset, my research went from understanding the broader context to gathering more detailed local information, in analysis, the process was reversed.

Preliminary analysis of information (creating concepts)

Preliminary coding of interview data and other data gathered from the field involved the following process. Once a specific category was identified, I automatically began to search for it among each new data set as the analysis proceeded. This is why the preliminary analytical process is called cumulative – there is a tendency for the same coding categories to come up again and again. For example, one category that finds expression in all the cases is intermediation. By this is meant the role played by a variety of players in mediating between the community and the public system – that is, the health system, the self-help group programme or the farming system. A second category that recurrs throughout my research is that of local administrative capacity. The primary data record numerous cases from the three study sites where local administrators have little autonomy to satisfy local development priorities.

Secondary analysis

In the second part of the analysis, the goal is to begin cementing together the various levels of data collection to form a larger picture of the patterns of human behaviour. It is called secondary analysis because it involves putting together already analysed bits of information to form larger conceptual patterns – that is, analysis of analysis. I no longer worked with my fieldnotes directly but was concerned with the potential relationship between one analytical concept and another. For example, the relationship between local administrative capacity and the delivery of improved services to citizens. However, patterns were not always the same in the three cases or even in the same case as individuals are influenced by different contextual factors at various times in their lives. For example, even local government functionaries have different behaviour patterns dependent on social conditioning.

Creating and testing theory

Ethnographic research consists of an ongoing process of developing theory (from earlier theories of a researcher or other researchers) and testing that theory. The creation of theory in my research occurs every time a linkage is suggested between one analytical concept and another – for example, between the concept of intermediation and community participation which is itself drawn from theorisation in the literature. My theory came to be 'tested' when I look to see how usefully it fits a different situation. The process of theory-building has been a cross-disciplinary exercise – an approach recommended by sociology of development scholars (Harriss, 2002). Although e-governance is often considered a technological innovation, a critical review of development and governance ideas has helped to understand the complexity of improving the living conditions of communities.

Some methodological issues and challenges that have arisen in my research

I have faced numerous methodological issues and challenges during the course of my research. First, my research involved numerous types of interactions with people. Often, for example, I found myself acting as a distant spectator observing a busy telecentre or primary health centre at peak times during the day. At other times, my research position was that of participant observer, for example, when I attended a training session for rural self-help groups and interacted with the trainees. I also sometimes held a position of action researcher, using findings from my research to provide feedback and thereby shape decisions made by policy-makers. In Kerala, for example, I have been invited to media briefing sessions and conferences where I have found myself interacting with senior policy-makers.

Second, the long-term duration of the research has meant sustained intellectual effort and theorising around one topic area. Fieldwork during the initial period of PhD research was more in-depth consisting of about three trips each of about two months' duration from the period 1989 to 1992. Thereafter, research has involved one or two periods of fieldwork per year in each of the three study sites and each trip has been of roughly six weeks' duration. The gap between trips has meant that concepts and research questions that were thought to be relevant at one time in a project have become irrelevant or trivial. For example, the concept of e-literacy which was a key criterion on which the Akshaya project's impact was measured in 2005 came to be superseded later on by a desire to introduce commercial and socially relevant activities. Similarly, the significant effort made to strengthen local administrative capacity in Gujarat in the mid-1990s was short-lived superseded by a technology-driven mandate to promote citizen-centric e-governance applications.

Third, while a longitudinal research design may seem essential for studying the interaction between e-governance projects and local processes of governance, this had cost and funding implications which I had to address. During the PhD fieldwork period, I was successful in obtaining funding for trips from an IT company. Following this, I applied to several funding bodies to secure travel money to continue with my research. Most of the funding lasted for three years which meant that I had to follow a regular cycle of application preparation to ensure continuity with the research.

Fourth, while a cross-disciplinary approach to the study of e-governance for development has provided scope for critical analysis, it also alerts the researcher to many other strands of literature which may be relevant. For example, the specific manifestation of development in practice is often concerned with a particular sector such as agriculture, rural development or health. There is a dearth of policy literature in each of these sectors that I can draw on to gain a more in-depth understanding of how communities develop, for example, the work of health systems specialists.

These methodological issues and challenges will remain with me for some years to come as I see my research on e-governance for development as part of a long-term commitment. I plan to remain focused on depth rather than breadth strongly defending the approach advocated by critical development scholars to study relatively small geographic areas over time. Carrying out qualitative longitudinal research is demanding both in cost and time but vital for building up a base of knowledge about the contexts of e-governance implementation.

Without such a knowledge base, we are neither able to assess the real developmental value of an e-governance application, nor able to assess relevance of experience from one context to another. Before describing the case studies, the next chapter provides a review of changes that have occurred in India's policy environment both in terms of economic and political reform. This then leads to a discussion of the ideology that supports e-governance in India.

References

Fife, W. (2005) *Doing Fieldwork: Ethnographic methods for research in developing countries and beyond,* Palgrave Macmillan, Hants. Available at www1.worldbank.org/publicsector/bnpp/egovupdate.htm

Harriss, J. (2002) The Case for Cross-Disciplinary Approaches in International Development, *World Development,* 30, 3, pp. 487–496.

Madon, S. (1992) The Impact of Computer-Based Information Systems on Rural Development: A case study in India. PhD Thesis, Department of Computing, Imperial College, London.

Spradley, J. (1979) *The Ethnographic Interview,* Holt, Rinehart and Winston, New York.

Spradley, J. (1980) *Participant Observation,* Holt, Rinehart and Winston, New York.

6
India: Development, Governance and e-Governance

This chapter traces India's policy focus since the country adopted market liberalisation in 1991. By the end of the 1990s, with the opening up of the economy, deregulation and privatisation, India's economic position has been strengthened attracting higher levels of domestic and foreign investments, particularly in the IT sector. This growth, however, has benefited mainly the urban educated minority with evidence of increasing poverty and inequality in the country, particularly in rural areas. Under the neoliberal policy agenda, good governance prescriptions have been prioritised as essential for promoting socio-economic development. e-Governance has become an increasingly significant element of this policy agenda with the latest drive devoted to promoting these applications in rural settings. However, the ideology driving this agenda appears to be driven by the market rather than by a social policy mandate questioning the relevance of e-governance applications for promoting development.

At the time of Independence, India's economic profile was distressing. There had hardly been any growth in the previous half century, and both agriculture and industry were characterised by severe market distortions (Jalan, 1991, 2004). Against this background, there was unanimous agreement among political leaders, nationalists and industrialists that the state should take direct responsibility for the country's development. There was broad consensus on many strategic issues such as the role of the public sector, the discouragement of foreign investment in the country, the development of heavy industries and the need for centralised planning. Throughout the 1980s and 1990s, the Indian economy grew at an average annual rate of approximately 4%, adjusted for population growth and an average of 6% per year in the 1990s (Ahluwalia, 2002).

However, these gains were not sufficient to offset the burdens caused by a rising population and excessive fiscal deficit. In 1991, India was in a deep balance of payment crisis and this resulted in the introduction by the government of new trade, fiscal and industrial policy initiatives (Dandekar, 2004). By 2004, India had managed to generate one of the strongest balance of payments positions in the developing world and enjoyed the comfort of having a high level of foreign exchange reserves that were sufficient to cope with not one but several domestic or external shocks (such as during 2002–3 when India simultaneously experienced a bad drought, border tensions and high oil prices due to the war in Iraq). This transformation in India's economic position was facilitated by a deliberate pragmatic approach to exchange rate management taken by policy-makers in India as against the policy prescriptions of international economists and institutions which favoured countries making a choice between two extremes of having fixed exchange rates or a fully floating exchange rate without any central bank intervention (Jalan, 2004). The experience of several countries which had conformed to such prescriptions had been dismal whereas India's exchange rate policy was to adopt flexible exchange rate but not a free float with the central bank able to intervene in markets as and when needed. In addition to sharp increases in reserves and generally systematic movements in exchange rates, this policy move strengthened the confidence levels of domestic and foreign investors.

Since 1991, a spate of reforms has given impetus particularly to investment in the ICT sector. This was a period of rapid development of technology-based industry in India with growing levels of expertise in IT, injection of venture capitalism and increasing amounts of foreign investment in this sector. As part of this policy agenda, the Indian government took significant steps to promote ICTs with a focus on software development for export, telecommunications policy reform, privatisation of the national long-distance and mobile phone markets and development of a more comprehensive approach to ICTs. By the end of the 1990s, with the opening up of the economy, deregulation and privatisation, India became a favoured destination for software development due to cheap labour and highly skilled manpower. Building on the argument that information technology could enable developing countries to leapfrog stages of development (Davison *et al.*, 2000; Steinmueller, 2001), the Report of the National Task Force on IT and Software Development published in 1998 prescribed investment in IT to promote economic development. Many Panglossian views of the Indian economy were published coining official rhetoric about 'Shining India', 'Outsourced India' (The Hindu, 2004).

While it is true that India has made great strides in rates of economic growth and in its role in the global software export industry, the extent to which the recent liberalisation and growth has benefited the poorest sections of the population is contentious. Discrepancy in interpretation of statistics has led to heated debates in the Indian press and academia about the tensions between economic growth amidst increasing poverty and deprivation in the country. The various claims have largely been political. Advocates of the economic reforms back National Accounts Statistics growth estimates and argue that consumption is estimated to have grown at approximately 3.2% a year since the economic reforms of the early 1990s (Bhalla, 2001; Deaton, 2002; Deaton and Kozel, 2005). In contrast, opponents of the economic reforms in India argue that the growth of real consumption is exaggerated in the National Accounts arguing instead that the actual poverty reduction after 1993–4 has been much less than the earlier official estimates (Dev and Ravi, 2007; Himanshu Sen, 2004). More recently, data from the 2004–5 survey have become available which suggest that although the fall in the number of poor, mainly in rural areas, has continued, the absolute number of the broader category of poor people has only reduced very slightly. Per capita income for this group of the population remains low and over a quarter of the population still lives below the poverty line[1] (UNDP, 2002; World Bank, 2005; Bhaskar and Gupta, 2007). More recently, data from the 2004–5 survey have become available which suggests that although the fall in the number of poor, mainly in rural areas, has continued, the absolute number of the broader category of poor people has only reduced very slightly (Dev and Ravi, 2007; Himanshu Sen, 2004). Per capita income for this group of the population remains low and over a quarter of the population still lives below the poverty line (Bhaskar and Gupta, 2007; UNDP, 2002; World Bank, 2005).

Economic growth, then, has been accompanied by increasing inequality with a rising urban-rural divide and widening regional disparities (Deaton and Dreze, 2002). Liberalisation resulted in the opening up of a variety of controls but also to a shrinking of the development budget. At the same time, the budget increased taxation on essentials for the poor such as kerosene for cooking, fertilizers and pulses along with withdrawal of the minimum price support for wheat, rice and essential crops (Slater, 2002). There was a drastic reduction in government expenditure in the countryside, particularly in rural technologies such as irrigation pumps, which contributed not only to a crisis of rural infrastructure but also to a squeeze in the purchasing power of the rural poor resulting in a decline in per capita food absorption (Patnaik, 2005). What is also clear is that the process of reform initiated in the 1990s in India has hardly touched the agricultural sector which has experienced declining levels of both public and private investment (Chibber and Eldersveld, 2000; Hanumantha Rao, 2004). In India, an estimated 70% of the population, comprising mainly the lower range of the income spectrum, relies on agriculture for a living (ILO, 2004). Despite the more optimistic picture derived from national statistics, poverty has become more concentrated in the country's lagging states, in its rural areas and among its disadvantaged people many of whom are small-scale farmers or casual labourers. People of scheduled castes and scheduled tribes who together constitute approximately 24% of India's total population are more likely to be poor than those of other social groups because of their low status and because gender biases continue to operate as social obstacles that exclude them from opportunity (Harriss-White, 2003; World Bank, 2004).

As a consequence of a reduced development budget, investments in various elements of social policy such as health reform, agrarian reform, food procurement and distribution, education, employment, reservations and national anti-poverty programmes have declined (Ghosh, 2004). Growing inequality has increased social tensions showing up in the form of violence against minorities and voter backlash. Governments were voted out of power in Madhya Pradesh in 2003 and Andhra Pradesh in 2004 due to a backlash by peasant farmers and other vulnerable groups against the macro-economic reform agenda being pursued by the government in these two states. More recently, the promotion of industrial development and the interests of corporations have resulted in a widespread sense of marginalisation felt by many people in India. In October 2007, this resulted in a month-long march by activists and grassroots organisations on behalf of 25,000 landless peasants from 15 states in India who are among the poorest and most powerless members of India's vast population (The Independent, 2007). As a result of the march, the Indian government announced it would set up a national task force charged with overseeing land reform in the country – it remains to be seen whether policy promises will translate into genuine results on the ground.

Over the past decade, the Indian policy environment has been largely focused on aspects of governance reform and problems with India's overall development were identified as due to inefficiencies in the functioning of the government at all levels and solutions were proposed through reform initiatives. Many of these reform prescriptions were articulated in the Tenth Five-Year Plan document (2002–7) (GOI, 2002) under the heading of 'good governance' and are increasingly perceived as central for addressing India's overall development.

Governance reform in India

The concern about state-society relations in India has a long tradition dating back to the leading lights of India's anti-colonial struggles who all spoke about the importance of good government and suggested that power had to be used for and by 'the people'. For example, Mahatma Gandhi pointed to the village or cluster of villages while Ambedkar[2] looked to the district and state level institutions to break the power of locally dominant classes (GOI, 1978; John, 2007). By the 1960s, the question of corruption was forcing itself onto the national political agenda and the Report of the Santhanam Committee of 1964 on the prevention of corruption recommended the setting up of a system of Chief Vigilance Officer to review corruption (GOI, 1964, p. 189). The relevance of these efforts for reducing corruption was highlighted again in the 1970s and 1980s as concerns grew about the abuse of executive power and the criminalisation of politics. By the end of the 1980s, Rajiv Gandhi (who was prime minister at the time) was convinced that decentralisation of power was essential to create a more accountable system of governance and built this agenda into his election slogan. But nothing much changed under Gandhi despite various efforts to introduce decentralised structures and monitoring tools and it was left to Narasimha Rao (the next prime minister) in the 1990s to turn promises into policies.

In order to ease the impact of neoliberal restructuring on the poor majority, the government began to face strong pressure to compensate voters through development programmes and through the decentralisation of social policy. In 1993, the Government of India passed a series of constitutional reforms (the 73rd and 74th amendments) aimed at improving the performance and accountability of local government bodies in India (Govinda Rao and Singh, 2005; Narayan and Sanjay, 2007; Palanithurai, 2007). Decentralised local government which was earlier recognised as a most suitable mechanism to increase people's participation in policy formulation and implementation, particularly the weaker sections of the population, was now made statutory. At the village level, the gram sabha was legally constituted as a forum for all eligible voters and had to meet once every three months with the object of electing a village council (gram panchayat). These structures had to be functional and could not be abolished by state governments. Despite these advances, however, in practice, many panchayats are powerless with studies in India consistently highlighting the fact that the panchayat's ability to undertake the function of decentralised planning and governance is undermined by (1) centralising tendencies of state government in part to compensate for the increasing financial dependence of states on central government (2) the incentive structure of the bureaucracy which provides little motivation for functionaries at lower administrative tiers to improve their work performance and (3) rural inequalities rooted in land holdings, caste, religion and gender (Ghatak and Ghatak, 2002; Jha, 2000; Mukarji, 1999).

Experience with adherence to decentralised governance legislation has been varied across the country. Some states such as Kerala, Tamil Nadu, Maharashtra, Gujarat and Karnakata are highly developed with respect to decentralised governance structures. In these states, local elections are held routinely and the gram sabha is convened regularly. However, in other states of the country, there has been less commitment to establish and enforce local governance structures (Jafri, 2001; Slater and Watson, 1989). Establishing institutions to reform local governance structures is one step; however, experience shows that there is also need to produce people who are able to participate effectively in these structures. Decentralised local governance structures work most effectively in states such as Kerala or West Bengal where a supportive political culture exists and where general education levels are higher. These states continue to make steady progress in the implementation of reforms to strengthen local governance institutions through increased resource flows to panchayats or by empowering gram sabhas to demand accountability from elected representatives and government officials. Kerala, for example, has put 90% of development spending in the hands of its panchayats, reducing the role of the Collector (the most senior administrator at the district level) to a mere regulator – over seeing land records and advising the panchayats. But in most states, especially the Hindi-speaking belt where poverty levels are greatest, panchayats have not been granted adequate powers and resources and their impact remains modest (Robinson, 2005). The lack of power of the panchayats has encouraged local elites to capture decentralised organisations and their resources resulting in an inability of local government organisations to respond to the needs and priorities of community members (The Economist, 2008b).

Johnson *et al.* (2007) conducted research in the states of Andhra Pradesh and Madhya Pradesh to understand the impact that local governance structures have on the ability of government to implement anti-poverty programmes in rural India. A major finding from their study was that political decentralisation can only work if people are politically aware, supporting the experience from Kerala discussed earlier. If this is not the case, it is better to reduce the role of locally elected bodies in favour of local administration as more power in the hands of local government could be abused by powerful elite groups. In Madhya Pradesh, the government had conferred far greater responsibility to locally elected bodies, especially at village level. However, the general level of awareness and motivation of people about the programme and their participation in it was poor which meant that its economic impact was minimal. On the other hand, in Andhra Pradesh, the government worked extensively through the state bureaucracy and line departments, effectively bypassing the locally elected institutions. The wide publicity given by the government about the programme meant that its content and function were widely understood in rural areas strengthening peoples' capacity to get involved in local development initiatives.

India's neoliberal economic and political restructuring agenda has affected the direction of governance reform. In particular, the focus has been on reducing the role of government in all aspects of economic planning by broadening the role of civil society and community involvement in public affairs. There are signs that civil society in India is slowly being broadened. Sections of the public presenting complaints through the structures of political society has become more routinised (Haque, 2002). However, the advantages of civil society are seldom enjoyed by the very poor as the bulk of these people tend to avail of public services through the intermediation of either an administrator, political representative or NGO. The practice of working through NGOs and village-level community organisations has firmly taken root in India in various areas of developmental activity such as human rights, democracy, rural development, womens' development and health which had, until this time, been the preserve of the state. This has also been a solution favoured by multi-lateral agencies like the World Bank in pursuance of good governance goals based on the assumption that these local organisations are closer to citizens and therefore more capable of understanding and responding to their needs. The number of NGOs in India quadrupled in the 1980s and 1990s (from about 40,000 to nearly 200,000) (Jayal, 2001; Lal and Purohit, 2007). Government funding to NGOs has also increased substantially. In 1986, the Government of India established the Council for Advancement of People's Action and Rural Technology (CAPART) as an autonomous nodal agency for channelling development funds from the government to NGOs working in rural development sectors like rural technology, water supply, watershed management and social forestry. An NGO working in this sector is PRADAN established in 1983 to enhance the livelihood capacities of the poor giving them access to sustainable income opportunities. The NGO has a governing body comprised of honorary members all of whom are professionals from government, private organisations and research institutes. PRADAN plays the role of facilitator leveraging finances from government agencies at the district, state and central levels as well as from banks.

A large number of NGOs are increasingly concerned with mobilising the community to demand the right to information (Sivakumar, 2004). For example, the Mazdoor Kisan Shakti Sangathan in demanding the right to information in Rajasthan (Mishra, 2003) or the work of the Tarun Bharat Sangh in generating the natural water sources of the Alwar district in Rajasthan (Kumar and Kandpal, 2003). However, to the extent that mobilisation requires awareness, and the creation of awareness involves local political activity, various scholars have pointed out that unless NGOs have a long-term commitment to a particular locality, they invariably find themselves as outsiders unable to penetrate the local social and political milieu (Alsop and Kurey, 2005; Harriss, 2004). In their study of local organisations in India, Alsop and Kurey notice a lack of coordination between the various players and note that there is considerable duplication of mandated functions in all sectors and at all levels. These scholars focused on local organisations in three sectors such as womens' development, rural drinking water supply and watershed development in the states of Karnataka, Madhya Pradesh and Uttaranchal. Their findings showed that local administrative government bodies remain deeply involved and are largely effective in the execution of projects. Elected local government at gram, taluk and district panchayat levels, however, have only limited roles and are often ineffective in performing their assigned functions. Community level organisations function as extension of project implementation structures distributing short-term benefits to members. The presence of NGOs was low with most acting merely as contractors for government programmes.

An overtly neoliberal governance agenda has been pursued in India with support from the international development community resulting in the existence of parallel structures of governance. The older administrative structure continues to exist comprising of various tiers of bureaucracy (The Economist, 2008). In addition, new governance arrangements and contractual relationships between the administration and NGOs are proliferating. e-Governance has become an increasingly significant element of this policy agenda. In the Indian government's Tenth Five-Year Plan document (2002–7), under the chapter dedicated to 'good governance', specific mention was made to the promotion of e-governance in the country.

e-Governance in India

An important aspect of technology policy in the late 1980s was to actively promote computer applications which had a perceived catalytic effect on development (GOI, 1985). A massive programme of computerisation was launched in government administrative departments which created a large market for the products of the industry. Following liberalisation of the economy, state-of-the-art computers became available at about one-third of the 1983 price (Singhal and Rogers, 1989; Heeks, 1990). Applications during the 1970s, 1980s and early 1990s focused on automation of internal government functions rather than on improving citizen service delivery. The National Informatics Centre created by the Department of Electronics (and later transferred to the Planning Commission) was set up to establish informatics services for the government at central, state and district levels to improve decision-making processes for development planning. A major bottleneck to usage of computers at local administration level during the Seventh Five-Year Plan period (1985–90) was the weak telecommunications infrastructure in India, especially in rural areas. In 1985, the government created a new Department of Telecommunications announcing a telecommunications policy which permitted foreign collaboration with the Indian private sector towards manufacturing indigenous telecommunications equipment with a focus on the installation of rural automatic exchanges which could tolerate electrical power surges, extreme temperature variation, high humidity and dusty environments. A nationwide computer network called NICNET was created by the NIC to exchange information among government ministries and departments. The main NIC set-up in Delhi is linked to computers in state capitals which are in turn linked to hundreds of district-level computers installed at District Information Centres.

One of the major constraints for national economic planning in the 1980s had been identified as the inadequate or non-availability of comprehensive data (GOI, 1988). But the rapid advancement in computerisation by this time provided possibilities to transmit data about program implementation from the field level up to central government for monitoring and evaluation. This opportunity prompted the NIC to design and develop two computer applications for installation at all the 436 district agencies in the country to improve the efficiency and effectiveness of rural development programmes. First, the District Information System (DISNIC) which aimed to improve district-level planning in the panchayat offices. Second, the Computerised Rural Information Systems Project (CRISP) specifically aimed at improving the efficiency and effectiveness of anti-poverty programmes to be installed in the District Rural Development Agencies (DRDAs). The impact of these systems, however, was reported as minimal in terms of both efficiency and effectiveness (Madon, 1992; Pradan, 1990). They were designed and developed by a team of specialists in New Delhi but failed to take account of different information requirements of individual states. Moreover, the systems were implemented without adequate attention given to human resource and capacity-building at the district level in terms of providing enough data entry staff and developing skills to use data for improving planning (Madon, 1993). Nevertheless, in later years, I found that many of the district agencies had developed some in-house capability to use the technology for routine reporting to higher levels and for generating information for internal analysis. Both the DISNIC and CRISP systems continue to operate[3] although the CRISP project has changed significantly in its orientation. The main emphasis of the project has turned to the promotion of new e-governance applications for rural citizens and only a small element of the project, renamed RuralSoft since 2000, remains dedicated to strengthening district-level rural development planning and monitoring.

The emergence of India as a global player in software development, IT and call centre operations provided a catalyst for more investment in government information systems projects to improve systems of administration (Gill, 2004). The 1998 Department of IT Report of the National Task Force on IT and Software Development recommended the preparation of Five-Year IT Plans by every department in central and state governments earmarking 1–3% of their budget for applying IT to streamline their functioning. It gave the various ministries and departments three months to issue all necessary instructions and amendments to procedures. But in the rush to implement the policy, there was very little opportunity for analysing the information requirements for various levels of decision-making within individual government departments and agencies (Ghatak, 2007). With the introduction of neoliberal policies came the strong belief that IT could lead to the overall betterment of society by improving the quality of governance (Das and Chandrashekhar, 2006; Kalam, 2008). The National E-Governance Action Plan (NeGP) 2003–7 report was prepared jointly by the Department of IT (EGovernance Division) and the

Department of Administrative Reforms and Public Grievances with support from the World Bank (Dataquest, 2005). The plan advised that e-governance services should be outsourced and that full potentiality of the private sector should be exploited. An ambitious outlay of over Rs 12,000 crores (approximately US$2.6 billion) was earmarked over four years to support public and private investment aimed at improving the interface between the government and citizens. The NeGP website prominently displays 'mission mode' projects as an essential feature of the action plan.[4] Such projects have been launched based on their likely impact in terms of numbers of users and applications provided to citizens.

Over the past few years, various e-governance frameworks have been developed in India to support this e-governance policy drive. For example, the Department of IT commissioned the eTechnology Group@IMRB to develop a model drawing on various international e-readiness models and adapting them to take into account India's particular requirement to establish ICT infrastructure and to make major structural changes to the economic and political set up (eTechnology Group@IMRB, 2003). Similarly, the e-Governance Assessment Framework (EAF) was developed to assess the value of the increasing investments made on e-governance projects in terms of service orientation, technology architecture, replicability and sustainability in various states across the country (Rama Rao *et al.*, 2004). Numerous studies were undertaken to compare how states were progressing with e-governance ranking them from 1 to 5 and identifying frontline states like Andhra Pradesh and Karnataka and laggards like West Bengal and Madhya Pradesh (GOI, 2004, 2007).

The Andhra Pradesh government was a pioneer in the delivery of ICT services to citizens in 1999 through its deployment of eSeva[5] centres for the payment of utilities in the twin cities of Hyderabad and Secunderabad (Walsham and Krishna, 2005). Following Andhra Pradesh's example, parallel initiatives have been undertaken by many other state governments with several recent publications showcasing e-governance projects in India (Bose, 2006; Sinha, 2006; The Economist, 2008a; Vayunandan and Mathew, 2003). Indeed, e-governance projects are now plentiful in India, as are academic conferences and books on the subject. An example is the volume by Gupta and Bagga (2008) which documents several e-governance initiatives in India in terms of the projects' vision, objectives, services offered, technological architecture, project management and implementation challenges. Volumes such as these are largely descriptive although some analysis has been undertaken of savings in time and cost incurred to users following the deployment of e-services initiatives (Bhatnagar, 2004; Madon and Kiran, 2003; World Bank, 2007).

The majority of early e-governance initiatives reflected an urban policy bias with middle-class urbanites being the target beneficiaries of projects such as e-services to facilitate the payment of bills and other government dues, and the procuring of registration certificates such as land registration documents (Walsham and Krishna, 2005). However, more recently, the Indian government has focused its policy attention to the promotion of rural e-governance applications.

e-Governance in rural India

The Indian government has recently decided to invest significant amounts of money on rural e-governance projects, specifically telecentres, speculating that this investment could help in reducing poverty (Garai and Shadrach, 2006). Although telecentres have been established in Latin America and Africa, their most prolific growth appears to be in India (Sood, 2003) with estimates made in 2007 that 8961 telecentres existed in the country (i4donline, 2007[6]; Rangaswamy, 2006). Findings from studies conducted on six currently operating rural e-governance projects in India are summarised below.

Sustainable Access in Rural India (SARI), Madurai, Tamil Nadu – commenced in 2001

This project aimed at rural social, economic and political development by providing comprehensive information and communication services at kiosks set up for this purpose in rural communities. The kiosks, owned by private entrepreneurs, offer a number of services including basic computer education, e-mail, web browsing, e-government services such as provision of income and caste certificates and registration for birth and death – all of which are important to citizens wishing access to various government programmes. The services offered also include applying for pensions and making complaints through an online form. Kumar and Best (2006) found that villages used the kiosks far less for certificates than for other services because of the need to submit additional documents for obtaining certificates and because subsequent verification had to take place in the applicant's village requiring the citizen to interact directly with the taluk officials. Citizens therefore preferred to use traditional approach for obtaining certificates. The study also commented on the inability of the kiosks to diffuse widely within their communities. The kiosks attracted users mainly from the higher socio-economic strata within their communities and failed to upgrade their content to make it more relevant to a wider section of the village population. Blattman and Jensen's (2003) study showed that there is a local demand for expert agricultural advice – for example on pests and diseases or on new seeds and techniques – but that often farmers were locked into relations with particular brokers because of having borrowed money from them previously for seeds and fertilizers.

eChoupal, rural Madhya Pradesh – commenced in 2000

This is India's largest commercial ICT project launched by India Tobacco Company Ltd. This company primarily procures and exports agricultural commodities in raw or processed form and is India's largest overall agricultural exporter. Traditionally, the lack of basic physical infrastructure and the geographic dispersion of farmers in rural India have meant that traders played an important role in acting as middlemen to ensure the quality of produce, and to act as brokers of financial capital for seeds and other inputs. With the opening up of Indian agricultural markets in 1996–7 under the World Trade Organization's rules, Indian Tobacco Company (ITC) faced increasing competition from large, low-cost suppliers of agricultural products in the US, Brazil and other countries (Harris and Rajora, 2006). Whilst traders have information on price fluctuations through their contact with larger markets and export companies, farmers have not been able to predict such changes. ITC introduced eChoupals as village internet kiosks run by a local farmer entrepreneur providing price information to other local farmers enabling them to sell their produce directly to ITC thereby bypassing the middlemen. Despite the fact that the project has already proved to be profitable and self-sustaining, Kumar (2004) found that caste affiliations, political alignments and even the size of farm holdings were important factors influencing access to the eChoupals by small and marginal farmers and agricultural labourers. Also, the eChoupals had only been established in the larger and more prosperous villages rather than in the poorer and remoter parts of rural India.

Gyandoot, Dhar district, Madhya Pradesh – commenced in 2000

Gyandoot – a project initiated in a drought-prone rural district of Madhya Pradesh – aimed to provide immediate, transparent access to local government data and to reduce the amount of time and money people spend trying to communicate with government officials through the establishment of telecentres. These centres are either entrepreneur-owned or panchayat-owned and offer information and services to the local community for a nominal fee. Information includes a listing of people below the poverty line and prices of several agricultural products beyond the local market while services include a public complaint line for reporting government problems and applications for various certificates. In their study, Cecchini and Raina (2005) found that usage of Gyandoot was low because of poor accessibility of the centres to many villagers, lack of awareness about the project among the poor and marginalised within the community, lack of ownership of the project among the local community and lack of support given by local administrators and political representatives. Sreekumar's (2007) study identifies that despite the claims made that Gyandoot achieved success in active networking of villages in Dhar district, the project has only been able to reach particular segments of the community. Existing power relations in the village constitute an important influence on issues of inclusion. While the active support and collaboration of the village elites is solicited for the project to survive, Sreekumar observes that this only serves to reproduce traditional lines of social inequalities and reinforce rural power hierarchies rather than eliminating them.

**MSSRF Information Village Research Project,
Pondicherry – commenced in 1997**

The Information Village Research Project was initiated by the M.S. Swaminathan Research Foundation (MSSRF) to understand how ICTs could add value to existing networks of knowledge and information flows in villages with a focus on the poorest of the poor and women. Various services/content were made available through village volunteers at the knowledge centres including daily weather updates, news, employment and education news, agriculture information, information on government schemes and entitlements, health-related information, computer training and computer-assisted learning. The project has resulted in information being disseminated to more people, for example, information about government schemes (Kanungo, 2003). Punathambekar (2005) stresses the importance placed in this project on collaborating with existing social organisations such as self-help groups and youth associations. The project focused on achieving a high degree of social sustainability in terms of focusing on the poorest of the poor and addressing gender and caste issues in the local community. However, this strategy has placed severe financial constraints on the project as no revenues are generated locally by the centres resulting in the project being completely dependent on external funding. The strategy of targeting the poorest of the poor, while socially inclusive, has placed financial constraints on the project as these are the sections of the population least able to pay for services. This calls into question the long-term sustainability of projects such as MSSRF which have an overtly redistributive agenda.

Rural E-Seva, West Godavari, Andhra Pradesh – commenced in 2002

The Rural E-Seva project was established by the district administration setting up web-enabled rural ICT kiosks run by a mix of entrepreneurs and self-help groups trained by the District Rural Development Agency. The aim of the project was to serve as payment points for citizens for government bills and for other government services such as the filing of complaints and grievances, issuance of certificates, applying for government schemes and beneficiary loans, to access the district authority bulletin board to learn about meetings and other information (Raju, 2004). This project is one of the few e-governance projects that appears to be financially sustainable, partly because it was developed at a very low cost with some support from the National Informatics Centre and partly because of the use of local engineering students to develop software.

At the same time, IIITB (2005) raises questions regarding the degree to which the project has been institutionalised. While the project benefited from the enthusiasm and support of government officials during its pilot phase, Dileepkumar notes that the e-governance services being offered through this project remain dependent on the District Collector – that is, on a special relationship between the District Collector and the electricity company. This makes the long term sustainability of the project uncertain unless there is an attempt to strengthen linkages between the district administration and various utility and service agencies. This in turn would require a certain degree of administrative reorganisation, for example, creating back-end databases and streamlining procedures, to occur in parallel with the digitisation of the system.

Bhoomi, Karnataka – commenced in 2003

Land records computerisation was started by the Indian government during 1988–9. Since then, a number of Indian states have embarked on computerisation of land records projects of which the Bhoomi project in Karnataka has been the most successful. In the context of Karnataka, as in the rest of India, land records were traditionally kept by village accountants who had the power to record, manipulate and change land records – a life and death issue for small farmers – most of whom owned little land. Village accountants held a powerful position because they not only maintained land records but also used their monopoly position to advance corrupt practices such as bribes (Bhatnagar, 2004). With the Bhoomi system, farmers now have access to genuine certificates for the procurement of loans without harassment by bank staff. Whereas changes in land ownership were earlier an instrument for rural corruption, land records are now in the public domain and can easily be verified by anyone. However, the system has been criticised for being biased towards large farmers and landowners (who were eligible to apply for credit) over smaller and landless farmers. By eliminating the role of the village accountant who was a crucial intermediary for small farmers and landless labourers in accessing various facilities such as state-sponsored development programmes and bank loans, the Bhoomi project has appeared to worsen rather than improve living conditions of the poor (Prakash and De, 2007; Thomas, 2009).

These six rural e-governance projects in India share two common features in terms of ownership patterns and operation. First, although in some cases there are alternative models of kiosk ownership such as involving the panchayat, there is a tendency for kiosks to be owned and staffed by private entrepreneurs. Second, in all the six projects, e-governances service provision is facilitated by the kiosk staff rather than citizens directly interacting with the technology to obtain services. Third, each of the projects described above has been running for over five years yet none of them have shown any direct linkage to improving the living conditions of the communities they are serving

(Bagga *et al.*, 2005). Some useful learning can be distilled from each of the cases, with support from other studies on rural e-governance projects in India (IIITB, 2005), as to why this is so. For example, the cases described above and other studies (Kaushik and Singh, 2004; Kuriyan *et al.*, 2006) confirm the susceptibility of vulnerable groups such as small farmers to exclusion from the benefits of e-governance projects. In some cases, e-governance projects have resulted in community members finding that they are worse off as a result of the project as traditional access to local resources through human intermediaries has been removed (Gopakumar, 2006). Further studies and critical analysis of e-governance implementation is clearly required to assist future policy in promoting equity in service provision if earlier mistakes are to be avoided (Keniston, 2002). However, the likelihood of research findings feeding into policy seems unlikely under the latest NeGP policy directive for promoting e-governance in rural India through the establishment of Common Service Centres (CSCs).

The CSCs scheme was approved by the Government of India in 2005 with the aim of scaling up e-governance implementation in rural India. Infrastructure Leasing and Financial Services (IL&FS) has been nominated as the national level service agency. The scheme aims to set up 100,000 common service centres in 600,000 villages of India.[7] To facilitate the financial sustainability of these centres, the government envisages the inclusion of private sector players at sub-state level to be selected through a tendering process by individual states (Das and Chandrashekhar, 2006; Dhar, 2005; Gupta and Sridevi, 2008). These private players, called Service Centre Agencies (SCAs), will be charged with providing business and technical support to the CSCs. The criteria for selection of agents is that they must be financially strong showing a turnover of more than Rs 100 crores (US$210,615) and have a background in rural distribution networks from a technical side. One SCA may typically support 100 or more CSCs in a district or region delivering a package of government and localised services as required by citizens in a range of sectors including agriculture, animal husbandry, health, education, utilities, panchayat matters, tourism, transport and entertainment. At least two SCAs would operate in a state to prevent any single agency monopolising implementation. So far, 22 states have contracted agents that are either infrastructure or IT companies to support the implementation of CSCs. Some of these agents, for example, SREI Infrastructure, CMC Computers, Reliance and 3i Infotech are operating in five or more states.

In the CSCs scheme, equity in service provision has been addressed by the Government of India in two ways. First, certain parameters have been fixed by the central government for SCAs such as the obligation to provide universal access to villagers. Second, recognising that rural areas are not viable locations for investment, the government has guaranteed to provide a minimum monthly revenue of around Rs 3000 (approximately US$63) to each SCA to underwrite the potential loss that would be incurred for providing services in rural areas. However, almost uniformly across the states in India (excepting Jharkhand, West Bengal and Bihar), SCAs have been less concerned with securing a guaranteed income and more interested in securing the centres. In fact, through a process of reverse bidding, SCAs have paid the government to secure the centres, rather than the government compensating the SCAs. The implications of this action although good for ensuring the financial sustainability of the centres are serious for the provision of social services to rural poor communities. When the CSCs project was launched, the aim was that each centre would serve approximately six villages offering government and private services in an integrated manner. It was expected that the CSCs would be run either by village-level entrepreneurs or by members of self-help groups backed financially by NGOs or banks. However, the process of reverse bidding by SCAs has blurred this objective. These agents find themselves no longer obliged to provide government services and are free to channel their energy towards tapping the rural demand base for financial services and providing marketing chains for the selling of commercial products. Indeed, being predominantly commercial organisations, SCAs are more in touch with this type of service provision rather than social services aimed at improving rural livelihoods and welfare.

It may be too soon to comment on the success of the CSCs scheme. However, it is clear that the entire project is driven by a commercial and technological bias. The centres are likely to focus on tapping the rural demand base for the selling of commercial products and services rather than on providing essential social services to rural poor communities. Technology has been identified as important in supporting access to rural markets. The government has approved a scheme for establishing state-wide area networks across all the states over a period of five years to be monitored by representatives from the Department of IT and the National Informatics Centre (Ghatak, 2007). These networks are expected to extend data connectivity to block levels in all states. The block level nodes in turn will have a provision to extend connectivity further to village level using contemporary wireless technology.

e-Governance for development in India: A synthesis

Despite all this activity in the area of e-governance in India, there remain big question marks about what kind of development will be provided through these applications. National development priorities in India have shifted from their earlier bias towards social development through large-scale decentralised planning to the more recent bias towards achieving economic growth. However, as reviewed earlier, official estimates of poverty reduction since 1990s based on growth in national accounts have been too optimistic, particularly for rural

India. While it is clear that although the proportion of the population living below the poverty line has fallen, per capita income remains low and over a quarter of the population still lives below the poverty line. Structural adjustment policies that were introduced in the early 1990s in the wake of the fiscal deficit had led to borrowings from the IMF and the World Bank. This led to the opening up of the market and to the easing of a variety of controls but also resulted in the whittling away of development budgets in successive five year plans – for example, as reflected in the government's budget for the year 2002–3 in which a commitment was made to further opening up the agricultural sector, increasing allocations for the telecommunications sector, and the slashing of taxes on IT-related goods and cell phones. The global financial crisis is likely to concentrate policy attention in India on achieving economic rather than social development in order to mitigate effects which have already been felt in terms of reduced export earnings, a drastic decline in industrial growth and employment, a depreciation of the rupee, a reduction in foreign exchange reserves and a downturn in stock market and other indicators (Centre for Development Studies, 2008).

In a country where more than 70% of the population is dependent on the land to survive, the benefits of economic liberalisation have so far not touched the majority of the population. The Tenth Five-Year Plan (2002–7) and the approach paper to the eleventh plan (GOI, 2006) demonstrate a strong technology-driven vision of development with phrases such as knowledge society and IT-driven development (Bagchi *et al.*, 2006). e-Governance constitutes an important element of this vision although critics have cautioned that expenditure in implementing these projects may compromise expenditure in other important social development areas such as water supply and sanitation, public distribution system, housing, and healthcare which affect the rural livelihoods and living conditions of the poor in India (Keniston and Kumar, 2004). Indeed, the vision that e-governance can promote development has been clearly articulated by the ex-President of India, Sri Abdul Kalam (2008). This vision has two dimensions. First, that technology can promote development by improving administrative systems such that they contribute more to national development rather than merely being entangled in files. Second, that e-governance can lead to the betterment of society by satisfying the demand for products and services which can be used to generate income, increase productivity and improve social welfare.

Whether this vision is pure rhetoric or can become a reality depends on how we theorise the relationship between governance and development. Drawing on discussions in earlier chapters, the following comments are offered on Abdul Kalam's visions. His first vision of e-governance for development is dependent not on the successful development of technology alone, but also on the ability of local governance and administration to direct usage of technology to locally relevant needs. This ability has been supported more in theory than in practice. A central tenet of earlier governance reform initiatives was the establishment of a decentralised structure of power and resource allocation to local administrative and political bodies. But while these structures were put in place, the extent of real devolution of power and responsibilities was limited. The more recent economic and political restructuring policies under the guise of 'good governance' have precipitated a reduction of the state's role in providing government information and services and encouraged the inclusion of new players in welfare provision such as the private sector and non-governmental agencies. Abdul Kalam's second vision of e-governance for development is also not merely dependent on the deployment of technology. e-Governance projects designed to improve the interface between government and citizens will ultimately be influenced by the interplay between local administrative, political and social systems.

In the rest of this book, I use my theorisation of development and governance to analyse three cases of e-governance for development each from a different state in India.

Glossary

CSCs – Common Service Centres
District panchayat – district council
Gram panchayat – village council
NeGP – National E-Governance Plan
NIC – National Informatics Centre
SCAs – Service Centre Agencies
Taluk panchayat – taluk (village cluster) council

References

Ahluwalia, M. (2002) Economic Reforms in India since 1991: Has gradualism worked? *Journal of Economic Perspectives,* 16, 3, pp. 67–88.

Alsop, R. and Kurey, B. (2005) *Local Organizations in Decentralized Development: Their functions and performance in India,* World Bank, Washington DC.

Bagchi, A.K., Banerjee, D. and Chakraborty, A. (2006) A Critique of the Approach Paper for Eleventh Plan, *Economic & Political Weekly,* XLI: 31, 5–11 August.

Bagga, R.K., Keniston, K. and Mathur, R.R. (2005) State, ICT and Development: The Indian Context. In *State, IT and Development: The Indian Context,* edited by R.K. Bagga, K. Keniston and R.R. Mathur, Sage Publications, New Delhi, pp. 25–37.

Bhalla, S. (2001) Recounting the Poor: Poverty in India, 1983–1999, *Economic and Political Weekly,* 25 January, pp. 338–349.

Bhaskar, V. and Gupta, B. (2007) India's Development in the Era of Growth, *Oxford Review of Economic Policy,* 23, 2, pp. 135–142.

Bhatnagar, S.C. (2004) *E-Government – from Vision to Implementation: A practical guide with case studies,* Sage Publications, New Delhi.

Blattman, C. and Jensen, R. (2003) Assessing the Need and Potential of Community Networking for Development in Rural India, *The Information Society,* 19, pp. 349–364.

Bose, H. (ed.) (2006) *EGovernance in India: Issues and cases,* The Icfai University Press, New Delhi.

Cecchini, S. and Raina, M. (2005) Electronic Government and the Rural Poor: The case of Gyandoot, *Information Technologies and International Development,* 2, 2, pp. 65–75.

Centre for Development Studies (2008) Report on the Global Financial Crisis and Kerala Economy: Impact and mitigation measures. Centre for Development Studies, Trivandrum, Kerala, India, December.

Chibber, P. and Eldersveld, S. (2000) Local Elites and Popular Support for Economic Reform in China and India, *Comparative Political Studies,* 33, 3, pp. 350–373.

Dandekar, V.M. (2004) Forty Years after Independence. In *The Indian Economy – Problems and prospects,* edited by B. Jalan, Penguin Books, India, pp. 38–92.

Das, S.R. and Chandrashekhar, R. (2006) Capacity-Building for EGovernance in India. In *EGovernance in India: Issues and cases,* edited by J. Bose, The Icfai University Press, Hyderabad, pp. 81–106.

Dataquest. (2005) $500 mn. World Bank Support for NEGAP, 16 April. Available at http://dqindia/ciol.com/content/eGovernance/2005/105041603.asp

Davison, R., Vogel, D., Harris, R. and Jones, N. (2000) Technology Leapfrogging in Developing Countries – An inevitable luxury? *EJISDC,* 1, 5, pp. 1–10.

Deaton, A. (2002) Is World Poverty Falling? *Finance and Development,* 39, 2, pp. 1–6.

Deaton, A. and Dreze, J. (2002) Poverty and Inequality in India: A re-examination, Working Paper No. 107, Centre for Development Economics, Delhi School of Economics, New Delhi.

Deaton, A. and Kozel, V. (2005) Data and Dogma: The great Indian poverty debate, *World Bank Research Observer,* 20, pp. 177–199.

Dev, S.M. and Ravi, C. (2007) Poverty and Inequality: All India and States, 1983–2005, *Economic and Political Weekly,* 10 February, pp. 509–521.

Dhar, A. (2005) Citizen Service Centres: Ensuring efficient delivery of services, *E:gov,* 1, 5, pp. 6–10.

The Economist (2008) Battling the Babu Raj, 8 March. The Hindu (2004) India – Shining Bright, Sunday 11 January 2004.

The Economist (2008a) E for Express, Special Report Technology and Government, 14 February.

The Economist (2008b) Briefing: India's Civil Service, 8 March.

eGov. (2005) Citizen Service Centres: Ensuring efficient delivery of services, 1, 5, pp. 6–7.

eTechnology Group@IMRB (2003) EGovernance Readiness Assessment. Available at www.imrb.com

Garai, A. and Shadrach, B. (2006) Taking ICT to Every Indian Village: Opportunities and challenges, OneWorld South Asia, New Delhi.

Ghatak, M. and Ghatak, M. (2002) Recent Reforms in the Panchayat System in West Bengal: Towards greater participatory governance, *Economic and Political Weekly,* 5 January, pp. 45–58.

Ghatak, S. (2007) CSCs: An overview, *i4d,* 5, 8, pp. 6–8.

Ghosh, J. (2004) Social Policy in Indian Development. In *Social Policy in a Development Context,* edited by T. Mkandawire, Palgrave Macmillan, Hants.

Gill, S.S. (2004) *Information Revolution and India,* Rupa & Co., New Delhi.

GOI. (1964) Report of the High Level Committee on Power, Ministry of Irrigation and Power, New Delhi.

GOI. (1978) Report of the Committee on Panchayati Raj Institutions (Ashoka Mehta Committee), Department of Rural Development, New Delhi.

GOI. (1985) Seventh Five Year Plan 1985–1990. Government of India, Planning Commission, New Delhi.

GOI. (1988) Report of the Committee of the Study Group on the Information Gap, Government of India, Planning Commission, New Delhi.

GOI. (2002) Tenth Five-Year Plan (2002–07), Planning Commission, Government of India, New Delhi.

GOI. (2004) India: E-Readiness Assessment Report 2003, Department of Information Technology and National Council of Applied Economic Research, New Delhi.

GOI. (2006) Towards Faster and More Inclusive Growth: An approach to the 11th Five Year Plan, 14 June, Planning Commission, Government of India, New Delhi.

GOI. (2007) India: E-Readiness Assessment Report 2005, Department of Information Technology and National Council of Applied Economic Research, New Delhi.

Gopakumar, K. (2006) EGovernance Services through Telecentres – Role of human intermediary and issues of trust, Proceedings of the 2006 International Conference on ICT and Development, Berkeley, CA.

Govinda Rao, M. and Singh, N. (2005) India's Federal Institutions and Economic Reform. In *Public Institutions in India: Performance and Design,* edited by D. Kapur and P. Bhanu Mehta, Oxford University Press, New Delhi.

Gupta, P. and Bagga, R.K. (eds) (2008) *Compendium of eGovernance Initiatives in India,* Universities Press, Hyderabad, India.

Gupta, P. and Sridevi, A. (2008) eGovernance Approach in India: The National eGovernance Plan, NeGP. In *Compendium of eGovernance Initiatives in India,* edited by P. Gupta and R.K. Bagga, Universities Press, Hyderabad, India, pp. 8–24.

Hanumantha Rao, C.H. (2004) Agriculture: Policy and performance. In *The Indian Economy – Problems and prospects,* edited by B. Jalan, Penguin Books, India, pp. 127–156.

Haque, M.A. (2002) E-Governance in India: Its impacts on relations among citizens, politicians and public servants, *International Review of Administrative Sciences,* 68, 2, pp. 231–250.

Harris, R. and Rajora, R. (2006) Empowering the Poor: Information and Communications Technology for Governance and Poverty Reduction – A study of rural development projects in India, UNDP-APDIP, Elsevier.

Harriss, J. (2004) India: Ambedkar and democracy, *LSE Magazine,* Summer 2004, pp. 16–17.

Harriss-White, B. (2003) *India Working: Essays on society and economy,* Cambridge University Press, Cambridge.

Heeks, R. (1990) Technology Policy-Making as a Social and Political Process: Liberalising India's Software Policy, *Technology Analysis and Strategic Management,* 2, pp. 275–291.

Himanshu Sen, A. (2004) Poverty and Inequality in India: Getting close to the truth, *Economic and Political Weekly,* (in two parts), 18 September, pp. 4247–4263 and 25 September, pp. 4361–4375. The Hindu (2004) India…Shining Bright, 11 January.

The Hindu (2004) India – Shining Bright, Sunday 11 January 2004.

IIITB. (2005) Information and Communication Technologies for Development: A comparative analysis of impacts and costs from India. Indian Institute of Information Technology, Bangalore. Report for a project funded by the Department of Information Technology, Government of India and Infosys Technologies, Bangalore. Available at http://www.iiitb.ac.in/ICTforD/ict4d.htm

ILO. (2004) World Employment Report 2004–5: Employment, Productivity and Poverty, International Labour Organization, Geneva, p. 147.

The Independent (2007) The March of the Dispossessed, Tuesday 30th October.

Jafri, A. (2001) Promise and Problems of Panchayati Raj: Experiences from Madhya Pradesh. In *Public Health and the Poverty of Reforms: The South Asian predicament,* edited by I. Qadeer, K. Sen and K.R. Nayar, Sage Publications, New Delhi.

Jalan, B. (1991) *India's Economic Crisis: The way ahead,* Oxford University Press, New Delhi.

Jalan, B. (2004) Introduction. In *The Indian Economy – Problems and prospects,* edited by B. Jalan, Penguin Books, India, pp. ix–1.

Jayal, N. (2001) Reinventing the State: The emergence of alternative models of govern-ance in India in the 1990s. In *Democratic Governance in India: Challenges of poverty, development, and identity,* edited by N. Jayal and S. Pai, Sage Publications, New Delhi.

Jha, S. (2000) Fiscal Decentralisation in India: Strengths, limitations and prospects for Panchayati Raj Institutions. Background Paper No. 2, World Bank unpublished, 'Overview of Rural Decentralisation in India', Volume 3.

John, M.S. (2007) Gandhi and the Contemporary Discourse on Decentralisation. In *Local Governance in India: Ideas, challenges and strategies,* edited by T.M. Joseph, Concept Publishing Company, New Delhi, pp. 20–32.

Johnson, C., Deshingkar, P., Farrington, J. and Start, D. (2007) Does Devolution Deliver? Institutional and political dimensions of self-help programmes in India, *IDS Bulletin,* 38, 1, pp. 33–45.

Kalam, A.P.J. (2008) A Vision of Citizen-Centric EGovernance for India. In *Compendium of eGovernance Initiatives in India,* edited by P. Gupta and R.K. Bagga, Universities Press, Hyderabad, India, pp. 3–8.

Kanungo, S. (2003) Information Village: Bridging the digital divide in rural India. In *The Digital Challenge: Information Technology in the Development Context,* edited by S. Krishna and S. Madon, Ashgate, Hants, pp. 103–124.

Kaushik, P.D. and Singh, N. (2004) Information Technology and Broad-Based Development: Preliminary lessons from North India, *World Development,* 32, 4, pp. 591–607.

Keniston, K. (2002) Grassroots ICT Projects in India: Some preliminary hypotheses, *ASCI Journal of Management,* 31, 1–2, pp. 1–9.

Keniston, K. and Kumar, D. (eds) (2004) *IT Experience in India: Bridging the digital divide,* Sage Publications, New Delhi.

Kumar, P. and Kandpal, B.M. (2003) Project on Reviving and Constructing Small Water Harvesting Systems in Rajasthan, SIDA Evaluation 03/40, Department of Asia.

Kumar, R. (2004) eChoupals: A study of the financial sustainability of village internet centres in rural Madhya Pradesh, *Information Technology and International Development,* 2, 1, pp. 45–73.

Kumar, R. and Best, M. (2006) Impact and Sustainability of E-Government Services in Developing Countries: Lessons learnt from Tamil Nadu, India, *The Information Society,* 22, 1, pp. 1–12.

Kuriyan, R., Toyama, K. and Ray, I. (2006) Integrating Social Development and Financial Sustainability: The challenges of rural computer kiosks in Kerala, Proceedings of the 2006 International Conference on ICT and Development, Berkeley, CA.

Lal, R. and Purohit, H.C. (eds) (2007) *Rural Development and NGO,* Shree Publications, New Delhi.

Madon, S. (1992) The Impact of Computer-Based Information Systems on Rural Development: A case study in India, *Journal of Information Technology,* 7, pp. 20–29.

Madon, S. (1993) Introducing Administrative Reforms through the Application of Computer-based Information Systems: A case study in India, *Public Administration and Development,* 13, pp. 37–48.

Madon, S. and Kiran, G.R. (2003) Information Technology for Citizen-Government Interface: A study of FRIENDS project in Kerala. World Bank Global Knowledge Sharing Program (GKSP). Available at www1.worldbank.org/publicsector/bnpp/egovupdate.htm

Mishra, N. (2003) People's Right to Information Movement: Lessons from Rajasthan. Human Development Resource Centre Discussion Paper Series, No. 4, UNDP, New Delhi.

Mukarji, N. (1999) The Third Stratum. In *Decentralisation and Local Politics: Readings in Indian Government and Politics*, edited by S.N. Jha and P.C. Mathur, Sage Publications, London, pp. 70–82.

Narayan, J. and Sanjay, P. (2007) Democracy and Decentralisation. In *Local Governance in India: Ideas, challenges and strategies*, edited by T.M. Joseph, Concept Publishing Company, New Delhi, pp. 3–20.

Palanithurai, G. (2007) Panchayats: Relevance and Potentials. In *Local Governance in India: Ideas, challenges and strategies*, edited by T.M. Joseph, Concept Publishing Company, New Delhi, pp. 78–98.

Patnaik, P. (2005) The Crisis in India's Countryside. Paper presented at the India: Implementing Pluralism and Democracy Conference, November 11–13, Centre of Comparative Constitutionalism, University of Chicago. Available at http://ccc.uchicago.edu/docs/india/patnaik.pdf

Pradan, A.K. (1990) Use of Computerisation in District Administration – A case study in Panchmahals district, Indian Institute of Management, Ahmedabad.

Prakash, A. and De', R. (2007) Importance of Development Context in ICT4D Projects: A study of computerisation of land records, *Information Technology & People*, 20, 3, pp. 262–282.

Punathambekar, A. (2005) MSSRF's Information Village Research Project, Pondicherry.

Raju, K.A. (2004) A Case for Harnessing Information Technology for Rural Development, *The International Information & Library Review*, 6, 3, pp. 233–240.

Rama Rao, T.P., Venkata Rao, V., Bhatnagar, S.C. and Satyanarayana, J. (2004) EGovernance Assessment Framework EAF Version 2.0, Centre for Electronic Governance, Indian Institute of Management, Ahmedabad and National Institute for Smart Governance, Hyderabad, Prepared for the EGovernance and E-Rural Group, Department of IT, Government of India.

Rangaswamy, N. (2006) Social Entrepreneurship as Critical Agency: A study of rural internet kiosks, *Proceedings of the 2006 International Conference on ICT and Development*, Berkeley, CA.

Robinson, M. (2005) A Decade of Panchayati Raj Reforms: The challenge of democratic decentralisation in India. In *Decentralisation and Local Governance*, edited by L.C. Jain, Orient Longman, New Delhi, pp. 10–31.

Singhal, A.K. and Rogers, E.M. (1989) *India's Information Revolution*, Sage Publications, New Delhi.

Sinha, R.P. (2006) *EGovernance in India: Initiatives and issues*, Concept Publishing Company, New Delhi.

Sivakumar, S.K. (2004) A Battle for Information, *Frontline*, 21, 26.

Slater, J. (2002) Ever So Slowly, *Far Eastern Economic Review*, 14 March, pp. 48–49.

Slater, R. and Watson, J. (1989) Democratic Decentralization or Political Consolidation: The case of local government reform in Karnataka, *Public Administration and Development*, 9, pp. 147–157.

Sood, A.D. (2003) Information Nodes in the Rural Landscape, *I4D*, 1, 1, pp. 14–22.

Sreekumar, T.T. (2007) Decrypting EGovernance: Narratives, Power Play and Participation in the Gyandoot Intranet, *EJISDC,* 32, 4, pp. 1–24.

Steinmueller, W.E. (2001) ICTs and the Possibilities for Leapfrogging by Developing Countries, *International Labour Review,* 140, 2, pp. 193–210.

Thomas, P. (2009) *Bhoomi, Gyan Ganga,* EGovernance and the Right to Information: ICTs and development in India, *Telematics and Informatics,* 26, 1, pp. 20–31.

UNDP. (2002) Human Development Indicators 2002. Available at http://hdr.undp.org/reports/global/2002/en/indicator/indicator.cfm?File=indic_298_2_1.html

Vayunandan, E. and Mathew, D. (eds) (2003) *Good Governance Initiatives in India*, Prentice-Hall, New Delhi.

Walsham, G. and Krishna, S. (2005) Implementing Public Information Systems in Developing Countries: Learning from a success story, *Information Technology for Development,* 11, 2, pp. 123–140.

World Bank (2004) India: Sustaining reform, reducing poverty, World Bank, Washington DC.

World Bank (2005) World Bank World Development Indicators 2005, World Bank, Washington DC.

World Bank (2007) Impact Assessment Study of Computerized Service Delivery Projects from India and Chile, IT @ WB Staff Working Paper No. 2.

Available at http://www-wds.worldbank.org/external/default/WDSContentServer/WDSP/IB/2008/04/08/000333038_20080408052408/Rendered/PDF/421470WPOBox327349B01Public1/pdf

7
MIS for Rural Self-Employment Programmes in Gujarat

Rural poverty remains a serious challenge in India despite a policy thrust in the 1990s to revamp rural development programmes. In 1999, with influence from the international development community, a rural self-employment programme called the SGSY was introduced based on providing credit to self-help groups constituted from among the poor. Various concerns were identified with the SGSY related to selection of group members and schemes, capacity-building among self-help group members and integration between agencies. This chapter presents a longitudinal case study of the role of MIS for monitoring the SGSY in Gujarat. The state plays an important role in setting the performance criteria against which we hold public officials accountable. The research provides an opportunity for critical reflection on the extent to which the performance criteria in the MIS reflect ground-level realities of rural poverty alleviation. Government fieldworkers play an instrumental role in forming and sustaining self-help groups yet their 'intelligence' about the process of social mobilisation of rural poor communities is not embedded in the formal MIS. Under these circumstances, the extent to which the MIS can promote development by improving the administration of the SGSY remains doubtful.

While the growth of income and wealth among the affluent in India has continued unabated, poverty remains widespread in rural parts of the country (IFAD, 2001). The Indian Constitution and all the Plan documents since the 1950s pledged for improving the conditions of the rural poor with community development, integrated rural development, livelihood approaches and a variety of participatory paradigms all scrambling for policy space. However, by the 1960s, it was realised that the focus on national economic development programmes alone was inadequate as significant sections of the rural population were unable to improve their living conditions. The approach taken in India was to launch specific programmes called the Integrated Rural Development Programme (IRDP) which targeted the poorest of the poor (Deb, 1986).[1] These

programmes provided rural poor households with subsidy and credit to facilitate the purchase of an income-generating asset so that, with appropriate infrastructure and linkages, the rural poor family could lift itself out of poverty.
The programme was to be administered in a decentralised manner through the
District Rural Development Agency and was launched in 1978.

However, despite this programme, the government's attention was concentrated on the urban minority resulting in a worsening of the employment situation and poverty in rural areas. From the 1990s onwards, there has been a
turnaround in terms of sectoral priorities with many donor agencies placing
the rural economy at the centre of their development agenda whether for delivering economic growth, as a source of livelihood for small holders and landless
workers, for entrepreneurship in the emerging rural non-farm local economy,
or for providing environmental services such as preserving biodiversity (World
Bank, 2007). This policy thrust has given fresh impetus for many developing
countries to revamp their rural development programmes, particularly those
targeted at the poorest of the poor. It has also led to the adoption of a new
ideology of targeting assistance not to individual households, but to groups.

The IRDP, operational from 1978 until 1999 as India's flagship rural development programme, was replaced with the Swarnjayanti Gram Swarozgar Yojana
(SGSY) which is a self-employment scheme financed by the centre and the
respective state government in the ratio 75:25. Envisaged in the design of the
SGSY were macro influences from the international development community
encouraging 'good governance' ideals such as sound project management, participation of people, involvement of civil society and microenterprise. Based
on these principles, the success of the Grameen Bank model of microfinance
to rural poor communities became an exemplar for other developing countries to follow[2] (Bhatnagar, 1996). Moving away from the earlier approach
of targeting individual households, the SGSY scheme proposed to alleviate
poverty through the formation of self-help groups (SHGs) – each containing
approximately 10–20 rural poor members of the community[3] who have volunteered to organise themselves into a group for eradicating poverty of its
members. The underlying objective of the scheme is to help the poor to build
their self-confidence by enabling them to carry out internal lending to other
group members and eventually to obtain micro-credit from banks for entrepreneurial development (GOI, 1999). While the DRDA remained responsible
for the overall coordination of the SGSY, grassroots organisations and NGOs
were increasingly promoted as implementing agents for community development projects (Jain, 1985). Despite these intentions, however, the scheme has
been beset with problems like faulty selection of SHG members and schemes,
poor capacity-building among SHG members, and lack of integration of various agencies involved in scheme implementation (Shylendra and Bhirdikar,
2005; Sud, 2003).

A national development scheme like the SGSY is dependent on having in place an effective monitoring system which can feed local relevant information to policy-makers – an e-governance application commonly referred to as e-administration. This type of application was discussed in the previous chapter as constituting a key dimension in the vision of e-governance for development put forward by the former President of India, Sri Abdul Kalam. To date, almost 1.3 million SHGs have been formed in India under the SGSY programme making this MIS one of the most strategic e-administration projects in the world. The historical background and current status of this application is described below.

MIS implementation for rural development monitoring in India

The first MIS called the Computerized Rural Information Systems Project (CRISP) was introduced for the IRDP programme in 1988. The objective of the system was to improve the efficiency and effectiveness of the programme. CRISP was a menu-driven system for monitoring the IRDP that had been designed by the National Informatics Centre in New Delhi. During the period 1989 to 1992, my doctoral research involved studying the impact of CRISP on the programme. After installation, however, various resource, design, political and cultural issues were identified which hampered usage of the system in its early years (Madon, 1992a, b). In particular, the system had been designed and developed by the central government to reflect physical and financial targets and achievements under the IRDP in a uniform manner across the country (i.e., numbers of households targeted and assisted, and amount of funds earmarked and spent). These centrally defined reporting formats did not correspond well with the physical and financial reporting requirements of different states. These problems led to underutilisation of the system and reports continued to be prepared manually by local administrators in the prescribed format.

By 1991, Madon's study found that while district staff had abandoned the menu-driven system, they were starting to design more locally relevant reporting formats for providing data about physical and financial targets and achievements to the state headquarters. The authority to make these changes in usage came from the Government of Gujarat in response to the way in which the original CRISP system had been designed and developed without much consultation with the state government. The state administration initiated a sequence of training sessions for DRDA officials specifically on using the computer to generate reports and for simple analysis (Madon, 1993). These computerised formats enabled district staff to increase the efficiency of routine monthly reporting. District staff also began to show interest in designing simple analytical tools for monitoring the IRDP using spreadsheets and databases (Madon and Walsham, 1995). The findings suggested that local DRDA administrators welcomed the possibility of exercising discretion in the development of alternative performance criteria for local analysis of the IRDP. One example of this type of local adaptation was for the assessment of poverty based not just on income but also on environmental factors such as whether the locality is in a drought-prone area. Another more complex type of analytical application was to match rural poor households to income-generating schemes taking into account local linkages, for example, fodder for grazing and marketing outlets for the selling of produce (Madon, 1993). The development of locally generated performance criteria provided many DRDAs with an opportunity to experiment with poverty alleviation strategies specific to their local context.

Sadly, however, these encouraging trends in usage of MIS for improving local planning and administration were short-lived. By early 2000, there were few signs remaining of such usage in the DRDAs of Gujarat. The demise of interest in local MIS usage coincided with a policy bias against e-administration in favour of e-services applications. As the role of the bureaucracy came to be undermined under the 'good governance' ideology, more policy attention and resources were diverted to e-governance applications that had an overtly citizen-centric orientation. Sub-district levels saw the arrival of One-Day Governance centres providing citizens with computerised entitlement certificates for a small fee. In 2001, the Mahiti Shakti community information centre[4] began as a pilot in Panchmahals district of Gujarat. Eighty centres were set up, each owned by a private entrepreneur under licence from the government to interface with citizens and government departments within a radius of approximately 20 km. Various government forms could be obtained from these centres and advice was given to citizens about how to complete them and apply for assistance under different schemes. To support these e-services applications, Gujarat became the first state in the country to achieve wide-area network connectivity up to sub-district level.[5]

As policy priority shifted to e-services, this led to neglect in developing back-end applications for improving government administration and in ensuring that services being provided to citizens were locally relevant (Gupta and Agrawal, 2005). When the IRDP was replaced by the SGSY, the monitoring system put in place by the central government was based on physical and financial targets and achievements. The original formats for reporting that were prescribed in 1999 when the programme commenced were revamped in 2007 to include further categorisation of group members in terms of their ethnic composition and socio-economic status to compile aggregate statistics for government reports (GOI, 2007). There are currently 15 formats to be completed by district staff as shown in Table 7.1.

Kalam has a vision that e-governance applications can promote development by improving the administration of national development programmes such as the SGSY. To what extent is this vision realistic? This question is

Table 7.1   SGSY reporting formats

Format	Details
1	Monthly statement of total funds received from central and state government by the district DRDAs
1A	Monthly statement of expenditure on the programme classified into expenditure on NGOs/facilitators, capacity-building of SHGs, infrastructure, marketing, revolving funds, formation of federations for marketing of goods
2	Monthly statement of number of SHGs formed, defunct, passed grades 1 and 2, taken up economic activity and classified into women's groups, below poverty line groups
2A	Monthly statement of number of SHG members assisted for economic activities classified into minority status
2B	Monthly statement of number of SHG members trained categorised into minority status
3 & 3A	Monthly statements of subsidy and credit disbursed to SHGs and to weaker sections
3B	Monthly statement of number of SHGs given revolving fund
4	Monthly statement of numbers of loan applications submitted, sanctioned, disbursed, pending and rejected
5	Monthly statement of credit disbursed by banks and meetings held at various administrative levels
6	Quarterly statement of number of SHG members assisted for different sectoral activities
6A	Quarterly statement of expenditure on SHGs
7	Quarterly statement of product profiles showing numbers of SHGs involved, offer price, marketing mechanisms, potential
8 & 8A	Quarterly statements of special projects expenditure

Source: (GOI, 2007).

addressed by describing the implementation of the SGSY programme in Gujarat.

Implementing SGSY in Gujarat – ground-level realities

Gujarat is a small state accounting for only 5% of India's population, but it has been the strong arm of the nation's industrial and trade performance projected by the Planning Commission in its Tenth Five-Year Plan to be one of the fastest growing states (Dholakia, 2008). But despite the rate of growth in the Gujarat economy, there has been a deceleration in some of the major human development indicators since the early 1990s, for example, indices of gender inequality in education, health and participation indices (Hirway and Mahadevia, 2008). Two major reasons for this have been identified. First, while the secondary and tertiary sectors have done well over the past few decades, the primary sector, particularly agriculture, has lagged behind with highly fluctuating income. Since over 50% of the state's workforce remains dependent on agriculture, a lag in this sector is a matter of concern for the sustainability of growth as well as poverty reduction in the state. Second, evidence shows that human health has been adversely affected by environmental depletion and degradation. For example, the incidence of water-borne diseases has increased significantly in the state mainly due to the shortage of potable water. Environmental degradation has also affected education and literacy in the state as well as the livelihood and employment of the people. This situation has perpetuated the incidence of droughts which increase instability of employment and livelihood of the rural agricultural population (Dholakia, 2008).

The change in leadership from a Congress to a BJP[6] government in 2001 heralded a new policy agenda in Gujarat state with the Chief Minister Narendra Modi deeply committed to correcting the imbalance in development (Hindustan Times, 2007). While Gujarat has always focused on industrial production, this has been combined in recent years with a focus on the social sectors. In particular, effort has been directed towards providing vital infrastructure such as water harvesting structures and electricity to rural areas. The district of Surat located in south Gujarat provides a good example of the concerted effort made by the Modi administration towards promoting rural development. The district has a predominantly agricultural economy with high rainfall. However, only 49% of cultivable land is provided with irrigation facility. Hence, the average production of major crops is approximately 30% below their potential production. The large community of farmers from the district belong to the small and marginal category and to boost their crop production and productivity, the state government increased input subsidies to them for various components such as seeds, fodder and plant protection equipment. From 2005, various community-based agriculture and irrigation projects were promoted through fairs and demonstrations such as projects to conserve rainwater, to build check dams, community wells and lift irrigation schemes and to introduce organic farming technologies. As a result of these efforts, new crops of vegetables like cabbage, cauliflower and lady's fingers have been introduced and are exported in bulk routinely to Mumbai and London. These efforts have lifted farmers from survival status providing a large number of small and marginal farmers with secure housing, a motorbike, cell phone, television and CD player.

Despite these advances in raising agricultural productivity, however, rural poverty in Surat remains high with many parts of the district showing no significant reduction in the percentage of people below the poverty line over the past five years. The bulk of deprivation exists in the tribal belt of the district and to target this area more closely, it was decided in September 2007 to split Surat into two districts, Surat and Tapi. Surat district now comprises of nine talukas (a taluka being a subdivision of a district), while Tapi district consists of the remaining five talukas with approximately 90% of the tribal population. A major reason for the persistence of poverty in the tribal talukas is that the majority of poor, particularly women, are forced to seek loans from moneylenders for personal contingencies despite the existence of the SGSY scheme. As the study by Breman and Shah (2005) reveals, moneylenders remain the major source for credit in rural Gujarat with interest rates varying from 30–50% a year. The study found that a large segment of the population remains to be covered by microfinance schemes such as the SGSY and this finding was supported by my field visit to Tapi in 2008 which revealed that only 5% of the total population of those below the poverty line (BPLs) get benefit under the scheme. Moreover, where the SGSY is in operation, the majority of borrowing tends to be for consumption purposes rather than for productive purposes to generate income.

The research has identified that a critical issue explaining the high incidence of poverty in Tapi district relates to the survival of the SHG. My research shows that while many groups are being formed, the vast majority do not survive for more than a year. For this reason, from 2003–7, the Tapi district administration had instructed fieldworkers not to form any new groups as it was noticed that 75% of them were becoming inactive after one year of operation. Table 7.2 shows that the total number of SHGs over the period 2003 to 2008 has remained stagnant.

From the SHGs that have remained active, an almost insignificant number have started to generate revenue. According to the SGSY guidelines, once groups have stabilised, the next stage is to fund income-generating activities. The choice of key activities involves analysing the profile of the group to ascertain the most appropriate type of activity given the background and skills of the members, the local infrastructure and markets. For this exercise, both programmes recommend the involvement of the gram panchayat as crucial. However, although the SGSY has been running for nine years in Gujarat, Table 7.3 shows that in all three talukas there are very few groups at the stage of embarking on economic activity.

Table 7.2 Total number of SHGs over past 6 years in 3 talukas of Surat

Taluka	2003	2004	2005	2006	2007	2008
Songadh	875	875	720	720	857	875
Ucchal	587	587	487	487	527	561
Vyara	1,035	1,035	750	750	890	1,034

Source: Official figures obtained from Surat DRDA during fieldwork conducted in March 2008.

Table 7.3   Number of SHGs at various stages of the Sakhi Mandal programme, March 2008

	SHGs doing internal lending		SHGs with credit link		Grade 1 SHGs		Grade 2 SHGs		SHGs in economic activity	
	No.	%	No.	%	No.	%	No.	%	No.	%
Songadh	80	9.1	0	0	0	0	0	0	1	0.1
Ucchal	35	6.2	0	0	0	0	0	0	2	0.4
Vyara	81	7.8	0	0	32	5.7	0	0	2	0.2

Source: Official figures obtained from Surat District Panchayat during fieldwork conducted in March 2008.

Recognising that the SGSY was not effective in reducing poverty in rural parts of the state, in 2007 the Gujarat government decided to supplement the SGSY with another scheme called Sakhi Mandal.[7] This scheme is specifically designed to extend the reach of self-employment programmes in Gujarat by targeting poor women in the hinterland of the state. The programme, guaranteed to run until end of January 2010, provides an initial subsidy of Rs 5000 (US$103) to each SHG making no distinction between members who are below or above the poverty line classifying them all as 'poor'. The Rural Development Department in consultation with the NABARD (National Bank for Agriculture and Rural Development) acts as the nodal agency for the programme's implementation and monitoring. For the Sakhi Mandal programme, some new reporting formats have been developed jointly by the state Department of Rural Development and NABARD to track groups that gain access to microfinance through the banks and to grade groups in terms of their credit worthiness and activity levels. Some additional Sakhi Mandal formats have been designed by the state government to provide more detail about group formation and internal lending stages of the project in order to identify problems in the early stages of the project such as the formation of poor quality groups that are not credit worthy for bank linkage.

The two schemes, SGSY and Sakhi Mandal, currently operate in parallel in Gujarat. While similar in spirit, the strategy for implementing the Sakhi Mandal scheme has been different. The SGSY scheme is implemented by the field-level staff working under the DRDA. However, these workers face increasing demands by higher administrative authorities and are often unable to devote adequate time conducting field visits within the community. For the whole of Surat district, for example, only one extension officer and eight village level workers have been deployed from the DRDA staff to implement a programme of this scale. To address the need for more front-line workers, the central government actively encourages that NGOs be involved in the formation and sustenance of the SHGs. In contrast, with Sakhi Mandal, the Government of Gujarat considers that a better strategy for implementing the project is to draw on the large outreach and strength of the government machinery. The scheme currently functions using the project staff of the central government Integrated Child Development Scheme (ICDS) which includes staff at district, taluka and village cluster levels plus an army of 34,406 anganwadi workers and 33,789 anganwadi helpers at the village level. The term 'anganwadi' refers to field workers who are specially trained in various aspects of health, nutrition and child development. The majority of anganwadi workers are either matriculates or VIII standard passes. They are normally aged between 18 and 40, command credibility within the local community and are therefore motivated to support community development. The Gujarat government felt that this field-level support was required to run a programme of this scale and complexity recognising that group formation is not a one-time activity but a process that could take a few years to stabilise.

The role of the anganwadi workers is to help identify community members for group formation and to help build their confidence by imparting training in holding regular meetings, understanding norms of savings and credit, maintaining good bookkeeping records and learning about leadership skills (Government of Gujarat, 2007). The Sakhi Mandal scheme operates a three-tiered training and capacity-building programme for the SHGs starting with training a cadre of resource persons who will train anganwadi workers to train group members. Each Sakhi Mandal group has a president to lead the group and a secretary who does bookkeeping. The idea was that two members of the group would receive training and then impart this knowledge to the others in the group. I visited two training courses for Sakhi Mandal groups in Songadh taluka – one on leadership training, the other on bookkeeping skills. Each group consisted of between 15 and 20 members and each member has been saving approximately Rs 50 (US$1) per month for the past 6 months and has been issued with a passbook. Many of the women in the SHG work as teachers and put aside these savings by economising from their income or cutting costs from the family budget.

Most of the SHG members are poor, illiterate and lack confidence which necessitates extensive handholding by the anganwadi workers during the first year of formation. Indeed, most of these women might be coming out of their houses for the first time and generating self-belief in them requires a concerted effort from the field worker. In the Sakhi Mandal scheme, the experience and village-level connections of the anganwadi workers place them well ahead of NGO field workers who are perceived as occasional visitors to the villages due to the contractual nature of their connection with the village. This is clear in Table 7.4 where I compare the status of activity between SHGs formed by

Table 7.4 New SHGs formed under Sakhi Mandals by government staff versus NGOs since the scheme started in 2007

	No. of SHGs doing internal lending		No. of SHGs with credit link		Grade 1 SHGs		Grade 2 SHGs		No. of SHGs doing economic activity	
	ICDS	NGOs	ICDS	NGOs	ICDS	NGOs	ICDS	NGOs	ICDS	NGOs
Songadh	80	0	0	0	0	0	0	0	1	0
Ucchal	35	0	0	0	0	0	0	0	2	0
Vyara	81	0	0	0	32	0	0	0	2	0

Source: Official figures obtained from Surat District Panchayat during fieldwork conducted in March 2008.

anganwadi workers (under the ICDS scheme) and SHGs formed by NGOs. The table shows the involvement of ICDS government machinery (i.e., the anganwadi workers at field level) versus the almost zero involvement of NGOs in the formation of new SHGs in the three talukas visited. Although the anganwadi workers encourage the SHGs to start interlending for personal borrowing rather than going to moneylenders, the data show that the number of SHGs engaging in this activity as a percentage of the total is still very small. Another reason to encourage interlending is to gain points so that the banks would be more inclined to grant a loan for starting economic activities in the future. However, the data show that no groups have as yet established a credit link with banks and very few have started to get involved in internal lending, let alone economic activity. This is despite the fact that many of the groups had existed earlier under the SGSY scheme.

The NGO sector in Gujarat has also shown its limitations in terms of its presence and outreach with regards to the implementation of SGSY. For example, an NGO working in Surat is the BAIF Development Research Foundation created in 1967 to assist self-employed rural families to obtain gainful employment to improve their living conditions. In Gujarat, the NGO works through its sister organisation GRISERV (Gujarat Rural Institute for Socio-Economic Reconstruction Vadodara) which was formed in 1985. However, its outreach is small covering only approximately 10% of villages in the state. The Government of Gujarat proposes that the majority of SHGs (90% of total) should be formed through anganwadi workers and only 10% by NGOs under supervision of government workers and with the district-level committee having powers of selecting/removing NGOs.

Table 7.4 shows that only a limited number of SHGs are currently undertaking economic activity. Only relatively recently have there been attempts to link groups to relevant income-generating activities within a locality. I visited Andavari Dhur gram panchayat in Vyara taluka where a farmers club has been held for the past four years. In this agricultural area, only 2–3% of the youth go onto university. Most leave college to start farming activity. A farmers' club has been running twice a month for farmers in the catchment of 8–10 km and a second club has been set up around 15 km away by NABARD bank with plans to start up a third club in the area shortly. Local farmers reported that each club meeting is attended by about seven to eight female SHG members in the area and that various issues are discussed at the club meetings related to raising the productivity of local crops and accessing more lucrative markets

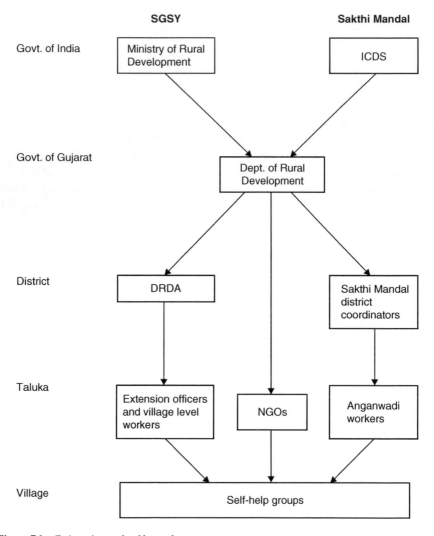

Figure 7.1   Gujarat's rural self-employment programmes

for the selling of produce. A second income-generating activity is the gober gas[8] community programme, which I visited. This programme has been running for one year in Bhidputrak village in Ucchal taluka and delivers gas directly to 121 households once a day and produces organic compost to increase farmer productivity. This project has given work to three groups of SHGs in rotation with each group working for ten days to water the soil and spread the compost.

My fieldwork in Gujarat has provided me with an understanding of the ground-level realities of implementing a rural self-employment programme in a relatively backward area. To be effective in terms of poverty alleviation, the programme requires integration at various levels such as between ministries and agencies at different tiers of government and between front-line workers and community self-help groups as shown in Figure 7.1. In the next section, we consider the extent to which the vision that e-administration can promote development by improving planning and administration is realistic.

MIS for improving rural development in Gujarat: A commentary

The development priorities of Gujarat state have shifted over the years from an earlier emphasis on entrepreneurship to a more balanced approach. The Modi government has stood firmly against excessive economic growth policies and has moved more towards balancing economic gains with social priorities. In particular, the current administration recognises the need for public spending in the rural sector. There have been many macro-level influences on the state government. First, in terms of rural development planning, there has been a change in philosophy within India from a household target-orientation to a group-based ideology. This change has been influenced by macro influences from the international development community which encourage community participation and credit mobilisation schemes. A second influence on the state government is related to structures of governance for implementing rural development programmes. There has been increasing global pressure to downsize the role of government and encourage the involvement of civil society in development interventions. These pressures have, in turn, affected the implementation of programmes. With the SGSY programme, there has been a steady increase in the number of NGOs who have been contracted by the government to form and nurture self-help groups. A third and related influence on the state government has been through the e-governance policy rhetoric of the international development community. The focus of this policy has been to move away from back-end type e-administration applications to front-end citizen-centric applications. The aim of e-administration applications has been to use tools and techniques to improve the efficiency of project management rather than to improve programme effectiveness.

Improving systems of governance, however, is not a managerial or technological issue but a social activity. After eight years of implementing the SGSY
programme, my study reveals that the majority of self-help group have not
yet started to engage in internal lending, credit linking with banks or microfinance activity. On the contrary, I found that most of the SHGs, once formed,
often fall apart with little accumulated learning documented about why this
happens and how to prevent it. The strength of SHGs depends crucially on
front-line fieldworkers who are government employees working under the district administration or directly recruited by the central government. In either
case, these fieldworkers have an intimate knowledge of the culture that exists
within the community and can facilitate the strengthening of organisational
and political resources within a group and between groups. The rural poor
in Gujarat face erratic income streams due to their vulnerability to external
shocks that may occur such as natural disasters, climate change and global
economic crises. Moreover, studies conducted in other developing countries
have shown that engaging in microfinance activity may create stress for rural
poor women within their household (Ahmed *et al.*, 2000). However, the MIS
that exists for monitoring this programme offers little input to policy-makers
regarding real-life contingencies – a disjuncture coined by Heeks as 'design-
reality gap' (Heeks, 2002). The state plays an important role in creating this
disjuncture by setting the performance criteria against which public officials
are held accountable sometimes creating a bias towards particular policy prescriptions. For example, if the performance of a government programme such
as the SGSY is measured by the number of self-help groups formed, this may
suggest a policy move to encourage further group formation even though this
move offers no guarantee that the most vulnerable community members will
necessarily be included.

In theory, the SGSY was considered a process-oriented scheme. It was recognised by the government that social mobilisation and community organisation require a process-oriented rather than a target-oriented approach (GOI,
1999). However, in practice, the programme remains target-based. An example
from the Sakhi Mandal programme demonstrates the futility of a monitoring
system that is based solely on physical and financial targets. During my last
visit to Surat district in March 2008, I was told by the Sakhi Mandal district coordinator that targets set for programme expenditure are currently
not being met. If this is taken as the key performance indicator for Sakhi
Mandal, the programme is clearly underperforming. However, performance
can be interpreted differently if other more qualitative indicators are used,
for example, that provide information about solidarity within a group. This
interpretation could tell a different story about the programme's impact – one
that reflects more closely the ground-level realities and complexities of poverty alleviation.

This discrepancy between performance targets and the identification of relevant qualitative indicators for the rural self-employment programme signals a wider problem with regards to the lack of capacity of local administrators to plan and implement programmes. Capacity-building, in its wider sense, relates to ways of managing rural development that transcend individual programmes. Field staff repeatedly emphasised the importance of recording information about solidarity-building of individual SHGs as this was something far more permanent than recording information about whether the group was formed under SGSY, Sakhi Mandal or any other future scheme that may be introduced by different administrations. But this way of thinking is at odds with the development planning apparatus. Sakhi Mandal has its own staff employed directly by the ICDS department (the anganwadi workers). The SGSY programme has its own staff deployed by the DRDA (the village-level workers and extension officers). The few NGOs working on rural self-employment schemes in Gujarat have their own machinery. All of these staff works on the same SHGs but according to the guidelines prescribed by their ministry or agency.

The task of building capacity for understanding processes of development relies on tapping the 'intelligence' of local fieldworkers about ground-level realities. In Gujarat, the policy influence of the Modi administration on basic rural infrastructure and development has been a positive move. A combination of inputs are required for poverty alleviation to support the formation of SHGs such as employment opportunities and the promotion of other community development schemes including infrastructure, water, energy and sanitation. Over the next few years, there is every indication that the present administration will continue with its coordinated approach to work for the upliftment of the rural poor. This policy direction in Gujarat is combined with the realisation that those perceived as mundane grassroots field workers are really the greatest asset in community development projects, a finding which is supported through other studies on rural self-employment schemes in India (Ashley and Maxwell, 2001; Meenakshisundaram, 2005). For example, being a local villager, the anganwadi worker has a clear understanding of the issues confronting families in the locality. This understanding enables her to empathise with group members and work for their needs. The involvement of local political bodies at the gram and taluka panchayat levels has so far been minimal in the rural self-employment programmes in Gujarat. However, once key activities have been identified, their role will become more important in identifying local markets and intermediary agencies for obtaining access to finance, inputs and markets. The renewed acceptance of local government workers and political representatives as important players in rural development planning has been a bold step taken by the Gujarat administration and negates the advice given by the international development community about reducing the role of government and involving civil society players more actively in development planning.

A third aspect of local-level capacity-building relates to local autonomy for planning and implementing schemes. So far, decentralisation has been supported more in theory than in practice. Despite the passing of legislation for decentralising the planning and administration of development programmes, in reality only deregulation has been achieved. The extent of real devolution of power and responsibilities has been limited. As described earlier, some discretion had been accorded to district DRDA staff in the early 1990s to develop alternative criteria for evaluating programme implementation. However, with the diversion of policy interest away from e-administration towards e-services, the opportunity to learn about locally relevant performance indicators was lost. As discussed earlier, decentralisation is not a purely administrative issue. It requires that local administrators have the opportunity and resources to strengthen their interface with fieldworkers and the local community. Despite the scale of the SGSY programme in India and its existence for almost a decade, there is a general paucity of research/analysis carried out on key aspects of the programme such as on the formation, sustainability and productivity of SHGs.

Glossary

Anganwadi workers – government workers trained in various aspects of health, nutrition and child development
BJP – a major political party in India
CRISP – Computerized Rural Information Systems Project
DRDA – District Rural Development Agency
Gram Panchayat – the village council
ICDS – Central government Integrated Child Development Scheme
IRDP – Integrated Rural Development Programme
Livelihood approach – an approach to programme development that focuses on understanding the interaction between various factors that influence the livelihoods of poor people
Mahiti Shakti – telecentre project implemented in certain districts of Gujarat
One-Day Governance – an e-service application that provides registration documents and certificates to citizens
Sakhi Mandal – a rural self-employment programme launched by the Gujarat government in 2007
SGSY – Swarnjayanti Gram Swarozgar Yojana is India's current flagship rural development programme
SHG – self-help group comprising between 11–20 persons
Taluka – a subdivision of the district, there are 15 talukas in Surat district

References

Ahmed, S., Adams, A., Chowdhury, M. and Bhuiya, A. (2000) Micro-Credit and Emotional Well-Being: Experience of poor rural women from Matlab, Bangladesh, *World Development,* 29, 11, pp. 1957–1966.

Ashley, C. and Maxwell, S. (2001) Rethinking Rural Development, *Development Policy Review,* 18, 4, pp. 395–425.

Bhatnagar, S.C. (1996) Applications of Information Technology in Grameen Bank. In *Global Information Technology and Socio-economic Development,* edited by M. Odedra-Straub, Ivy League Publishing, New Hampshire, USA, pp. 95–106.

Breman, J. and Shah, C. (2005) Microfinance and the Poor in Gujarat, *IDPAD Newsletter,* III, 2, July–December.

Deb, K. (1986) *Rural Development in India since Independence,* Oriental University Press, London.

Dholakia, R. (2008) Macroeconomic Framework for Development in Gujarat. In *Gujarat: Perspectives of the future,* edited by R. Swaminathan, Academic Foundation, New Delhi, pp. 105–151.

GOI. (1999) Swarnjayanti Gram Swarozgar Yojana (SGSY) Guidelines, Government of India, Ministry of Rural Development, New Delhi.

GOI. (2007) Revision of Monitoring Formats for Reporting Monthly Progress Reports under SGSY, Internal document of Ministry of Rural Development, Department of Rural Development, Krishi Bhavan, New Delhi.

Government of Gujarat (2007) Sakhi Mandals, Government of Gujarat, Panchayats, Rural Housing and Rural Development Department, Sachivalaya, Gandhinagar.

Gupta, P. and Agrawal, S.M. (2005) Rural Telecom: A case study on Gyan Ganga Project, Indian Institute of Management (online). Available at http://www.iimahd.ernet.in/ctps/pdf/Gyan%20Ganga%20Report.pdf

Heeks, R. (2002) Information Systems and Developing Countries: Failure, success and local improvisations, *The Information Society,* 18, 2, pp. 101–112.

Hindustan Times (2007) Development Is Synonymous with Gujarat: Narendra Modi, 12 October.

Hirway, I. and Mahadevia, D. (2008) Human Development and Gender Development in Gujarat: Some issues. In *Gujarat: Perspectives of the future,* edited by R. Swaminathan, Academic Foundation, New Delhi, pp. 151–195.

IFAD. (2001) Rural Poverty Report 2001: The challenge of ending rural poverty, Oxford University Press, Oxford.

Jain, L.C. (1985) *Grass without Roots: Rural development under government auspices,* Sage Publications, New Delhi.

Madon, S. (1992a) The Impact of Computer-Based Information Systems on Rural Development: A case study in India. Thesis submitted for the degree of Doctor of Philosophy, Department of Computing, Imperial College, London.

Madon, S. (1992b) The Impact of Computer-Based Information Systems on Rural Development: A case study in India, *Journal of Information Technology,* 7, pp. 20–29.

Madon, S. (1993) Computer-Based Information Systems for Development Planning: Managing human resources, *European Journal of Information Systems,* 2, 1, pp. 49–55.

Madon, S. (2006) IT-Based Government Reform Initiatives in the Indian State of Gujarat, *Journal of International Development,* 18, 6, pp. 877–888.

Madon, S. and Walsham, G. (1995) Decentralised Information Systems for Development Planning in India: Context/process interaction, *Information Infrastructure and Policy,* 4, 2, pp. 163–179.

Meenakshisundaram, S. (2005) Rural Development for Panchayati Raj. In *Decentralisation and Local Governance,* edited by L.C. Jain, Orient Longman, New Delhi, pp. 417–434.

Shylendra, H.S. and Bhirdikar, K. (2005) 'Good Governance' and Poverty Alleviation Programmes: A critical analysis of the Swarnajayanti Gram Swarozgar Yojana, *International Journal of Rural Management,* 1, 2, pp. 203–221.

Sud, N. (2003) Experience of SGSY in Gujarat: From process-oriented theory to *deterministic* practice, *Economic and Political Weekly,* 38, 39, pp. 4085–4087.

World Bank (2007) Agriculture for Development, World Development Report 2008, World Bank, Washington DC.

8
Telecentres for Rural Outreach in Kerala

Kerala's focus on social and community services over economic growth has resulted in poor economic growth, a narrow industrial and agricultural base and unemployment. Since the late 1990s, Kerala has opened up to international investment and influence in development activities. Part of the state's governance reform agenda has included the Akshaya telecentre project which aims to promote community development in rural areas. This chapter describes the genesis and evolution of this project in its original pilot district of Malappuram. In recent years, a specific focus of the project has been to assist the district's small farming community. The study shows that unless moderated by the state, the project tends to favour economic entrepreneurship over social development priorities. At the local level, government officers, political representatives and telecentre entrepreneurs play a crucial role in interfacing with the community. Finally, the chapter concludes that more than the technology, the Akshaya project has provided a useful social space for integrating local administrative, political and social systems.

Agriculture is fundamental to growth and poverty reduction in many ways – as an economic activity, as a livelihood and as a provider of environmental services (Eswaran and Kotwal, 2006; Kotwal and Ramswami, 1998; World Bank, 2007). In India, it had become clear by the mid-1960s that there was no alternative to technological change in agriculture for achieving self-sufficiency in grains. The allocation of funds for rural development was always disproportionately low with agriculture seen as a relatively small productive sector and the future viability of small farms and petty commodity production increasingly called into question due to technological complexity, greater connectedness to markets and the globalisation of commodity chains (Ashley and Maxwell, 2001). Nevertheless, public investment in agriculture was stepped up significantly and new technology raised the profitability of investment for the farmers, particularly noticeable in terms of the acceleration in the growth rate of output of pulses and oilseeds in the 1970s and 1980s (Hanumantha Rao, 2004).

However, in terms of growth of labour productivity, these have been modest. As an example, the agricultural sector generates incomes on average only one-fifth of those in the rest of the economy (Bhaskar and Gupta, 2007; Roy, 2007). Despite the slow growth in agriculture, the sector continues to have a huge influence on the economy as a whole because it continues to affect the majority of the population. Employment has continued to grow in Indian agriculture albeit at a much smaller rate than either industry or services. In absolute terms, in 2004 nearly 60% of the population was in agriculture and nearly 80% of India's below-poverty-line population lived in rural areas directly or indirectly dependent on agriculture.

In recent years, the Government of India has recognised the potential of ICT for enhancing farmer productivity launching various initiatives for this purpose. The emphasis of government support in agriculture has traditionally been on providing inputs (such as funds, seeds, fertilizers) rather than on other aspects of the supply chain such as marketing, transport and logistics. Classified as e-services applications, projects were launched to provide information and services to farmers to assist them in producing, selling and marketing their crops. In March 2000, the Ministry of Agriculture sanctioned the Agricultural Marketing Information Network (AGMARKNET) project to be implemented by the National Informatics Centre. AGMARKNET is a national portal designed to connect farmers to all important agricultural produce markets in India to strengthen their bargaining position with up-to-date price information.[1] A second initiative launched by the Ministry of Agriculture called KissanKerala is a call centre project[2] formally launched in 2005. This project is designed to deliver extension services to the farming community via the telecommunications infrastructure. KissanKerala provides an instant service to farmers with agricultural extension officers and other domain experts responding to issues they raise by telephone and the internet in the local language. Both AGMARKNET and KissanKerala can be classified as e-governance applications as they aim to provide information and services to farmers.

Another type of ICT application is the telecentre. Telecentres have become an important aspect of India's e-governance strategy. Over the past five years, approximately 10,000 rural centres have been set up in the country aimed at increasing productivity, generating income and improving social welfare (i4donline, 2007). Telecentres are sometimes referred to as 'multi-purpose community centres' because they provide a range of services related to different domains and sectors such as agriculture, education, business and health.[3] Agriculture is identified as a key sector where telecentres can play a major role in providing agricultural support services to farmers on a commercial basis (Harris *et al.*, 2003). One such project discussed earlier is eChoupal launched by the India Tobacco Company (ITC) in the Indian state of Madhya Pradesh in 2000. ITC introduced telecentres run by local entrepreneurs who provided price information to farmers which allowed them to sell their produce directly to the company, rather than through middlemen. Evidence shows, however, that the benefit to farmers has been very much dependent on local social factors such as caste affiliation, political alignments and size of farm holdings. Few benefits were derived from the project for small and marginal farmers,[4] or agricultural labourers (Kumar, 2004).

This chapter explores the role that the Akshaya project in Kerala has played in overall community development in the district of Malappuram. In particular, I focus on one of the more recent aims of this telecentre project which has been to support small and marginal farmers in Kerala to increase their productivity and thereby generate income. Before describing the project, let us briefly review Kerala's unique development trajectory.

Kerala's unique development context

Kerala lies on the south-western tip of India and is a small but densely populated state (GOI, 2008). Nearly 28% of the land area is covered by forests which forms the resource base for many industries. Kerala receives ample rainfall from its two monsoons and its breathtaking terrain makes it a great tourist destination. Over the past 50 years, the state has achieved a remarkable transformation from an extremely poor state with caste and conflicts to a state with high levels of social indicators, a rich agrarian economy, a high degree of urbanisation and infrastructure development, and high foreign exchange remittances from migrant workers. The growth rate of the population is the lowest in India and Kerala leads other states in the country in education, particularly for women.

The state has a reputation for being 'leftist' particularly in terms of social development and this is linked to its long history of political mobilisation and social movements (Chathukulam and John, 2007; Heller, 1996, 1999; Kannan, 2000; Parayil, 2000; Thomas, 2007). An extensive literature exists about how the state contradicted the neoliberal doctrine of rapid economic growth being the sole determinant of improvements in standards of living of ordinary people (Isaac and Tharakan, 1995). This, in turn, has had the effect of keeping private and voluntary initiatives distant from the public realm (Joseph and Chathukulam, 2007). Kerala has been active in areas of land reform, social welfare, education and legislation for the formal and informal labour market (Franke and Chasin, 2000; Tornquist, 2000). The state has been committed to decentralisation and the process put in place has been the most extensive in the country in terms of powers and funds devolved (Jha, 2002; Mathew, 2007; Sharma, 2007). Through the People's Planning Campaign introduced in 1996, responsibilities and one-third of plan resources of the state were transferred to the local governments (Rajasekharan, 2007). Activities of volunteer groups such as the People's Science Movement were actively supported by the state to empower backward communities and to promote democracy and sustainable development within the state (Sharma, 2007; Thomas, 2000).

However, the predominance of social and community services over economic growth has also been the major cause of revenue deficits and fiscal strain in Kerala. While the remittances boom which began in the 1970s compensated for the state's poor economic situation, it has done little to improve the narrow domestic agricultural and industrial base. As a result of the decline in traditional industries, the unemployment rate has remained high in the state, particularly among the educated population. While some growth has taken place in the tertiary sector, the primary and secondary sectors have languished and even registered negative growth rates (The Hindu, 2006). Within agriculture, since the mid-1970s, there has been a movement away from labour-intensive annual crops to less labour-intensive commercial crops whose products are exposed to international competition (Viswanathan, 2007). Crop promotional agencies have provided institutional support to ensure increased levels of income generation and employment to farmers due to the relative profitability of these crops and local farming communities were mobilised for the setting up of associations in some village panchayats (John and Chathukulam, 2002). Notwithstanding these achievements, from the early 1990s, Kerala started to lose its comparative advantage in the export of traditional commodities such as pepper, cardamom, ginger, cashew, coir, tea and coffee. Furthermore, there was a reduction in levels of public investment in agriculture, allied infrastructure and technological development such as irrigation and crop-specific technologies (Jeromi, 2003; Viswanathan, 2007). The declining size of operational holdings led to a proliferation of small and marginal holdings across the major commercial crops and a growing dependence on hired labour, a shortage of skilled/unskilled labourers in the midst of growing rural unemployment and dwindling institutional support mechanisms (George, 1993; Tharamangalam, 1998; Veron, 2001).

With poor economic growth rates, a weak agricultural sector and high unemployment, the Kerala government was forced to seek an alternative approach to development within the state. Since the late 1990s, partly in response to India's recent neoliberal economic reforms, it has been recognised that the state, though still dominated by leftist ideology, cannot withstand the trend towards an increased role for international investment and influence in development activities (Joseph and Chathukulam, 2007). In 2002, the state government received funds from the Asian Development Bank under its Modernising Government & Fiscal Reforms Programme (MGP) aimed at implementing good governance policy prescriptions in the state (MGP, 2003). This agenda included initiatives to modernise the government machinery including computerisation of local panchayats and other local bodies through the use of

ICTs. Also included in the agenda were e-services applications, for example, a project called FRIENDS[5] that provided citizens with the convenience of a single-window system for paying a variety of government bills all under one roof (Madon and Kiran, 2003). These applications were first implemented at district headquarters and major towns in the state. In the second phase, a project called Akshaya[6] was launched not only with the objective of providing an outreach for IT training and government services (such as bill payment) to rural citizens, but also to promote overall development in terms of generating income, raising productivity and providing a range of social services. Akshaya was piloted in the district of Malappuram in north Kerala in 2002 and since then has been rolled out to all the districts in the state. My involvement with the project started in 2002 just at the time when the project was being conceived and even before any telecentres were physically established. This has provided me with a good opportunity to study its evolution over time.

Akshaya's role in promoting community development and local farming activity

The Akshaya project is now in its sixth year of implementation and forms an interesting study of the complexity involved with the notion of telecentres acting as conduits for development. The project was conceived in what is considered to be Kerala's most backward district of Malappuram in north Kerala in April 2002. This mainly Muslim-dominated rural district has a population of approximately 3 million residents – 70% of whom are farmers. It has the lowest human development index in the state but at the same time has the largest number of emigrants resulting in high purchasing power from external remittances (KSITM, 2002). In April 2002, the 100 gram panchayat members of Malappuram district made a proposal to the Kerala IT Minister to use their budget allocation for imparting district-wide computer literacy. The state government supported the proposal and suggested the idea of a telecentre project for imparting computer literacy and for promoting community development and entrepreneurship through a variety of commercial and social services.

A series of workshops took place at the district and block levels in the months following the official launch to gain acceptance of the project among local agencies and politicians, as well as among the community. The Kerala State IT Mission (KSITM) headed by the IT Minister and IT Secretary planned and supported the project. Each centre was to be located within a 3 km distance from any household.[7] All the centres were franchised to private entrepreneurs, some of whom had previously owned internet cafes or computer training centres. New entrepreneurs were selected through a government tender announcement in consultation with the gram panchayat based on social commitment and entrepreneurial talent. Each telecentre was created at a cost of about

Rs 200,000 (US$4114) to the entrepreneur, normally through a subsidised bank loan facilitated by the government. The rent and equipment purchase of computers for each centre was to be the responsibility of the entrepreneurs although the government facilitated loans for this and organised an IT fair in 2003 at which entrepreneurs could lobby to negotiate a good price for equipment. The government planned for a massive wireless infrastructure to enable broadband connectivity to all locations controlled through a network operating centre.

From early 2003, there were 630 telecentres that were operational with between 5–19 computers and other peripherals per centre. The initial phase of the project was devoted to e-literacy in which one person from every family was eligible to receive basic ICT training from their local centre. Each trainee paid Rs 20 (US$0.41) to the telecentre franchisee for the course while the remaining 86% of the cost was subsidised by the government with the gram panchayat making the largest contribution. By the end of the e-literacy phase in December 2003, approximately 500,000 people (mostly women) had received training consisting of 10 CD-ROM based training modules – each module of 90 minutes duration. Most entrepreneurs had recuperated approximately 50% of their initial investment through this activity and the Akshaya project began to receive publicity as Malappuram became the first district in India to achieve 100% e-literacy.[8] The project entered its second phase in 2004. Training continued to generate a modest revenue stream with demand from approximately 40% of persons trained under the e-literacy programme for further training in IT, particularly on office software packages, language skills and on a CD-based educational programme for school leaving students developed by KSITM called e-Vidya.[9] Some entrepreneurs began to generate revenue by satisfying local demand for other services such as digital photography, photo album-making (particularly during the wedding season), digital astrology and kids and women's clubs (Rangaswamy, 2006). Some entrepreneurs made their telecentre the hub for collating and disseminating information about particular health ailments that prevailed in their locality such as dengue fever.[10] Another popular source of revenue for the telecentre was data digitisation of local panchayat records. Entrepreneurs charged the local panchayat a fee for digitising land records, employee records and for maintaining databases for other village-level administrative matters. While the majority of telecentres remained financially sustainable, about one-third of them were closed down at this stage as many entrepreneurs were unable to initiate revenue-generating activities (Madon, 2005).

In 2004, in the aftermath of the e-literacy phase, the strategy of the Kerala government was to focus on generating commercial activities by attracting local companies. Six activity streams were identified for the district including among others data digitisation, multimedia, servicing the local IT park and selling financial services. Centres were designated to specialise in one of these streams so that in each gram panchayat, all the commercial specialisations were covered. In September 2004, local companies were invited to attend the Akshaya Enterprise Connect meeting to publicise the launching of Akshaya as a commercial hub for local entrepreneurship. However, although the meeting was well-attended, a low level of corporate confidence was shown by companies for using the Akshaya centres. One reason for this was that any contract that was made for the selling of products and services through the centres was between the company and the entrepreneur. As KSITM did not underwrite the contract, this gave no legal security to the company. Technical and administrative delays in delivering high-speed internet connectivity to the centres also adversely affected the start-up commercial activities. In terms of the Kerala government's social agenda for the telecentre, some modest experiments took place commissioning content-providers to generate locally relevant applications in sectors such as agriculture, health, tourism, education and others although the software created remained very much prototypes within the KSITM. Later on in 2004, a door-to-door health-mapping exercise was piloted at Cheekode panchayat using medicinal monitoring devices and questionnaires to collect data about health status among the local community. The data were entered at the local Akshaya telecentre and later analysed by health specialists to identify risk groups and to direct individuals identified with abnormalities for further diagnosis. However, the exercise was abandoned a few months later as the health-mapping exercise had been conducted without consulting the health administration and therefore lacked legitimacy (Madon, 2005).

In 2005, the two main activities in Akshaya centres were communications with family members abroad[11] (Pal *et al.,* 2006) as well as training. In 2006, two more services were launched in the centres. First, a programme called Internet for the Masses which provided ten hours of advanced ICT training for professionals such as school teachers and government officers. Second, a facility called e-Pay modeled on the FRIENDS bill payment system introduced in district headquarters. Entrepreneurs charged citizens Rs 10 (US$0.2) per bill transaction which provided them with a modest but regular income stream. More than revenue, however, e-Pay has encouraged a regular flow of local residents to frequent the centres making the entrepreneur and his centre a community hub. From mid-2007, there was an increase in the linkages made between the Akshaya telecentres and local government departments. For example, citizens were now able to register at the Akshaya centres for rural self-employment schemes such as SGSY and other government development schemes.

By July 2008, Akshaya had stabilised with 342 centres, although in reality I was told that a more accurate number of well-performing centres was 212. Many of the earlier centres identified as non-productive were closed down by mutual consent with the entrepreneur. According to the Akshaya field office in Malappuram, this number was considered adequate to serve the local community with the argument that earlier there were too many centres. In three panchayats, however, there were no Akshaya centres offering services to citizens. The Akshaya field office in Malappuram consists of 14 staff plus 4 block coordinators who monitor the centres at field level addressing any issues that arise. The centres are graded annually from a scale A to D in terms of financial sustainability, locally generated activities and social commitment. In my last trip to Malappuram in July 2008, approximately 50% of telecentre activity was devoted to training in ICT or other courses (mainly Arabic and English), approximately 20% to e-Pay activity and approximately 10% to data digitisation for the local panchayat, browsing and providing a meeting house for clubs. The remaining 10–20% of activity was devoted to supporting the local farming community which I describe in the remainder of this chapter.

This activity for local farmers commenced under the label of e-Krishi[12] – a project supported under the UN ICT for Development initiative within the Government of India's e-governance framework and had an implementation time frame of 2003–7. The project is implemented by KSITM in collaboration with the Indian Institute of Information Technology and Management, Kerala and the agriculture department. Officially launched in 2005, the project aims to boost agricultural productivity by using the Akshaya centres to reach the masses of farming community in Malappuram. e-Krishi provides a web-based platform for creating a virtual services gateway to connect farmers with buyers, input providers (e.g., seeds, fertilizers, pesticides), warehouse facility providers, bankers, insurers and others.[13] In Malappuram, however, the take-up of e-Krishi by the farming community has been poor. While there are benefits of an improved supply chain management using ICT for large farmers, in Malappuram most farmers belong to the small or marginal category and have low production levels aiming at self-sufficiency rather than commercial gain. Competitive markets remain inaccessible to these farmers due to the domination of bigger players who have institutional backing from agricultural marketing boards.

While the e-Krishi portal is not of particular relevance to the local farming community of Malappuram, the label 'e-Krishi' continues to be adopted by the Akshaya entrepreneurs to describe various ways in which the centres are used as an outreach to support particularly small and marginal farmers. These different types of support are coordinated through the running of Bhoomi Clubs[14] in the telecentres. As of July 2008, 67 of the 212 telecentres host a Bhoomi Club regularly. These clubs consist of between 150–300 farmer members although some Akshaya centres reported as many as 500 members. From these, entrepreneurs reported that approximately 40–50 farmers come regularly every month. Of the farmers registered in the Bhoomi Club, approximately 85% belong to the small and marginal category. For this category of farmer, the marketplace is the local community. Here, buyers and sellers all know each other and are cognizant of local market prices without the need for an e-Krishi type portal. In fact, for the small farmer, there are risks of selling produce to an outside market since there is no legally binding contract to safeguard the farmer if the buyer defaults. Membership of the Bhoomi Club is free and farmers congregate monthly at the Akshaya centres to discuss issues affecting their livelihoods and to seek advice regarding farming practices, latest crop prices and marketing issues. The Akshaya centre acts as a hub to bring together farmers, the local panchayat and the agricultural extension officer. The Bhoomi Club also serves as a collection point for products that are delivered by clusters of local farmers, and as an exchange point for bringing together buyers and sellers of products. For example, many entrepreneurs have started to earn revenue by logging details of farmers within their catchment area and making this information available to prospective buyers for a fee. The telecentres also routinely serve as a focal point for the pooling and allocation of wage labour to farmers. In some cases, the entrepreneur has formed tie-ups with local fertilizer companies for selling fertilizer to farmers for a small profit.

In some telecentres, the entrepreneur has shown initiative in helping the local farmers address some of their needs. In one Akshaya centre visited, for

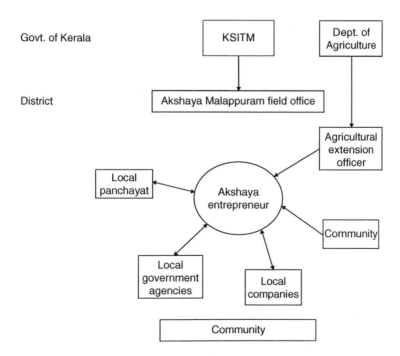

Figure 8.1 Kerala's Akshaya telecentre project

example, the entrepreneur has helped small farmers and below-poverty-line women to acquire loans from a local bank. Before the advent of the telecentres, a local merchant would give an advance to a small farmer for producing any crop as they would be denied loans from banks. However, by accepting the loan, the farmer would be trapped into selling his produce only to that merchant. The Akshaya entrepreneur has enabled the farmer to break this rela tionship of dependency with the local merchant.

My fieldwork with the Akshaya project provides a rich understanding of the important role played by state government departments and by local social, political and administrative players as illustrated in Figure 8.1. Taking these ground-level realities into consideration help us to reflect on the vision of improving community development through telecentres.

Telecentres for promoting community development in Kerala: A commentary

The Kerala government has shown a commitment to addressing both economic and social aspects of community development through the Akshaya telecentre project. At the outset, the Kerala government ensured that the project was portrayed as socially inclusive through participation of local political representatives, particularly in the selection of entrepreneurs. Active grassroots campaigning in the initial phases of the project created community awareness and interest in e-literacy. In terms of promoting commercial activities, training has proved to be lucrative for many centres. With other commercial activities, success has depended on the talent of the entrepreneur in identifying local demand and providing niche services. A recent initiative undertaken in about one-third of the Akshaya centres for improving economic productivity is the setting up of the Bhoomi Club. In the centres where it operates, the club has helped build solidarity among the rural poor farmers and to increase the income of these small cultivators. It has given them an integrated forum for presenting their produce for purchase, for getting farmers together for training and for conducting a regular agricultural clinic.

To a much greater extent than elsewhere in India, the Kerala government has shown its commitment to using telecentres for balancing both economic and social priorities. The state's strong legacy of redistributive social policy and decentralisation shaped the ideological orientation of Akshaya. The state government gave a clear signal of its commitment to the project by providing good support to entrepreneurs and by the symbolic move in 2003 made by the erstwhile Director of KSITM to take up the post of Malappuram District Collector[15] to oversee the project implementation. At that time, I was in involved in many debates that were taking place within KSITM about the right balance between economic and social objectives. However, there have been times when political influences have resulted in less state direction, for example from 2004 to 2006 (Kuriyan *et al.*, 2006). During these years, there was a growing tendency for business-driven entrepreneurship in many centres. Such activity attracted a more educated local clientele who were attracted to new high-technology courses being offered. Without state direction, entrepreneurs continued to make a good profit but the project proved irrelevant for the majority of community members.

Unless moderated by the state government, the tendency to favour economic entrepreneurship over social priorities (which is already prevalent in some of the roll-out districts of the Akshaya project), may distort the original mission of the project. The implementation strategy in the roll-out districts has been different from Malappuram. There are fewer centres, each serving a larger catchment area. This has resulted in problems of access for some community members who live in remote locations. In addition, in terms of identifying entrepreneurs, emphasis is now placed on financial means and entrepreneurial experience rather than the earlier focus on social commitment. The current debate in India about the National eGovernance Programme (NeGP) discussed earlier has serious ramifications for Kerala's community development focus. So far, the Kerala government has resisted the NeGP strategy with CPI (M)[16] supporters arguing that the handing over of Akshaya centres to major corporates like Reliance will mostly benefit the private sector. The fear is that this will lead to the telecentres being run as retail outlets obscuring the project's ideological orientation towards social development.

Just as the state plays an important role in providing the ideological framing for telecentre projects, state support for establishing and nurturing effective local systems is vital in ensuring that the project remains relevant for the community. The Akshaya field office in Malappuram needs to be vigilant in terms of providing an effective monitoring system for the project by identifying and addressing day-to-day issues faced by entrepreneurs. Local government departments and panchayat offices play an important role in integrating the activities of the telecentre with existing social, administrative and political systems. In cases where the nexus of connections between these local systems is good, the benefits to the community are increased, for example, with the local panchayat members using the Bhoomi Club to extend their political base. However, in cases where the local panchayat is supportive neither of Akshaya nor of the Bhoomi Club, benefits to the community are reduced. Local government plays a crucial role in providing legitimacy for a range of development services to be run through telecentres. Earlier with the Akshaya project, I described how a health-mapping experiment was abandoned precisely because of lack of integration between the experiment and the local health-planning apparatus. With the running of the Bhoomi Club, the local agricultural extension officer is well-placed to serve as an intermediary because of his scientific domain knowledge and local expertise. This type of local agro-advisory service can be compared with the larger technology-mediated KissanKerala project discussed earlier. However, Gopakumar (2006) found that this e-service only became relevant to local farmers through the intermediation of the agricultural extension officer who was conversant with the scientific terminology used by the experts and could translate this to the farmer. Moreover, the agricultural advice of the local extension officer meant that local farmers could tap traditional knowledge bearers and social networks to extract information about new cropping patterns, pesticides or employment opportunities. Many a time, Gopakumar's study found that solutions to simpler or known queries could be handled by the extension officer without contacting the KissanKerala expert team via the website. If the query seems difficult to answer, the extension officer would post the query onto the web and provide relevant contextual information to make the query understandable. Similarly, when the response was received from the expert, the extension officer was able to translate and personalise the information given by the expert.

The telecentre entrepreneur also constitutes an important local agent for interfacing with the community. For example, Kuriyan *et al.* (2006) found that many entrepreneurs act as a government help desk to low-income customers providing information about a range of government services. The entrepreneur has also acted as a crucial intermediary in terms of building trust relations between the citizens and the state. Due to the fact that the entrepreneur was known and trusted by the village community during the initial phase of selection, a large percentage of women (as many as 80% in some centres) volunteered as trainees. Relations with the community are strengthened in cases where the telecentre entrepreneur has a good relationship with the local panchayat office and when the panchayat effectively represents the needs of the community. Experience to date with the Akshaya project demonstrates that there is great diversity of needs within the community depending on local contextual circumstances. Sometimes these needs are articulated by community members at the statutory gram sabha village-level meetings.[17] For example, despite the fact that the Bhoomi Club has enabled small cultivators to increase their income levels, there are no direct advantages for agricultural workers who own little or no land. For this category of the rural poor, poverty is bound up with the wage rate and special programmes and services may be needed to improve their living conditions.

Finally, the Akshaya telecentres have provided an opportunity for entrepreneurs and the local community to generate income, raise productivity and promote social welfare. However, evidence shows that more than technology, the telecentres have provided a social space for integrating local administrative, political and social systems that together combine to promote democratic development.

Glossary

AGMARKNET – India's national agricultural portal
Akshaya – Kerala's flagship telecentre project which commenced in 2002
Bhoomi Club – farmers' club
eChoupal – a telecentre project introduced in Madhya Pradesh to provide market information to sell products directly to companies thereby bypassing middlemen
e-Krishi – web-based portal to connect farmers with buyers, input providers, warehouse facility providers, banks and others
FRIENDS – a bill payment system operating in Kerala
Gram panchayat – village council
Kisan Call Centre – a project to deliver extension services to the farming community through the telecommunications infrastructure
KSITM – Kerala State IT Mission
SGSY – Swarnjayanti Gram Swarozgar Yojana – India's national rural self-employment programme

References

Ashley, C. and Maxwell, S. (2001) Rethinking Rural Development, *Development Policy Review*, 19, 4, pp. 395–425.

Bhaskar, V. and Gupta, B. (2007) India's Development in the Era of Growth, *Oxford Review of Economic Policy*, 23, 2, pp. 135–142.

Chathukulam, J. and John, M.S. (2007) Social Capital in Kerala: Mixed evidence from a village panchayat. In *Local Governance in India: Ideas, challenges and strategies,* edited by T.M. Joseph, Concept Publishing Company, New Delhi, pp. 311–342.

Eswaran, M. and Kotwal, A. (2006) The Role of Agriculture in Development. In *Understanding Poverty,* edited by A.V. Banerjee, R. Benabou and D. Mookherjee, Oxford University Press, Oxford, pp. 111–125.

Franke, R.W. and Chasin, B. (2000) Is the Kerala Model Sustainable? Lessons from the past, prospects for the future. In *Kerala – The Development Experience,* ed., G. Parayil, Zed Books, London.

George, K.K. (1993) Limits to Kerala Model of Development: An analysis of fiscal crisis and its implications. Monograph Series, Trivandrum, Centre for Development Studies.

GOI. (2008) Kerala Development Report, Planning Commission, Government of India, New Delhi.

Gopakumar, K. (2006) EGovernance Services through Telecentres: The role of human intermediary and issues of trust, Proceedings of the 2006 International Conference on ICT & Development, Berkeley, CA.

Hanumantha Rao, C.H. (2004) Agriculture: Policy and performance. In *The Indian Economy: Problems and prospects,* edited by B. Jalan, Penguin Books, New Delhi.

Harris, R.W., Kumar, A. and Balaji, V. (2003) Sustainable Telecentres: Two cases from India. In *The Digital Challenge: Information Technology in the Development Context,* edited by S. Krishna and S. Madon, Ashgate, Aldershot, Hants, pp. 124–136.

Heller, P. (1996) Social Capital as a Product of Class Mobilisation and State Intervention: Industrial workers in Kerala, India, *World Development*, 24, pp. 1055–1071.

Heller, P. (1999) *The Labour of Development: Workers and the transformation of capitalism in Kerala, India,* Cornell University Press, Ithaca, NY.

The Hindu (2006) 9.2% Growth Rate in 2004–5: Review, 9 February. Available at http://www.thehindu.com/2006/02/09/stories/2006020910620400.htm

i4donline (2007) Available at http://www.i4donline.net/August07/maping.pdf

Isaac, T. and Tharakan, M. (1995) Kerala: Towards a new agenda, *Economic & Political Weekly*, 30, 31–32, pp. 1993–2004.

Jeromi, P.D. (2003) What Ails Kerala's Economy: A sectoral exploration, *Economic & Political Weekly*, 38, 16, 19 April, pp. 1584–1600.

Jha, S. (2002) Strengthening Local Governments: Rural fiscal decentralisation in India, *Economic and Political Weekly*, 29 June, pp. 2611–2612.

John, M.S. and Chathukulam, J. (2002) Building Social Capital through State Initiative@ The case of participatory planning in Kerala. *Economic & Political Weekly*, 37, 20, 18 May, pp. 1939–1948.

Joseph, T.M. and Chathukulam, J. (2007) Paradigm Shift in Local Governance: The synergy between state and non-state actors in Kerala. In *Local Governance in India: Ideas, challenges and strategies,* edited by T.M. Joseph, Concept Publishing Company, New Delhi, pp. 562–583.

Kannan, K.P. (2000) Poverty Alleviation as Advancing Basic Human Capabilities: Kerala's achievements compared. In *Kerala – The Development Experience,* ed., G. Parayil, Zed Books, London.

Kotwal, A. and Ramswami, B. (1998) Economic Reforms of Agriculture and Rural Growth, *Policy Reform,* 2, pp. 369–402.

KSITM. (2002) Project Akshaya. Document released by the Kerala State IT Mission on the occasion of the inauguration of the project by the President of India on November 18th 2002, Department of Information Technology, Government of Kerala.

Kumar, R. (2004) eChoupals: A study of the financial sustainability of village internet centres in rural Madhya Pradesh, *Information Technology and International Development,* 2, 1, pp. 45–73.

Kuriyan, R., Toyama, K. and Ray, I. (2006) Integrating Social Development and Financial Sustainability: The challenge of rural computer kiosks in Kerala. Proceedings of the 2006 International Conference on ICT & Development, Berkeley, CA.

Madon, S. (2005) Governance Lessons from the Experience of Telecentres in Kerala, *European Journal of Information Systems,* 14, pp. 401–416.

Madon, S. and Kiran, G.R. (2003) Information Technology for Citizen-Government Interface: A study of FRIENDS project in Kerala. World Bank Global Knowledge Sharing Program (GKSP). Available at www1.worldbank.org/publicsector/bnpp/egovupdate.htm

Mathew, B. (2007) Emergence of New Institutions through Participatory Democracy, An evaluation of Kerala experiment. In *Local Governance in India: Ideas, challenges and strategies,* edited by T.M. Joseph, Concept Publishing Company, New Delhi, pp. 254–274.

MGP. (2003) Strategic Documents 1–5. Modernising Government Programme, Government of Kerala. Available at http://www.keralamgp.org

Pal, J., Nedevschi, S., Patra, R. and Brewer, E. (2006) A Multidisciplinary Approach to Open Access Village Telecenter Initiatives: The case of Akshaya, *E-Learning,* 3, 3, pp. 291–316.

Parayil, G. (2000) Introduction: Is Kerala's development experience a 'model'? In *Kerala – the Development Experience,* ed., G. Parayil, Zed Books, London.

Rajasekharan, K. (2007) Decentralisation in Kerala: Problems and prospects. In *Local Governance in India: Ideas, challenges and strategies,* edited by T.M. Joseph, Concept Publishing Company, New Delhi, pp. 274–297.

Rangaswamy, N. (2006) Social Entrepreneurship as Critical Agency: A study of rural internet kiosks, Proceedings of the 2006 International Conference on ICT & Development, Berkeley, CA.

Roy, T. (2007) A Delayed Revolution: Environment and agrarian change in India, *Oxford Review of Economic Policy,* 23, 2, pp. 239–250.

Sharma, R. (2007) From Kallesseri to the People's Plan Campaign: Issues in governance. In *Local Governance in India: Ideas, challenges and strategies,* edited by T.M. Joseph, Concept Publishing Company, New Delhi, pp. 239–254.

Tharamangalam, J. (1998) The Perils of Social Development without Economic Growth: The development debacle of Kerala, India, *Bulletin of Concerned Asian Scholars,* 30, 1, pp. 23–24.

Thomas, E.M. (2007) The Institution of Gram Sabha and the Creation of Social Capital in Kerala. In *Local Governance in India: Ideas, challenges and strategies,* edited by T.M. Joseph, Concept Publishing Company, New Delhi, pp. 297–311.

Thomas, I. (2000) Campaign for Democratic Decentralisation in Kerala – An assessment from the perspective of empowered democracy, Kerala State Planning Board, Thiruvananthapuram.

Tornquist, O. (2000) The New Popular Politics of Development: Kerala's experience. In *Kerala – The development experience,* ed., G. Parayil, Zed Books, London.

Veron, R. (2001) The 'New' Kerala Model: Lessons for sustainable development, *World Development,* 29, 4, pp. 601–617.

Viswanathan, P.K. (2007) People's Planning and Kerala's Agriculture: The missed linkage. In *Local Governance in India: Ideas, challenges and strategies,* edited by T.M. Joseph, Concept Publishing Company, New Delhi, pp. 342–363.

World Bank (2007) Agriculture for Development. World Development Report 2008, World Bank, Washington DC.

9
Health Information Systems in Rural Karnataka

Decentralisation of public healthcare delivery emerged as the way forward for improving health status in developing countries in the late 1970s with the primary health centre (PHC) as the agency that would coordinate various health programmes with other social development priorities at the local level. Karnataka is one of the pioneering states in India in terms of its commitment shown to enforcing the Panchayati Raj legislation and therefore constitutes an interesting case in which to study the role of PHC-level health information systems in improving community health. This chapter presents the case of Gumballi PHC which is one of 26 primary health centres run by the Karuna Trust NGO. The Karuna Trust model is based on integrating health with social welfare provision at the community level and on working 'with' government rather than creating alternative structures. The study shows the important role of local health fieldworkers, other key government workers and political representatives in providing a community-based system of healthcare for the rural poor community. Finally, the chapter provides comments on some of the key challenges for building capacity among primary health centre staff.

India has a vast healthcare sector comprising both the public and private sectors. Since over a quarter of the population in the country still lives below the poverty line (Bhaskar and Gupta, 2007; UNDP, 2002; World Bank, 2005), the public health infrastructure is of paramount importance for the country's overall development and provides health services at different levels. Primary health centres (PHCs) as the basic units of rural health are mandated to cover a population of 20,000 to 30,000. The concept of primary healthcare originated in discussions which took place in international development agencies in the late 1970s regarding how best to provide low-cost, equitable access to health services in developing countries (WHO, 1978). The earlier health system inherited by developing countries after independence had been organised as standalone programmes resulting in duplication of funding, wastage of resources and lack of coordination in terms of overall health planning. By the time of the Alma Ata Conference in 1978, a consensus had emerged under the banner 'Health for All' to establish primary health centres in order to bring decision-making closer to the community and to integrate information regarding health burdens and trends (Mills *et al.*, 1990). In the Indian context, primary health centres are expected to provide a wide range of services such as immunisation, disease control, treatment for illness and injury, health education, promotion of nutrition, basic sanitation and provision of mother and child family welfare services. Each PHC is a nodal centre for about five subcentres covering three to four villages each. Each subcentre covers a population of about 5000 and is operated by a male health worker (MHW) and female health worker called an auxiliary nurse midwife (ANM). While progress in improving health in India is visible in immunisation coverage (Ramani and Mavalankar, 2006) and family planning (Nag, 1992; Santhya, 2003), the provision of public health services has been poor with lack of staff, medicine and infrastructure being the common complaints noted from PHCs around the country (Ramani and Mavalankar, 2006). This poor performance has, in turn, been blamed on a number of factors related to weak governance structures and lack of capacity among local health workers resulting in non-accountability of staff and insensitivity to local community needs (GOI, 2002).

One of the fundamental elements of the 1978 Declaration was to emphasise primary healthcare within an overall social welfare-oriented development model. Many places including China, Costa Rica, Sri Lanka and the Indian state of Kerala followed this ideology in the 1980s with the aim of providing affordable and effective health systems (Halstead *et al.*, 1985). Over time, however, the social welfare-orientation was compromised by the imperative of cost-effectiveness. The emergence of the concept of 'selective primary healthcare' was advocated as a way of improving the efficacy of healthcare delivery by controlling a few specific diseases within a locality (Walsh and Warren, 1979). However, this proposal was critiqued by adherents of the primary care approach as too narrow a model for improving equity in healthcare provision for rural poor communities (Atkinson *et al.*, 2000; McPake, 2008; Sen, 2002). Since the 1990s, the health-reform agenda for developing countries has resulted in an increased role for the market and NGOs to improve the efficiency of healthcare provision (Mercer *et al.*, 2004; Oliveira-Cruz, 2008; WHO, 2003). User fees and insurance mechanisms have been widely implemented but equally criticised as evidence emerged of how poor communities were excluded from access to health services as they could not afford to pay the fees and premiums (Mackintosh and Tibandebage, 2004; Waddington and Enyimayew, 1989). India has started to experiment with the inclusion of NGOs and community health-insurance schemes as an alternative to the conventional government-run facilities (Singh, 2008).

A key aspect of the current health-reform package is to improve the management of healthcare delivery at the primary health-centre level. An increasingly important role has been accorded to the use of data as evidence for supporting various stages of health policy-making from planning and resource allocation, to implementation, to monitoring the health status of patients (Bowens and Zwi, 2005; Hornby and Pereira, 2002; InfoDev, 2006; Lippeveld *et al.*, 2000; Nehinda, 2002; Scott, 2005; WHO, 1994, 2004). For example, for public health spending to have the greatest impact on reducing mortality and disability, routine information is required about which diseases have the largest effect on reducing the health status of a population (the health burden) and how health expenditure is allocated to combat different diseases (expenditure mapping). There is also a need for non-routine data arising from epidemics that require immediate action, from periodic surveys, for example, on HIV prevalence among pregnant women and from climatic and other environmental variables on the spread of diseases (Bodvala, 2002). A major health-information systems initiative is the HISP (Health Information Systems Project), the software for which was developed in open source on a Microsoft platform by a University of Oslo team. HISP was first implemented in South Africa in 1994 at the primary healthcare level and has subsequently been adopted by various other countries in Africa and by several states in India.[1] There is little evidence, however, that health information systems have led to significant improvements in the planning and implementation of health programmes (Heeks, 2005; Madon *et al.*, 2007; Noir and Walsham, 2007). On the contrary, various information sources outside the formal information system have been identified as more relevant by those responsible for healthcare delivery (Miscione, 2007; Mutemwa, 2006). Miscione's ethnographic study of telemedicine in northern Peru shows how a local community's construction of health derives from its own norms and practices rather than from any systems imposed from outside.

One key issue identified in the literature on health systems relates to the lack of autonomy primary health centres have to manage their funds and take decisions about local health priorities, equitable healthcare provision and overall community needs (Bossert, 1998; Bossert, 2000; Bossert and Beauvais, 2002; Bossert and Kumar, 2002; Collins and Green, 1994). Bossert uses the term 'decision space' to refer to the range of effective choice available to local government officials as sanctioned by central government along a series of functional dimensions. While the formal decision space defines the specific rules of the game for decentralised agents, the actual or informal decision space may be defined by lack of enforcement of these rules allowing local government officials discretion to bend the rules. This lack of decision space among local health planners is aggravated by the prevalence of standalone, vertical[2] programmes targeted to address specific health problems. These programmes tend to have different reporting systems, each responding to the criteria set by donor agencies to allow them direct control over their resources (Braa *et al.,* 2004; Chilundo and Aanestad, 2004; Kimaro and Nhampossa, 2005; Madon *et al.,* 2007; Mosse and Sahay, 2005; Sahay and Walsham, 2006). At the same time, linkages between ill-health and reduced productivity levels[3] (Hulme and Lawson, 2006; WHO, 2001; World Bank, 2004) have diverted attention of global health policy discourse towards understanding the interconnections between poor health and other social indices such as income poverty, lack of education, malnutrition, poor sanitation and other variables (Doyal and Gough, 1991; Ellis, 2000; Johnson and Forsyth, 2002; Nussbaum, 2000).

India's recent effort to improve the social welfare-orientation of primary healthcare is exemplified by the recently constituted National Rural Health Mission (NRHM). In 2005, the Mission introduced an ambitious plan of action which is scheduled to run until 2012[4] and includes increasing public expenditure on health, reducing regional imbalances in health infrastructure provision, integrating resources and organisational structures, better deployment of health manpower, promoting decentralisation and community participation, and improving the management of health systems through the deployment of information technology. A key element of the plan is the devolution of funds directly to community/village level through a variety of mechanisms including a direct payment of Rs 700 (US$14.50) to a pregnant woman[5] provided that she agrees to have a hospital delivery rather than risk maternal death through a home delivery. A further allocation of Rs 75,000 (US$1554) is made to the PHC to address maintenance needs.[6] Special mechanisms have also been introduced to improve the interface between the primary health centre and the local community by involving the gram panchayat in public health activity. As part of this strategy, one female accredited social health activist (ASHA) has been allocated per 1000 population to assist the ANM. This health activist is chosen by and accountable to the village panchayat. A village health plan is prepared by the Village Health and Sanitation Committee (VHSC) of the panchayat through a local team including various key workers such as the male and female health workers, the ASHA social health activist, the anganwadi worker[7] and gram panchayat members. Each village receives an annual fund transfer from the government to the value of Rs 20,000 (US$512) for use on health-related matters. The meeting is supervised and directed by the ANM who acts as secretary of the VHSC.

In India, health is the responsibility of the state governments although there are a number of standalone vertical programmes designed to address specific diseases such as malaria, HIV/AIDS and TB which are handled by the central government and guided by the Millennium Development Goals.[8] In the next section, I review the policy of the state government of Karnataka. This state forms the context for my case study which focuses on one PHC and examines the ground-level realities faced by the health workers and community in delivering healthcare for the rural poor. My involvement in this project comes as part of a three-year academic exchange programme with the Indian Institute of Management, Bangalore and Imperial College, London.

Health information systems for improving public healthcare in rural Karnataka

The state of Karnataka is situated in the southern part of India with a population of approximately 70 million people. The state is divided into 26 districts and comprises 4 natural regions – each having its own distinctive characteristics. The Karnataka model of development has two pillars – technology-led growth and decentralised governance. Karnataka's rate of economic growth in the past 15 years has been approximately 5–6% higher than the rest of India – much of which can be attributed to growth in the IT industry (Narayana, 2008). Its capital, Bangalore, is one of the fastest growing cities in Asia and is home to industries such as aircraft building, telecommunications, aeronautics and machine manufacturing with biotechnology emerging as a new area bringing in an inflow of private and foreign direct investment. However, the development of the Bangalore region goes hand in hand with the persistence of Karnataka as one of the poorest states in India. It is India's second most arid state and many of its parts are backward with high levels of poverty and ill-health. The scale of unemployment, particularly the highly fluctuating situation in the unorganised sector, is due to continued droughts and poor infrastructure, for example related to irregular supplies of electricity (GOI, 2007; Kadekodi *et al.*, 2008). The Government of Karnataka has actively promoted decentralised governance structures throughout the state (Kadekodi *et al.*, 2008; Slater and Watson, 1989; World Bank, 2000). Karnataka was the first state in the country to comply with the changes proposed in the 73rd Constitutional Amendment to increase the participation of weaker sections of the population in the formulation and implementation of policy in different sectors including health (Chandran, 1993; Rajasekhar and Veerashekharappa, 2004). In addition, the state has introduced e-governance projects, for example, the much-acclaimed Bhoomi land records computerisation project and panchayat-level computerisation of records (Nayak *et al.*, 2007). However, recent evidence from six districts in Karnataka shows that many of the functions constitutionally assigned to gram panchayats are not fully undertaken because of inadequate power and resources accorded to these bodies (Besley *et al.*, 2008; Rajasekhar and Satapathy, 2007).

Karnataka has developed a widespread network of health services. The state capital, Bangalore, has many speciality hospitals but in terms of the public health infrastructure, the state is following the national pattern of centres and subcentres. Karnataka increasingly has a large number of NGOs/oluntary organisations involved in healthcare delivery, community health training, research, advocacy and networking. Since the early 1970s, the state has negotiated and received various grants and loans from international funding agencies for implementing national programmes such as malaria, leprosy, tuberculosis, blindness and AIDS. At the primary healthcare level in Karnataka, there are a total of 1800 PHCs and 8143 rural subcentres. Each PHC covers a population of approximately 30,000 dispersed into 35–40 villages providing both preventive care in terms of immunisation coverage and drug administration through household visits of the field health workers, and curative care in terms of patients coming to visit the ANM or medical doctor as outpatients.

In 1999, a Task Force was set up by the Karnataka government with the aim of improving the management and administration of the Department of Health and Family Welfare. In April 2001, the Task Force submitted its final report which, in addition to recommending the filling of health personnel vacancies and increasing the allotment of medicines for the PHCs, highlighted many organisational issues such as the difficult working conditions faced by ANMs and the highly bureaucratic monthly exercise of reporting. The report also addressed policy-related themes that went beyond medicine and public health such as lack of focus on equity, the widening gap between policy intent and implementation, decline of ethical values in the professional and health systems level, neglect of human resource development and the increasing cultural gap between providers and consumers of health (Government of Karnataka, 2001). Over the past few years, the Government of Karnataka has initiated several processes to improve the management of public healthcare in the state. In 2005, the World Bank commissioned the Indian Institute of Management, Bangalore (IIM-B) to produce an Information Systems Strategy Plan[9] which highlighted weaknesses in the information flows between various tiers of the health system and how that affected the decision-making process. Lack of information was identified as affecting inventory control resulting in the same amount of drugs given to all 1800 PHCs although each has specific needs. Poor quality data kept at the PHCs was identified as the main reason for independent surveys being conducted by the government or bilateral agencies for the compilation of statistical reports. The Strategy Plan made recommendations for improving management procedures at the PHC and introducing health information systems although there was little follow up of these action points.

A second recommendation made in the strategy report was to improve the management of healthcare provision by building partnerships with the private sector and with NGOs. In urban areas, this led to the handing over of high-technology hospitals to private agencies in the medical field such as the Apollo Group of Hospitals and the contracting out of non-clinical services. In rural areas, partnership relates to introducing new management structures for the PHCs in Karnataka (The Hindu, 2002). In 2002, all the PHCs in Karnataka were divided into two categories based on their performance, infrastructure and vacancies and eventually the management of the bottom half was offered to NGOs and medical colleges following approval by the zilla panchayat[10] and by a selection committee. The initial period of entrustment of the PHCs to the NGOs is five years with a review of its functioning after two years. The NGO is responsible for implementing all national and state health and family welfare programmes in the PHC employing its own personnel in accordance with the government staffing norms but having flexibility to fix the remuneration of its employees. During this period, the State Health and Family Welfare Department would retain powers to give directions to the agency and monitor the working of the PHC. All existing assets of the PHC and subcentres would be handed over to the NGO to maintain and return to the government at the end of the contract period.

The Karuna Trust[11] is one of the NGOs involved in a partnership with the government for managing the primary health centres in Karnataka. Formed in 1986 by Dr Sudarshan who is well-known in the field of primary healthcare and tribal development,[12] the Trust began as a response to the prevalence of leprosy in the taluka and through its efforts between the years 1987 to 2005 leprosy has reduced significantly. In 1996, the Trust assumed responsibility for running one PHC at Gumballi in the tribal taluka of Yelandur following a dialogue with the people of the PHC and based on approval from the gram, taluka and zilla panchayats. Since then, the Government of Karnataka has handed over the management of 26 PHCs in the state to Karuna Trust[13] – one in each district of the state. A guiding philosophy of the Trust is to provide access to basic healthcare including essential drugs throughout the year in a clean environment with no demands for bribes by staff. In terms of implementation, the Government of Karnataka provides Karuna Trust with 90% of salaries, administrative expenses and purchase of drugs through its state budget. The Trust recruits staff including medical officers, ANMs and MHWs, pharmacists, laboratory technicians, clerks and other support staff needed at the PHC and its subcentres and pays their salaries. All the PHCs managed by Karuna Trust are open 24 hours a day, 7 days a week and offer 24-hour emergency/casualty services, an outpatients department open 6 days per week, a 5–10 bed inpatient facility, 24-hour labour room, minor operating theatre, availability of essential medicines and laboratory tests. One of the basic stipulations for staff recruited by Karuna Trust is that they remain resident at the PHC or its subcentres in contrast with the situation found in other government-run PHCs where citizens encounter difficulties accessing medical staff.

The Karuna Trust has shown a willingness to follow up on the recommendations made in the Information Systems Strategy Plan document. A team at IIM-B has worked to modify the HISP system by offering Kannada text and voice interface to allow PHCs in rural areas to enter data on a routine basis for reporting. This system, initially called Karnataka Health Information System, has recently been renamed the Janaarogya Health Information System.[14] The software provides about 1000 elements and 26 reports with export options for sending data to district headquarters for consolidation and includes a regression tool which allows manipulation of data and production of graphs and pivot tables for analysis of data. The software was first installed in Gumballi in 2002 with a plan to complete installation and to input the past five years data in ten of the PHCs. Table 9.1 lists the reports that are currently required for each PHC to prepare.

The rest of the chapter describes healthcare provision in Gumballi PHC and Chamarajanagar district studied between 2006 and 2008. The majority of the population of Gumballi are below the poverty line.[15] The area is tribal with no facilities, infrastructure, electricity, water supply or drainage system. For example, not every household has a latrine; there is no power for about seven hours per day, although tap water is available for all households via bore well. The main occupation for the community is agriculture (mainly paddy and sugarcane) and both men and women go to the field to work to meet their basic household expenses. Land is owned by a few, with the majority of the population working as daily-wage agricultural labourers. There is no established education system present in the locality other than basic primary and secondary government schools and a school set up by the VGKK Trust[16] only for tribals located in BR Hills.

The PHC model adopted at Gumballi draws on the original Alma Ata philosophy of integrating primary health with social welfare provision at the community level. Apart from providing regular preventive and curative healthcare, Gumballi PHC operates as a polyclinic providing mental health services,[17] dental care and blindness control. These specialised facilities at Gumballi such as the mental health unit and eye clinic have attracted patients from outside the Gumballi catchment area. At Gumballi, the primary health centre is adjacent to a pre-university college providing arts, science and drama degrees, a community hall, a tailoring unit for self-help groups and a herbal garden for use in traditional healthcare such as ayurveda and homeopathy. The Karuna Trust is currently investigating anaemia among young children in rural Karnataka through extensive consultation with health field workers and other community representatives (Pasricha *et al.*, 2009). The Trust also strives to strengthen community participation in health affairs through the village-level committees set up under the NRHM and by helping to form and finance self-help groups so that they can avail themselves of healthcare facilities and take up productive activities. At present, there are approximately 60 self-help groups, although many are inactive. In all, the PHC serves 12 villages covering a population of approximately 20,187 through its 3 subcentres. Approximately 50–60 patients frequent the PHC everyday which is open 6 days a week from 9am to 5pm with a medical officer always present and other specialist doctors visiting on allocated days. On the doctor's day off, patients could visit the ANM at their local subcentre.

Table 9.1   PHC reporting formats

Format	Details
CNA	Monthly report of Community Needs Assessment
Communicable diseases	Monthly report of numbers of institutional deaths and cases due to communicable diseases
Dengue	Monthly report showing numbers of dengue cases
Dog bite	Monthly report showing numbers of dog bites
Snake bite	Monthly report showing numbers of snake bites
Form 6	Monthly report of services provided (e.g. antenatal, natal, immunisation, etc.)
Goitre	Monthly report showing numbers of goitre cases
Guinea worm	Monthly report showing numbers of guinea worm cases
H.S. Division	Monthly report showing figures for Hepatitis virus
ICDS	Monthly report providing data of cases assisted under the central government ICDS scheme
IEC	Monthly report showing numbers of education medium activities
Iodine deficiency	Monthly report showing numbers of iodine cases
Japanese Encephalitis	Monthly report showing numbers of Japanese Encephalitis cases
Leprosy	Monthly report showing numbers of leprosy cases
Malaria	Monthly report showing numbers of malaria cases
Revised TC	Monthly report showing logistics and microscopy stock for treating tuberculosis
Sankramika rogagalu	Monthly report showing figures for communicable diseases
School health	Monthly report showing figures of children assisted under the School Health Programme
Statistics	Monthly statistics showing numbers of inpatients, outpatients and inpatient deaths
TB	Monthly report for the National TB Programme showing cases identified, treatment activity, follow-up activity and outcome, plus drugs in stock
20-point programme	Monthly report showing data collected under the central government 20-point programme

Note: A monthly report is prepared by each subcentre detailing the same information.
Source: fieldwork October 2008.

At the subcentre level, there is one ANM and one male health worker assigned to three villages serving a population of between 3000–5000. The ANMs employed at Karuna PHCs are generally aged between 25–45 years, well-educated with several years of experience in the field. Most of these health workers are highly motivated to serve the community and inspired by Karuna Trust's involvement in integrated rural development work. The ANMs are either hired directly by Karuna post-training or recruited from a government-run PHC. Almost all of these workers are from surrounding towns and now resident at the subcentre. They had received training either at a government-accredited college or at the ANM college established by the VGKK at BR Hills in 2006. The college currently offers an intensive 18-month training course for 16-year old girls who have passed their school at a cost of Rs 40,000 (approximately US$831) to the student with the remaining cost subsidised by Karuna Trust. The VGKK syllabus is intensive and trainers specially appointed by the Trust focus on educating girls on how to provide a caring service to the public including how to cope with difficult communities. As part of their training, students receive four months practical experience working with the ANM at a tribal subcentre and six months experience at a tribal hospital. From the batch of students who completed their course in October 2008, all of the 30 students were offered and took up employment at Karuna PHCs with students from subsequent batches earmarked for working in Karuna-run subcentres.

By interacting with the ANMs, I was able to understand their very hectic work routine. The ANM travels in the field every day from 8.30am until 2pm visiting rural poor households and giving treatment under six government immunisation programmes. In one day, she visits 50–60 houses. Her time is spent talking with the community members in their homes with lots of questions to answer during each visit. The ANM makes summary notes of her visits in her field diary which she carries round with her. Many times, these health workers need to deal with sensitive cases. For example, if they suspect that a patient may have AIDS or TB, they cannot directly inform them of this but suggest they have some routine tests. In my discussions, ANMs related the difficult task of handling leprosy cases once detected as this disease is considered taboo with many households believing that it is an act of God and therefore those afflicted should not seek healthcare. Other diseases such as TB and HIV/AIDS have a social stigma attached to them and the ANM has to deal with patients who do not want others in the locality to know. Karuna has put in place a community-based model of health insurance based on an annual contribution of Rs 100 (US$2.07) per head by Karuna and a low premium chargeable to the citizen of Rs 22 (US$0.46) which includes treatment cover for up to 25 days per year (Karuna Trust, 2005). When the ANM detects a case of TB or HIV, the patients are referred to the taluka hospital for testing and counselling after which health insurance is taken out for them. Over and above household visits, the ANM together with the anganwadi worker conduct health awareness programmes in different subcentre locations to reach out to all the community, for example using videos and street plays to disseminate information about TB and about welfare and nutrition for mothers post delivery. After her field visit, every day between 3–5pm, the ANM manually completes 13 different registers recording details of various different vertical programmes.

The employees I interviewed at Gumballi and its subcentres were content with working at the Karuna PHC. While they could work for the same salary at a government-run PHC, they mentioned that conditions at the Karuna PHC were better in terms of workload, satisfaction and career progression, for example, by undertaking more advanced training for promotion to ANM supervisor and eventually to district nurse. Some suggestions were made by ANMs in terms of improving equipment and increasing staffing levels but in general most felt that the services they provide to the community including the quantity and quality of drugs and equipment at their disposal are sufficient for delivering basic healthcare. The ANMs felt that the newly established role of the ASHA worker (social health activist) would assist them in various duties. While the ASHA worker is not a paramedic, the 30-days training she will receive for providing ancillary support to the ANM, for example, by transporting a pregnant woman to the subcentre for delivery, will enable the ANM to concentrate on core work. I met several batches of ASHA students who were being trained to take up this position and would be assigned to an ANM within the next few months.

In Gumballi PHC, the Village Health and Sanitation Committee (VHSC) plays an important role in interfacing between the health system and the community. The committee includes various key village-level members such as ANMs, male health workers, anganwadi workers, gram panchayat member, SC/ST representatives and self-help groups from the village. The central government transfers funding directly to the committee into an account opened in the name of the anganwadi worker and the gram panchayat president for health-related expenses without the need for the PHC having to apply for funds to the district health authority. In some of the subcentres visited, the committee meets routinely every two months while in other subcentres the procedure is more informal with meetings convened only if there are issues to discuss. The forum has provided an opportunity for various issues related to health and village development to be discussed and a six-monthly or annual village health plan document to be drawn up to meet local priorities. Issues discussed at recent meetings have included electricity problems, TB patients not getting treated and children not going to school. Funding has been used to address priorities identified by the committee including fogging treatment to kill mosquitoes in the event of an epidemic such as chikungunya,[18] renovation work in the subcentre, travelling expenses for ANM to transport antenatal patients, and for sanitation works such as clearing drains using kerosene and testing for water-borne diseases. Local self-help groups typically number around 20–25 per village in Gumballi and the VHSC has identified for funding some of the activities they are engaged in such as managing watershed, dairying, harvesting and social forestry replanting to promote overall village development.

A greater degree of community engagement with the health system has led to citizens being more ready to seek healthcare. I administered a survey of health-seeking behaviour among community members in two subcentres covered by Gumballi PHC. In total, 18 persons from the community were interviewed either in their homes, at their place of work or in the village. About an equal number of men and women were interviewed and the aim was to identify community members who represented the occupational profile of the locality. The household survey was based on the assumption that a person's decision to attend the PHC was the composite result of socio-economic status, the location of services and the actions of healthcare providers. Table 9.2 summarises the data.

Most respondents were involved in agriculture as daily-wage labourers. All respondents confirmed good access to the PHC, either walkable access or a short bus journey away. The majority of respondents agreed that service at the PHC was good in terms of availability of medical staff, drugs and equipment and in terms of staff attitude although a small percentage of respondents commented that the infrastructure and facilities in at least three of the five subcentres needed to be improved. A question was asked to gauge the level of community outreach in terms of awareness about health ailments and diseases giving the example of TB. All respondents replied by showing a good understanding of symptoms and treatment. Overall, the survey suggested that members of the community in Gumballi were receptive to the services offered by the PHC.

A second survey was administered to seven Karuna Trust PHC staff comprising of three staff nurses, one laboratory technician, one field healthworker, one dentist and one computer operator. While generally content with their working conditions, the staff interviewed all complained about the current process of monitoring. The reporting system requires data to be entered into the Janaarogya software by a computer operator using the paper formats passed onto the PHC by the health fieldworkers. From the 13 registers that ANMs have to maintain at the subcentre, 18 separate formats are eventually prepared on the system. I was told that the system has improved the efficiency of preparing a variety of monthly reports at the PHC. However, the procedure for data entry

Table 9.2 Results of household survey on health-seeking behaviour

Socio-economic status (%)			PHC/subcentre access (%)		PHC/subcentre service (%)			Awareness of TB (%)	
Low	Medium	High	Good	Poor	Good	Medium	Poor	Good	Poor
70	20	10	100	0	85	15	0	100	0

is extremely ad hoc. Only when IIM-B staff visit the PHC and obtain the latest data files does data get entered into the system. Moreover, Janaarogya reports only on those data elements specified by the Karuna Trust as being relevant with regular revisions made by the Trust in both data elements and reporting formats confusing the PHC staff. The process of reporting relies on only some of the data elements from the field making it difficult to access other data for analysis. Staff also felt that the preparation of these formats was the typical bureaucratic review of performance that takes place to check why staff have

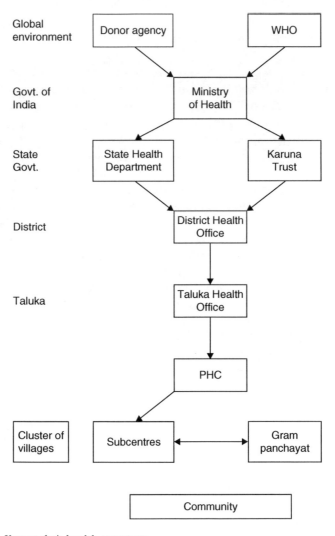

Figure 9.1   Karnataka's health structure

underperformed in terms of achieving targets for immunisation or treatment against specific diseases rather than of utility to the PHC for local analysis and learning. Recently, Karuna Trust has started to provide feedback to PHCs either by e-mail or by video conferencing on where performance needs to be improved based on targets and achievements although PHC staff feel that more guidance needs to be given about how to go about arranging outreach camps to create community awareness. For one of the prescribed reporting formats, Karuna has also introduced a more context-specific target for each PHC taking into account its demographic profile.

My fieldwork in Gumballi PHC reveals the complexity of providing healthcare to rural communities in India. Apart from international agencies and government bodies, Figure 9.1 shows the important role played by local administrative, political and social players in linking health with overall community development.

Health information systems in rural Karnataka: A commentary

At the policy level, the strongest influence both at national and state levels has come from the global health policy environment. The threat of global infections such as HIV/AIDS, tuberculosis and malaria has increased the need for evidence-based planning to comply with donor demands for increased accountability and to enable closer scrutinisation of progress towards the MDGs. These priorities have influenced choices made about the collection and usage of health information which are heavily biased towards quantitative data that describe health status of specific vertical programmes in terms of mortality, morbidity and burden of disease. This policy direction has had the effect of streamlining the implementation of healthcare but has compromised on providing the holistic healthcare intended by the original Alma Ata Declaration. There has also been increasing pressure to introduce market solutions for the delivery of healthcare resulting in a debate about whether such solutions compromise on the principle of providing equitable access to healthcare. The Karuna model of primary healthcare has offered an alternative to the mainstream PHC model while working within many of the broad parameters of the governance reform agenda set by the government. The Karuna model of healthcare provision is successful in providing equitable access to medical experts, drugs and equipment through improved resource allocation and inventory management. The model proposed by the Trust is based on the principle of working 'within' existing government structures rather than creating parallel structures. For example, the community model of healthcare provision that is currently in place is carefully structured so as to involve local political and administrative personnel.

There are two important lessons that arise from my study. The first relates to the crucial role played by the local health worker in healthcare provision supporting the findings from other studies on healthcare provision in developing countries (InfoDev, 2006; Jacucci *et al.*, 2006; James, 2007; Mosse and Byrne, 2005). In Gumballi, the ANM and male health workers, supported by other key village level government workers such as the anganwadi worker, form the core providers of healthcare to the community and it is almost impossible to visualise any alternative to this. Interestingly, even though the ANMs I interviewed work for Karuna PHCs, they see themselves as 'government workers'. The second important lesson relates to the linking of healthcare to other dimensions of community development as experimented by Karuna in the Gumballi polyclinic set up in which healthcare provision is linked to education and income generation. This model presents a welcome departure to the disease-focused way in which conventional PHCs are run. The linking of healthcare to community development also relates to new structures introduced to improve the interface between the community and the health system. The formalisation of the VHSC under the NRHM and other innovations introduced by the central government are positive steps taken to improve linkages between the health system, community needs and personal preferences. However, the constitution of formal committees such as the VHSC will not by themselves lead to improved health status among communities. What is needed is that the linkages established between health staff, other government and political representatives working at village level, and community members are nurtured and strengthened over time.

Health information systems can play an important role in this process. Rather than seen as a purely bureaucratic exercise, monitoring can improve the ability of local planners and decision-makers to learn from the past and thereby provide a better service. A process of community monitoring is currently being piloted across nine states in India as part of the NRHM.[19] Eleven parameters have been chosen covering different aspects of health issues and PHC functioning and the community monitoring exercise involves preparing a score card to give a snapshot of the performance at village and facilities level.

This discussion leads us to revisit the notion of capacity-building. Rather than a purely bureaucratic exercise, monitoring can improve the ability of local planners and decision-makers to learn from the past and thereby provide a better service. This is currently being attempted through several experiments at Gumballi. First, data from the PHC forms are being entered into the Janaarogya system demonstrating the utility of temporal analyses looking at trends in services and disease incidence. Second, a PHC profile is being conducted in Gumballi comparing this data with the state/national averages to track over time if the PHC is improving in terms of overall community health. Third, the technical efficiency of the PHC is being calculated by comparing inputs (such as number of staff, drugs and infrastructure) with outputs (such as field visits, immunisation coverage, deliveries, outpatients, and community sensitisation sessions). There are also examples of possible qualitative data usage by the PHC. First, the ANM uses her field diary as a memo for subsequent visits to the household. After verification by the PHC medical doctor, this information could be analysed in some systematic way. Second, the outpatients' register of drugs administered can be linked to an individual or household so that it can be used for profiling health conditions of patients. Third, the ANM's verbal feedback to the medical officer about issues arising from the VHSC meetings could be formalised so as to monitor whether priorities expressed regarding overall community development are being integrated into plans for action. A PHC set-up like Gumballi can also improve its capacity by learning about non-health aspects of the centre such as how the college and income-generating activities run by the PHC indirectly affect the health of the community.

Eventually, the issue of capacity-building is related to the wider issue of changing mindsets about decentralisation within the Indian administrative structure and hierarchy. HIS constitute a key element for improving management at PHC level by integrating the data sets of various disparate health programmes. However, capacity-building is not merely about data sets. It involves changes at the policy level, within the health administration and among the health professional community (Smith *et al.*, 2007). At the present time, even the senior-most person at the PHC level, the medical doctor, has little capacity to undertake local analysis of his own volition. He sees his role to implement programmes as directed from higher levels of administration and he does not have the requisite training or motivation for data analysis so is not in a strong position to query the existing way in which data are collected. Over the course of the next few years, I will continue to trace the changes in 'decision space' that are occurring at the PHC level and the interface that is developing between the PHC and the community. This is a growing interest among health systems scholars (Hyder *et al.*, 2007; MacKian, 2003). For example, in recent health-seeking behaviour literature, the concept of bridging ties from social capital theory is used to connect community structures to the capacity of the health system (Atkinson *et al.*, 2000; Baum, 1999; Campbell and Mzaidume, 2001; MacKian, 2003). A study of social capital within the community would also help to identify where formal institutions need to nurture informal networks and the role of intermediaries in facilitating this process. Of interest in the future will be studying the role played by the social health activist as she mediates between the health system and the community through her connections with the local panchayat.

Finally, the current global health-reform agenda calls for improved analysis of how disease patterns interact with other major trends affecting populations such as globalisation, urbanisation, environmental degradation and financial integration (Chronic Poverty Research Centre, 2004; Hulme and Lawson, 2006; Rienstra, 2002; UN, 2002). This wider perspective on health reform will require a radical change of mindset as the work of many health specialists still concentrates on genetic factors as determinants of health and disease susceptibility and pays little attention to income poverty, social inequality and vulnerability.[20]

Glossary

Alma Ata Declaration – promoted by the World Health Organization in 1978 to reform healthcare delivery in developing countries

Anganwadi worker – field workers who are specially trained in various aspects of health, nutrition and child development

ANM – auxiliary nurse midwife is a female field health worker based at the subcentre

ASHA – accredited social health activist

Ayurveda – a traditional system of healthcare

Gram panchayat – village council

HISP – Health Information Systems Project

ICDS – Integrated Child Development Scheme

IIM-B – Indian Institute of Management, Bangalore is a premier research and teaching institute with expertise in policy and management for both the private and public sectors

Kannada – the language spoken in Karnataka

Karnataka Panchayati Raj Act – an act passed by the Karnataka government to promote decentralised governance in the state

Karuna Trust – an NGO working in partnership with the Government of Karnataka currently managing 26 PHCs in the state

KHIS – Karnataka Health Information System

MHW – male health worker based at the subcentre

NRHM – National Rural Health Mission

PHC – primary health centre

SC/ST – Scheduled castes/Scheduled tribes are sections of the population regarded as underprivileged

Subcentre – health facility covering about three to four villages

Taluka – a subdivision of the district

VGKK – Vivekananda Girijana Kalyana Kendra is a trust dedicated to the upliftment of tribals in rural Karnataka

VHSC – Village Health and Sanitation Committee

WHO – World Health Organization

References

Atkinson, S., Medeiros, R., Oliviera, P.H. and Almeida, R. (2000) Going Down to the Local: Incorporating social organization and political culture into assessments of decentralized health care, *Social Science & Medicine*, 51, 4, pp. 619–636.

Baum, F. (1999) Social Capital: Is It Good for Your Health? Issues for a public health agenda, *Journal of Epidemiology and Community Health*, 53, pp. 195–196.

Besley, T., Pande, R. and Rao, V. (2008) The Political Economy of Gram Panchayats in South India. In *Development in Karnataka: Challenges of Governance, Equity and*

Empowerment, edited by G. Kakekodi, R. Kanbur and V. Rao, Academic Foundation, New Delhi, pp. 243–265.

Bhaskar, V. and Gupta, B. (2007) India's Development in the Era of Growth, *Oxford Review of Economic Policy*, 23, 2, pp. 135–142.

Bodvala, R. (2002) ICT Applications in Public Healthcare Systems in India: A review, *ASCI Journal of Management*, 31, 1, pp. 56–66.

Bossert, T. (1998) Analysing the Centralisation of Health Systems in Developing Countries: Decision space, innovation and performance, *Social Science and Medicine*, 47, pp. 1513–1527.

Bossert, T. (2000) Methodological Guidance for Applied Research on Decentralisation of Health Systems in Latin America. LACHSR Health Sector Initiative, Harvard School of Public Health, Cambridge, MA.

Bossert, T. and Beauvais, J. (2002) Decentralisation of Health Systems in Ghana, Zambia, Uganda and the Philippines: A Comparative analysis of decision space, *Health Policy and Planning*, 17, 1, pp. 14–31.

Bossert, T. and Kumar, S. (2002) Report of Decentralisation Team on Development of a Medium Term Health Sector Strategy and Expenditure Framework for Andhra Pradesh, International Health Group, Harvard School of Public Health, Harvard.

Bowens, S. and Zwi, A.B. (2005) Pathways to 'Evidence-Informed' Policy and Practice: A framework for action, *PLoS Med*, 2, 7: e166.

Braa, J., Monteiro, E. and Sahay, S. (2004) Networks of Action: Sustainable health information systems across developing countries, *MIS Quarterly*, 28, pp. 337–362.

Campbell, C. and Mzaidume, Z. (2001) Grassroots Participation, Peer Education and HIV Prevention by Sex Workers in South Africa, *American Journal of Public Health*, 91, pp. 1978–1986.

Chandran, S. (1993) Panchayati Raj and Health Care: The Karnataka Experience. In *People's Health in People's Hand: A model for Panchayati Raj*, edited by N.H. Antia and K. Bhatia, The Foundation for Research in Community Health, Mumbai.

Chilundo, B. and Aanestad, M. (2004) Negotiating Multiple Rationalities in the Process of Integrating the Information Systems of Disease-Specific Health Programmes, *EJISDC*, 20, 2, pp. 1–28.

Chronic Poverty Research Centre (2004) The Chronic Poverty Report 2004/05, Institute of Development Policy and Management. Available at http://www.chronicpoverty. org

Collins, C. and Green, A. (1994) Decentralisation and Primary Health Care: Some negative implications in developing countries, *International Journal of Health Science*, 24, pp. 459–475.

Doyal, L. and Gough, I. (1991) *A Theory of Human Need*, Macmillan, London.

Ellis, F. (2000) *Rural Livelihoods and Diversity in Developing Countries*, Oxford University Press, Oxford.

Government of India (2002) Tenth Five Year Plan (2002–2007), Planning Commission, New Delhi.

Government of India (2007) Karnataka Development Report, Planning Commission, Government of India, New Delhi.

Government of Karnataka (2001) Karnataka towards Equity, Quality and Integrity in Health, Final Report of the Task Force on Health and Family Welfare, Government of Karnataka.

Halstead, S.B., Walsh, J. and Warren, K. (1985) Good Health at Low Cost, Conference Report, Bellgaio Conference Centre, Rockefeller Foundation. Available at www. popline.org/docs/0862/271533.html

Heeks, R. (2005) Health Information Systems: Failure, success and improvisation, *International Journal of Medical Informatics*, 75, 2, pp. 125–137.

The Hindu (2002) Karnataka Entrusts Primary Health Centres to Voluntary Organisations, 14 October, Chennai.

Hornby, P. and Pereira, H.S. (2002) A Development Framework for Promoting Evidence-Based Policy Action: Drawing on experiences in Sri Lanka, *International Journal of Health Planning and Management*, 17, pp. 165–183.

Hulme, D. and Lawson, D. (2006) Health, Health Care, Poverty and Well Being: An overview for a developing country focus. Development Economics and Public Policy Working Paper Series, No. 19, Institute of Development Policy and Management, University of Manchester.

Hyder, A., Bloom, G., Leach, M., Syed, S. and Peters, D. (2007) Exploring Health Systems Research and Its Influence on Policy Processes in Low Income Countries, *BMC Public Health*, 7, pp. 309–321.

InfoDev. (2006) Improving Health, Connecting People: The role of ICTs in the health sector of developing countries. Working Paper No. 1. InfoDev, Healthlink and AfriAfya. Available at www.infodev.org/en/Publication.84.html

Jacucci, E., Shaw, V. and Braa, J. (2006) Standardization of Health Information Systems in South Africa: The challenge of local sustainability, *Information Technology for Development*, 12, 3, pp. 225–239.

James, K.S. (2007) Decentralisation and Its Impact on Health in India: A review of evidence. In *Local Governance in India: Ideas, challenges and strategies*, edited by T.M. Joseph, Concept Publishing Company, New Delhi, pp. 155–178.

Johnson, C. and Forsyth, T. (2002) In the Eyes of the State: Negotiating a 'Rights-Based Approach' to Forest Conservation in Thailand, *World Development*, 30, 9, pp. 1591–1605.

Kadekodi, G., Kanbur, R. and Rao, V. (2008) Assessing the 'Karnataka Model of Development'. In *Development in Karnataka: Challenges of Governance, Equity and Empowerment*, edited by G. Kakekodi, R. Kanbur and V. Rao, Academic Foundation, New Delhi, pp. 17–37.

Karuna Trust (2005) A Healthy Change: Community health insurance. Publication of the Karuna Trust, Chamarajanagar, Karnataka sponsored by UNDP India.

Kimaro, H. and Nhampossa, J. (2005) Analysing the Problem of Unsustainable Health Information Systems in Less-Developed Economies: Case studies from Tanzania and Mozambique, *Information Technology for Development*, 11, 3, pp. 273–298.

Lippeveld, T., Sauerborn, R. and Bodart, C. (2000) Design and Implementation of Health Information Systems, World Health Organization, Washington DC.

MacKian, S. (2003) A Review of Health Seeking Behaviour: Problems and prospects, University of Manchester, Health Systems Development Programme.

Mackintosh, M. and Tibandebage, P. (2004) Inequality and Redistribution in Health Care: Analytical issues for developmental social policy. In *Social Policy in a Development Context*, edited by Thandika Mkandawire, Palgrave Macmillan, Hants, pp. 143–175.

Madon, S., Sahay, S. and Sudan, R. (2007) E-Government Policy and Health Information Systems Implementation in Andhra Pradesh, India: Need for articulation of linkages between the macro and the micro, *The Information Society*, 23, pp. 327–344.

McPake, B. (2008) The Story of Primary Health Care: From Alma Ata to the present day, *id21 insights health*, 12, p. 3, May.

Mercer, A., Khan, M.H., Daulatuzzaman, M. and Reid, J. (2004) Effectiveness of an NGO Primary Health Care Programme in Rural Bangladesh: Evidence from the management information system, *Health Policy and Planning*, 19, 4, pp. 187–198.

Mills, A., Vaughan, P., Smith, D. and Tabibadeh, I. (eds) (1990) *Health Systems Decentralisation: Concepts, issues and country experience,* WHO, Geneva.

Miscione, G. (2007) Telemedicine in the Upper Amazon: Interplay with local health care practices, *MIS Quarterly,* 31, 2, pp. 403–425.

Mosse, E. and Byrne, E. (2005) The Role of Identity in Health Information Systems Development: A case analysis from Mozambique, *Information Technology for Development,* 11, 3, pp. 227–243.

Mosse, E. and Sahay, S. (2005) The Role of Communication Practices in the Strengthening of Counter Networks: Case of experience from the health care sector of Mozambique, *Information Technology for Development,* 11, 3, pp. 207–225.

Mutemwa, R. (2006) HMIS and Decision-Making in Zambia: Re-thinking information solutions for district health management in decentralised health systems, *Health Policy and Planning,* 21, 1, pp. 40–52.

Nag, M. (1992) Family Planning Success Stories in Bangladesh and India, Policy Research Working Papers, Population, Health and Nutrition, WPS 1041, Population and Human Resources Department, World Bank, Washington DC.

Narayana, M.R. (2008) ICT Sector and Economic Development: Evidence from Karnataka State. In *Development in Karnataka: Challenges of Governance, Equity and Empowerment,* edited by G. Kakekodi, R. Kanbur and V. Rao, Academic Foundation, New Delhi, pp. 291–323.

Nayak, M., Bhargava, B.S. and Subha, K. (2007) EGovernance at the Grassroots: The case of Belandur Grama Panchayat in Karnataka. In *Local Governance in India: Ideas, challenges and strategies,* edited by T.M. Joseph, Concept Publishing Company, New Delhi, pp. 384–407.

Nehinda, T.C. (2002) Research Capacity Strengthening in the South, *Soc Sci Med,* 54, pp. 1699–1711.

Noir, C. and Walsham, G. (2007) The Great Legitimizer: ICT as myth and ceremony in the Indian healthcare sector, *Information Technology and People,* 20, 4, pp. 313–334.

Nussbaum, M.C. (2000) *Women and Human Development: The capabilities approach,* Cambridge University Press, Cambridge.

Oliveira-Cruz, V. (2008) Financing Primary Health Care, *id21 insights health,* 12, pp. 1–2, May. Available at www.id21.org

Pasricha, S., Vijaykumar, V., Prashanth, N.S., Sudarshan, H., Biggs, B., Black, J. and Shet, A. (2009) A Community Based Field Research Project Investigating Anaemia Amongst Young Children Living In Rural Karnataka, India: A cross sectional study, *BMC Public Health,* 9, 59.

Rajasekhar, D. and Satapathy, S. (2007) The Functioning of Grama Panchayats in Karnataka. In *Local Governance in India: Ideas, challenges and strategies,* edited by T.M. Joseph, Concept Publishing Company, New Delhi, pp. 363–384.

Rajasekhar, D. and Veerashekharappa (2004) Role of Local Organisations in Water Supply and Sanitation Sector: A study in Karnataka and Uttaranchal States, India. A Project Report Prepared for the World Bank, Institute for Social and Economic Change, Bangalore.

Ramani, K.V. and Mavalankar, D. (2006) Health System in India: Opportunities and challenges for improvements, *Journal of Health Organization and Management,* 20, 6, pp. 560–572.

Rienstra, D. (2002) Health Is a Key to Development, *The Courier ACP-EU,* March–April, p. 205.

Sahay, S. and Walsham, G. (2006) Scaling of Health Information Systems in India: Challenges and approaches, *Information Technology for Development,* 12, 3, pp. 185–200.

Santhya, K.G. (2003) Changing Family Planning Scenario in India: An overview of recent evidence, Population Council, Regional Office for South and East Asia, New Delhi.

Scott, C. (2005) Measuring Up to the Measurement Problem: The role of statistics in evidence-based policymaking, PARIS 21 Partnership in Statistics for Development in the 21st Century, March, London School of Economics.

Sen, A.K. (2002) Why Health Equity? *Health Economics*, 11, pp. 659–666.

Singh, N. (2008) Decentralization and Public Delivery of Healthcare Services in India, *Health Affairs*, 27, 4, pp. 991–1001.

Slater, R. and Watson, J. (1989) Democratic Decentralization or Political Consolidation: The case of local government reform in Karnataka, *Public Administration and Development*, 9, pp. 147–157.

Smith, M., Madon, S., Anifalaje, A., Lazarro-Malecela, M. and Michael, E. (2007) Integrating Health Information Systems in Tanzania: Experience and challenges, *EJISDC*, 33, 1, pp. 1–21.

UN. (2002) Report of the World Summit on Sustainable Development, United Nations, New York.

UNDP. (2002) Human Development Indicators 2002. Available athttp://hdr.undp.org/reports/global/2002/en/indicator/indicator.cfm?File=indic_298_2_1.html

Waddington, C.J. and Enyimayew, K.A. (1989) A Price to Pay: The impact of user charges in Ashanti-Akim district Ghana, *International Journal of Health Planning and Management*, 4, pp. 17–47.

Walsh, J. and Warren, K. (1979) Selective Primary Health Care: An interim strategy for disease control, *New England Journal of Medicine*, 301, pp. 967–974.

WHO. (1978) Alma Ata Declaration, World Health Organization, Geneva.

WHO. (1994) Information Support for New Public Health Action at the District Level – Report of a WHO Expert Committee, World Health Organization, Technical Report Series No. 845, Geneva, pp. 1–31. Available at http://www.who.int/gb/ebwha/pdf_files/WHA56/ea5627.pdf

WHO. (2001) National Burden of Disease Studies: A practical guide, World Health Organization, Geneva.

WHO. (2003) World Health Report, WHO, Geneva.

WHO. (2004) World Report on Knowledge for Better Health: Strengthening Health Systems, WHO, Geneva.

World Bank (2000) Overview of Rural Decentralisation in India, Volume 1, World Bank, Washington DC.

World Bank (2004) World Development Report: Making services work for poor people, World Bank, Washington DC.

World Bank (2005) World Bank World Development Indicators 2005, World Bank, Washington DC.

Part III
Reflections and Implications

10
Conclusion

This book has provided an opportunity for a broader critical understanding of e-governance for development which is often concealed behind official consensus views. The perspective I have used for my critique and for analysing my three cases owes a lot to the work of scholars in the field of development studies, particularly those who have approached development and governance from a sociological perspective. My analysis has also been informed by fieldwork that I initially conducted in Gujarat in the late 1980s and have since reinforced through subsequent fieldworks in the states of Kerala and Karnataka. The cases I have presented are sites for my ongoing research on this topic and I hope they have provided the reader with a picture of the rich context within which rural e-governance projects are implemented in developing countries. Unfortunately, the complexity of the context within which e-governance projects are implemented is rarely traced in detail resulting in the project objectives losing all sense of actual reality. In this final chapter, I draw on salient points raised in the three cases. I have conceptualised each sector-specific e-governance application in terms of the influence of international development agencies on public policy-making, the implementation of the application within a specific context and the relevance of the project for improving the living conditions of beneficiary communities.

The three cases show variability in terms of lessons to be learnt with respect to the implementation of e-governance for development. The cases of Gujarat and Karnataka are similar in that they both relate to e-governance applications designed to improve the planning and administration of government services. In both cases, the policies of the state governments have been influenced by the trends in development and governance emanating from the international development community. In Gujarat this has manifested itself in the change in policy from targeting individual household to groups while in Karnataka the influence continues to be strong in terms of the continued focus on disease-specific programmes. In Kerala, the state government is pressurised by the trend in India towards contracting out the implementation of telecentres to large corporate organisations although so far this move has been resisted by the state government.

In terms of implementation, experience in Gujarat shows that although the self-employment programme will soon reach its tenth year of operation, many groups that had formed have broken apart with very little internal lending between group members and with most groups still not in a position to generate income from economic activities. A key lesson learnt here is that rural poverty alleviation is a difficult and long-term undertaking. Local government fieldworkers, rather than NGOs, have played a critical role in providing support to the community, in helping individuals to gain confidence and in building solidarity within the group. The MIS serves as a reporting tool for higher authorities to hold public officials accountable rather than a system for improving local planning and monitoring of the programme. The danger is that if the formal MIS is used as a surrogate to evaluate the performance of the SGSY, this may create a bias towards policy prescriptions that may not improve the developmental prospects of the rural poor. For the MIS to assist the intended beneficiaries, a system is needed which transcends individual programmes and which focuses instead on the life of individual self-help groups over time. Such a system will need to be highly flexible in character as it will rely on tapping the 'intelligence' of local fieldworkers to establish relevant criteria for monitoring.

A key lesson learnt from the Karnataka case study is that despite donor pressure, the improvement of health status within a local poor community does not concern only the monitoring of disease-related data. It is a complex task that requires a deep understanding of the local cultural context and the link between health and other community-related issues such as sanitation, nutrition, education and livelihoods. The key player in improving the health status of the local community is the government health fieldworker with the recent establishment of village-level committees presenting an opportunity for strengthening the interface between the formal health system and the community. While the HIS provides logistical support for the procurement of drugs, equipment and other resources for higher levels of administration, the vast amount of data collected from the field provide little decision support for health planning at the PHC level. Two experiments are being conducted to identify the utility of local data analysis for the PHC. First, a technical efficiency exercise at the Gumballi PHC correlating inputs such as staffing, equipment, drugs and procedures with outputs such as service delivery, immunisation and outreach. Second, an assessment of the 'performance' of the PHC in terms of health status of the community by providing a snapshot of overall community health to compare with the state or national average.

The Kerala telecentre project is designed to provide information and services to rural poor citizens to improve their livelihoods and welfare. The telecentres have enabled many entrepreneurs to generate income and have provided the local community with a range of commercial and government services. A key learning from this project has been the active role of government at various tiers. State government support has been crucial in branding the project as a 'legitimate' community development initiative in the eyes of the public. Without this branding, the project would have been perceived as a private sector initiative and would certainly have been boycotted given Kerala's historical focus on social rather than economic development. Support from local political bodies right from the start of the project has ensured that it remains accepted by the community. A second lesson from the Akshaya telecentre project relates to the objective of increasing the productivity of the small farming community in Malappuram. The case shows that rather than the technology, the centres have provided a social space for integrating government agricultural extension officers and political representatives. This social space has proved valuable for a range of activities including bringing together buyers and sellers, pooling and collecting wage labourers, procuring credit for small farmers and acquiring vital inputs needed for farming activity.

The lessons learnt from the three cases have implications for the achievement of Kalam's vision of e-governance for Indian development. In particular, there is need to address critical policy and management issues. Unless moderated, the tendency in public policy has been to favour economic growth over social development. Over the past few decades, despite great strides made by India in terms of economic growth and in terms of its participation in the global IT industry, the country's overall development has suffered. One of India's most successful business leaders, Nilekani, argues that the country's future rests on more than just economic growth with a growing imperative to focus on reforms and innovation in all areas of social development and public sector service (Nilekani, 2009). Indeed, rising inequality between sections of the population has undermined the contribution that growth alone can make to India's development. In a country where over 70% of the population is rural and dependent on the land to survive, stepping up investment in the social sectors – that is, agriculture, rural development, health and education is key to India's overall development. However, focusing attention on social development alone may not provide the answer. Indeed, the MDGs were introduced precisely to focus attention on social development goals. However, more than halfway to the 2015 Millennium Development Goals deadline, it is acknowledged that unless steps are taken, these goals will not be attained (The Guardian, 2008a). But the question that remains unanswered relates to exactly what steps are needed. Solutions are typically talked of in terms of providing more aid funding – for example, in terms of policy directives which channel more resources for additional frontline health staff, for infrastructure such as community wells, irrigation kits or bed nets for malaria. However, development experts argue that the extreme inequality existing in many parts of the developing world cannot be eliminated or reduced by policy changes alone (Mamman and Rees, 2007). Progress in addressing poverty depends as much on the management of development policies – on the human, organisational and institutional capacity needed to effectively administer development interventions.

The concept of capacity building discussed earlier now needs revisiting. My case studies support the suggestion made earlier that improving capacity is related not only to structure, skills and resources but also to altering mindsets and behaviour. On the one hand, a core theme in the good governance policy mandate is decentralisation which aims to devolve development planning to the local level to encourage integration between different aspects of community upliftment. For example, access to micro-credit schemes for rural poor women is often only one element of well-being and needs to be integrated with health planning, literacy programmes and other development priorities. On the other hand, some of the great successes in development planning, for example immunisation and family planning, often have vertical elements to them such as centralised targets. In the Karnataka case, almost all the funds are still targeted at disease-specific projects which although not an illegitimate focus does lead to fears that immunisation is diverting funds from strengthening health services and from integrating health equity with the larger issue of fairness and justice in other social arrangements.

However, the issue of capacity-building is not so much about whether a centralised or decentralised programme is good or bad per se. What is more important is to study how resources can be channelled to contribute more broadly to improving the capacity of development fieldworkers to handle the day-to-day challenges they face to alleviate poverty. Capacity-building within the local administration is generally referred to in terms of improving the efficiency of field functionaries in areas like report generation, budget preparation and auditing. Taken in its wider sense, however, capacity-building also refers to the possibilities for information generation and analysis in order that the local planning agency can address the dynamic, unpredictable and idiosyncratic elements of development planning that are often glossed over in the governance reform agenda. The interface between the local administration and the community needs to be nurtured and closely monitored. In the cases of Gujarat and Karnataka, this interface has been established through formally defined structures – for example, in Gujarat through the regular meetings between the anganwadi workers and the self-help groups and in Karnataka through the village-level committees. In both cases, however, these structures need to be continuously strengthened through informal contact with other government representatives, political bodies and community members. In the case of Kerala, the interface is not a formal set-up but has been established informally by the entrepreneur who invites the local agricultural extension officer to participate in Farmers' Club meetings. Strengthening the capacity of development fieldworkers, then, can be better described as a process that infiltrates across formal state institutions and informal societal structures. The importance of understanding the informal system within any human organisation has been repeatedly emphasised by scholars over the decades (Land, 2008; Land and Kennedy-McGregor, 1987). Indeed, most of what I have presented in this book relates to describing the informal environment within which the government agency or telecentre operates. Exploration of this environment provides crucial information about developmental issues although this information may be unstructured and qualitative in nature. Yet, in practice, this approach has remained marginal in international development discourse. Indeed, it has always been easier to develop e-governance applications which rely on obtaining and inputting quantitative data for measuring progress but which may or may not have a bearing on improving the living conditions of communities.

The economic uncertainties facing the world today provide even more reason to question accepted practices in development (Silva and Westrup, 2009). The economist Rodrik (2004) argues that 'the secret of economic growth lies in institutional innovations that are country specific and that come out of local knowledge and experimentation'. Rodrik's argument about institutional innovation has important implications for the way in which development programmes are managed. An argument often made is that managerialism in international development has encouraged a particular plan-driven type of approach which increasingly involves market solutions and ICT deployment (Cooke and Dar, 2008). An alternative approach to managing development proposed by Sen (2006) is that rather than taking the plan and its targets as given, information and initiatives must be sought from many sources. This calls for local adaptation with a constant search for what the problems are and how they can be addressed. In the three cases presented there are examples of non-routine information which, if recorded and analysed, could greatly enhance the planning capacity of development fieldworkers and the local administration. In the Gujarat case, non-routine information is regularly collected in the field diaries of the anganwadi workers and includes details of whether self-help groups were increasing in their levels of confidence and trust or experiencing problems related to bonding and internal lending. In Kerala, during the Farmers' Club meetings, the agricultural extension officer acquires non-routine information related to problems farmers are facing in cultivating, marketing and selling their produce and more generally about village amenities. The telecentre entrepreneur too is a custodian of non-routine information about how to obtain credit and other inputs for small farmers. In Karnataka, non-routine information is captured in the field diaries of health workers during their regular house visits and verified by the medical doctor. Non-routine information also includes the minutes of various village-level committees that take place and the monthly meetings Karuna Trust holds with PHC staff.

Building capacity among local administrators to use non-routine data for planning and local analysis requires a change of mindset among various tiers of the bureaucracy and indeed from the international development community. A wider view of managing development interventions is needed which places importance on understanding the human setting within which interventions are implemented. This approach requires a more humble and experimental attitude to development planning and relates to theories of organisational learning, particularly the distinction between single-loop and double-loop learning (Argyris, 1982; Argyris, 1990; Smith, 2001). Argyris' research focused on how an intervention in an organisation may increase the capacity for more creative and reflexive double-loop learning.[1] In the case of rural e-governance projects in India, this type of learning would imply that a local administrator confronts and challenges the basic assumptions behind pre-defined government targets and models of promoting development. This seems like an unrealistic proposition unless the local worker receives adequate institutional backing to do so. The distinction made by Johnson and Thomas (2007) between capacity and capability is useful. They argue that while individuals or organisations may have increased their capacity, they may still not have the necessary capability to implement change. For example, an organisational setting may supply opportunities for local analysis of information but not a great deal of support for change. In other cases, for example, in local government agencies in many parts of the developing world, the opportunities are not available and the individual is in no position to implement new ideas or the organisation may be too constrained externally.

Our discussion so far has centred on capacity-building as an important issue for promoting development. But at the same time, it is important that we do not reduce development to the capacity to achieve development goals. Development is a historical change process beyond any single organisation and involves clashes between competing visions or cultures (Sen, 2001). This type of approach suggests that inequality is caused by how members of a group relate to one another and how the group relates to other groups. At the same time, culture does not work in isolation from other social influences like caste, class and gender. So far, however, development agencies have found themselves under the strong influence of economists and financial experts and have tended to neglect the role of culture in promoting development (White, 2005).

Today e-governance constitutes an important element in India's policy environment although, as this book has shown, its role in strengthening planning systems and improving the delivery of services to citizens has so far been minimal due to a variety of policy, institutional, managerial and cultural issues. These issues are, of course, also evident in the context of e-governance implementation in industrialised countries with an up-to-date example being the National Programme for IT (NPfit), an initiative by the Department of Health in England. The cost of the programme and its problems of implementation have placed it at the centre of controversy with serious concern expressed over its scope, planning, budgeting, the low morale of NHS staff who are implementers of the project and the practical value of the system to patients (The Guardian, 2008b; Hendy *et al.*, 2005; The Telegraph, 2007). In the Indian context, the entire e-governance policy drive has resulted in projects being launched as more or less standalone implementations designed either to increase the efficiency of reporting and monitoring of government schemes, or to provide a more 'customer-facing' service to citizens in their routine interactions with government. For example, telecentre projects typically provide service to citizens for paying government bills and other dues. However, the efficacy of this service depends crucially on the quality of databases maintained within individual government departments. Similarly, the success of eGovernance projects aimed at strengthening the management of rural development programmes depends on the easy accessibility of applications forms and the assistance given to completing and submitting them through front-end rural outreach service kiosks. This close coupling between back-end administration and front-end service also leads us to think more creatively about technology usage. Standard prescriptions regarding the choice of appropriate communication channels for the dissemination of e-governance service should not be reduced to computers and the internet alone. The high rate of illiteracy, the popularity of TV and radio and the rich oral tradition of villagers emphasise the opportunity for an integrative multimedia approach including face-to-face interaction. In recent years, developing countries have achieved deeper mobile penetration than internet penetration with much speculation regarding the possible use of mobiles for the delivery of government services (Narayan, 2007).

Finally, the pace at which e-governance projects are launched in many developing countries is fast, leaving policy-makers little time to consider the opportunity cost of investment in e-governance projects as opposed to other key development priorities and to evaluate the societal outcome of the projects they have implemented (Hanney *et al.*, 2003). As a result, analysis and documentation of the untidy reality that characterises local development processes rarely finds management support. But eventually it is this kind of assessment exercise that will enable critical reflection about misconceived models of development and governance and about how local agents can inform decisions in uncertain contexts. The utilisation of research conducted on individual development interventions within particular cultural contexts can contribute to policies that may eventually lead to desired development goal (Court *et al.*, 2005; Crew and Young, 2002; Garret and Islam, 1998; Mosse, 1998; Surr *et al.*, 2002; Sutton, 1999).

The integration of research and policy raises methodological implications for scholars involved in this study domain. While case studies conducted over time are useful in providing scope for depth of analysis regarding the wider developmental impact of e-governance projects, there is need to ensure adherence to a systematic theoretical approach to say something general from the findings of individual cases. This can be achieved through consistency in adopting an overall theoretical lens for studying e-governance projects. While research may not have a direct impact on specific policies, it may still exert a powerful indirect influence by introducing a new conceptual framework for shaping the agenda-building and policy discourse. It is hoped that the current research may contribute to this activity. But there remains much more work to do for scholars who wish to follow such a critical approach as projects continue to evolve under new influences and constraints and in new areas. Above all, it is important to ensure that modern technological solutions such as e-governance for development are not privileged over gaining a deep understanding of the historical processes of development and governance that have evolved over time.

References

Argyris, C. (1982) *Reasoning, Learning and Action: Individual and organisational,* Jossey Bass, San Francisco.

Argyris, C. (1990) *Overcoming Organizational Defences: Facilitating organisational learning,* Jossey Bass, San Francisco.

Cooke, B. and Dar, S. (2008) Introduction: The New Development Management. In *The New Development Management: Critiquing the dual modernisation,* eds, B. Cooke and S. Dar, Zed Books, London.

Court, J., Howland, I. and Young, J. (2005) Research and Policy in International Development: Introduction. In *Bridging Research and Policy in Development: Evidence and the change process,* edited by J. Court, I. Howland and J. Young, ITDG Publishing, Rugby, pp. 3–25.

Crew, E. and Young, J. (2002) Bridging Research and Policy: Context, evidence and links, ODI Working Paper No. 173, Overseas Development Institute, London.

Garrett, J.L. and Islam, Y. (1998) Policy Research and the Policy Process: Do the twain every meet? *Gatekeeper Series,* 74, International Institute for Environment and Development, London.

The Guardian (2008a) All Out on Poverty. Supplement produced in association with the Department for International Development, 24 September. Available at guardian.co.uk/alloutonpoverty

The Guardian (2008b) Chaos as £13 bn. NHS Computer System falters. 10 August.

Hanney, S., Gonzalez-Block, M., Buxton, M. and Kogan, M. (2003) The Utilisation of Health Research in Policy-Making: Concepts, examples and methods of assessment, *Health Research Policy and Systems,* 23, 1, pp. 1–28.

Hendy, J., Reeves, B.C., Fulop, N., Hutchings, A. and Masseria, C. (2005) Challenges to Implementing the National Programme for Information Technology (NPfit): A qualitative study, *BMJ,* 331, pp. 331–336.

Johnson, H. and Thomas, A. (2007) Individual Learning and Building Organisational Capacity for Development, *Public Administration and Development,* 27, pp. 39–48.

Land, F. (2008) Frank Land's Reflections, DSSResources.Com. 16 March. Available at http://dssresources.com/reflections/land/land03162008.html

Land, F. and Kennedy-McGregor, M. (1987) Information and Information Systems: Concepts and perspectives. In *Information Analysis: Selected readings,* edited by R. Galliers, Addison-Wesley Publishing Company, Wokingham, UK.

Mamman, A. and Rees, C. (2007) Towards the Understanding of Development Policy Failures through the Eyes of Management and Organisational Theories: Research agenda, Management in Development Working Paper Series, No. 18, Institute for Development Policy and Management, University of Manchester.

Mosse, D. (1998) Process Documentation Research and Process Monitoring: Cases and issues. In *Development as Process: Concepts and methods for working with complexity,* edited by D. Mosse, J. Farrington and A. Rew, Routledge, London, pp. 31–55.

Narayan, G. (2007) Addressing the Digital Divide: E-Governance and M-Governance in a hub and spoke model, *The Electronic Journal of Information Systems in Developing Countries,* 31, 1, pp. 1–14.

Nilekani, N. (2009) *Imagining India: Ideas for a renewed nation,* Penguin Press.

Rodrik, D. (2004) *How to Make the Trade Regime Work for Development,* Harvard University Press, Cambridge, MA.

Sen, A. (2004) How Does Culture Matter? In *Culture and Public Action,* edited by V. Rao and M. Walton, Stanford University Press, Stanford, CA, pp. 37–59.

Sen, A. (2006) The Man without a Plan, *Foreign Affairs,* March/April, 85, 2, pp. 171–177.

Silva, L. and Westrup, C. (2009) Development and the Promise of Technological Change, *Information Technology for Development,* 15, 2, pp. 59–66.

Smith, M.K. (2001) Chris Argyris: Theories of Action, Double-Loop Learning and Organizational Learning, *The Encyclopedia of Informal Education.* Available at www.infed.org/thinkers/argyris.html

Surr, M., Barnett, A., Duncan, A. and Speight, M. (2002) Research for Poverty Reduction: DFID Research Policy Paper, Development Committee Meeting, 24 October.

Sutton, T. (1999) The Policy Process: An overview, *ODI Working Paper 118,* ODI, London.

The Telegraph (2007) Patients 'won't benefit from £12 bn. IT Project'. 17 April.

White, H. (2005) Challenges in Evaluating Development Effectiveness, *IDS Working Paper, 242,* Institute of Development Studies, Brighton, Sussex.

Notes

1 Introduction

1. www.itu.int/wsis/
2. http://go.worldbank.org/M1JHE0Z280
3. www.sdnp.undp.org/e-gov/mapping.html

2 What do we mean by development?

1. The term 'intermediate technology' was considered to be similar in meaning to the term 'appropriate technology' and referred to tools and technology that could be used in developing countries to increase productivity but which were considerably cheaper than developed-world technology, easier to maintain and use.
2. The focus of the discipline of cybernetics is the study of information, communication and control. It uses the scientific work on the physiology of the brain and nervous system as a core reference discipline. The application of cybernetic principles to the design of control systems for organisations is known through the work of Stafford Beer (1981).
3. Such as oil shocks, international debt and volatile currency fluctuations.
4. There are also innovations in other technology such as biotechnology.
5. See http://laptop.org
6. An alternative political philosophy that stands in between top-down socialism and neoliberalism.
7. A framework for planning and managing development projects in a clear, concise, logical and systematic way.
8. Heeks (2008) provides examples of these revolutionary opportunities which include using SMS technology to remind people to take immunisation, providing banking services for the unbanked, enabling the poor to create their own content on open source Web 2.0 platforms, create jobs selling accessories and prepaid phone cards, using the mobile phone to connect small producers to sellers.
9. Social networking sites like MySpace and Bebo and volunteer-created sources of knowledge such as Wikipedia and alternative news services and trading systems like eBay.

3 Linking governance and development

1. The decentralisation agenda included variants of deconcentration (the disbursal of agents to areas under the government's jurisdiction), deregulation (the transfer of functions to lower-level arenas), and devolution (the transfer of democratic and administrative powers to lower levels of government) (Rondinelli, 1981; Manor, 1999).
2. Indeed, Putnam acknowledged the existence of such an institutional framework to be the influencing factor in explaining high levels of civic engagement in north central Italy and backwardness of the Italian south.

3. This view finds support in the work of Gramsci and other earlier sociologists who discussed the concept of social space as categorised into civil society and political society – the former being the ensemble of individual and collective subjectivities, the latter referring more or less to the state and its apparatus but the two being inseparable in practice as they are in constant interplay.
4. Bourdieu suggested the idea of social capital in the context of an analysis of class differentiation.
5. 'Voice' and 'exit' are two important theoretical concepts developed by Albert O. Hirschman which apply to members of any type of organisation such as a business, a nation, or any other form of human grouping. According to Hirschman, members have two possible options when they perceive a decline in the quality of products/services – they can either exit (leave, emigrate) or voice (protest, communicate their concerns).

4   e-Governance for development

1. The productivity paradox was established by the MIT economist Robert Solow in the 1960s. The paradox was that despite investment in new technology in the workplaces across the US in the 1970s and 1980s, this had little impact on productivity and long-term growth of the economy. But already by the 1990s, while the paradox remained, the explanation for it changed. As there was a shift away from manufacturing to services in the US and Western Europe, it was recognised that it would take much longer for growth to be visible.
2. See http://www.infodev.org
3. See http://www1.worldbank.org/publicsector/egov/ and http://www.unpan.org/discover.asp
4. In Africa alone, over 20 projects were implemented over the past few years (Mayanja, 2003). In 1998, the Latin American and Caribbean region had fewer than 50 telecentres, while towards the end of 2002 numbers were estimated at more than 6500 (Delgadillo *et al.*, 2002). Sood (2003) found that telecentre installations are increasing at a faster rate within India than in other countries with over 30 such projects currently in existence.
5. Examples of such frameworks are (1) UNPAN (2004) E-Government Readiness Report www.unpan.org (2) Brown University (2004) Global E-Government Report www.insidepolitics.org/egovt05int.pdf (3) Centre for International Development Readiness for the Networked World www.readinessguide.org (4) Insead's Networked Readiness Index.
6. Most widely cited among these is the US Government's Performance Reference Model (PRM) according to which value is created along the entire chain of government service provision from inputs, activities, outputs and outcome. Other frameworks have been developed along similar lines. For example, in the UK refer to http://www.ogc.gov.uk/documents/HM_Treasury_-_measuring_the_expected_benefits_of_e-government.pdf and in India see http://egov.mit.gov.in
7. A panchayat is the name given to the elected council operating in the locality.
8. Theoretical notions of the linkage between structure and agency are not new in the social sciences. For example, structuration provides a useful theoretical lens for analysing the manner in which human interactions at the micro level become established (or not) as routinised practices over time and serve as macro structures that in turn enable or constrain human action and interactions (DeSanctis and Poole, 1994; Giddens, 1979, 1984; Orlikowski and Robey, 1991).

5   Researching e-governance for development

1. The Telegraph, 17 April 2007, 'Patients Won't Benefit from £12 bn. IT Project'.
   The Guardian, 10 August 2008, 'Chaos as £13 bn. NHS Computer System Falters'.
   The Daily Mail, 30 May 2008, 'The NHS and Its Great White Elephant'.

6   India: Development, governance and e-governance

1. The World Bank's definition of the poverty line for underdeveloped countries like India is US$1 per person per day.
2. Dr B.R. Ambedkar was an Indian nationalist and political leader. He spent his life fighting against social discrimination.
3. Refer to the DISNIC website at disnic.nic.in and the CRISP website at crisp.nic.in
4. India.gov.in/govt/national_egov_plan.php
5. E-Seva was the name given to the centres. Seva in Hindi means 'help'.
6. http://www/i4donline.net/August07/maping.pdf
7. A parallel initiative was started in July 2004 by the Government of India called Mission 2007 which aims to provide over 600,000 knowledge centres in villages across the country. A national alliance comprising of the private sector, civil society, bilateral agencies, academic and research institutions and government ministries has constituted seven task forces to implement the project (Dhar, 2005). Synergies between the two schemes are currently being explored. At present, the plan is that the MS Knowledge Centre Scheme will focus on the second phase of the NeGP scheme in terms of using the centres to deliver national development programmes.

7   MIS for rural self-employment programmes in Gujarat

1. The Integrated Rural Development Programme was also launched in other developing countries at this time.
2. The Grameen Bank project was initiated in Bangladesh in 1976 by Professor Mohammad Yunus to provide credit and banking services to the rural poor. See www.grameen-info.org
3. Rural poor members under SGSY must be confirmed as 'below poverty line' using the criteria set by the government.
4. Mahiti Shakti literally means 'Information is Power'.
5. This state-wide network is called GSWAN (Gujarat State Wide Area Network).
6. BJP is a major political party in India founded in 1980. The party has a strong nationalist/Hindu agenda reflecting both strong economic growth and social policies. The BJP in alliance with other parties was in power in India between 1998 and 2004.
7. Sakhi Mandal translates to 'self-help groups'.
8. This is a process of obtaining gas from the decomposition of organic cow dung.

8   Telecentres for rural outreach in Kerala

1. See agricoop.nic.in
2. See www.kissankerala.net

3. See UNESCO site at http://portal.unesco.org/ci/en/ev.php-URL_ID=5341&URL_DO=DO_TOPIC&URL_SECTION=201.html
4. Small and marginal farmers refers to farmers that have landholdings below 5 acres.
5. FRIENDS is an acronym for Fast, Reliable, Instant, Efficient, Network for Disbursement of Services.
6. Akshaya means 'infinity'.
7. This was in line with to the philosophy of social development in Kerala according to which civil amenities would be located within close proximity of citizens.
8. See official Akshaya website – http://210.212.236.212/akshaya/in_nrews.html
9. E-Vidya literally translates to e-learning.
10. This is a fever found in the tropics and Africa.
11. Since around 25% of the population live abroad as migrant labour, there is a need for cheap communication.
12. Krishi translates to 'agriculture'.
13. See www.e-krishi.org
14. These are farmers clubs.
15. District Collector is the highest government official in the district.
16. This is the local Communist party.
17. The Gram Sabha is a forum for all men and women in a village over 18 years of age.

9 Health information systems in rural Karnataka

1. See www.hisp.org
2. These vertical programmes are designed by donor agencies or government who set targets, implementation procedures and monitoring proformae to address specific diseases.
3. The World Health Organization define DALYs as Disability Adjusted Life Years. DALYs compute the sum of years of potential life lost due to premature mortality and the years of productive life lost due to disability.
4. See http://mohfw.nic.in/NRHM/Documents/NRHM%20Mission%20Document.pdf
5. This scheme is called Janani Surakshi Yojana.
6. This scheme is called Arogya Raksha Samitis.
7. Anganwadi workers are field workers who are specially trained in various aspects of health, nutrition and child development.
8. Three of the Millennium Development Goals (reducing infant mortality, reducing maternal morbidity, and tackling specific diseases such as AIDS, malaria and TB) directly focus on health.
9. See www.janaarogya.org/English/Janaarogya%20-%20Our%20Work.htm
10. Zilla panchayat is the District Panchayat.
11. See Karuna Trust website at www.karunatrust.org
12. Karuna Trust is a public charitable trust affiliated to the Vivekananda Girijana Kalyana Kendra (VGKK) which has been providing basic health care, education and livelihoods to tribal communities from B.R. Hills, Yelandur taluka, Chamarajanagar district for the past 27 years. See www.vgkk.org
13. Karuna Trust also manages nine PHCs in the Indian state of Arunachal Pradesh and six PHCs in Orissa state.
14. See www.janaarogya.org
15. 80% of the population of Gumballi is below poverty line.

16. The VGKK is located in 540 sq km in the protected forest area of B.R. Hills, serving a population of about 30,000 landless indigenous people. Under the auspices of the Social Welfare Department's Integrated Tribal Development Project, the VGKK offers courses to approximately 540 students per year.
17. Mental services at Gumballi PHC are provided with the help of the National Institute of Mental Health and Neuro Sciences based in Bangalore.
18. Chikungunya is a viral illness spread by infected mosquitoes.
19. See http://www.nrhmcommunityaction.org
20. The WHO's International Classification of Diseases (ICD) which is used to classify diseases and other health problems recorded on many types of health and vital records including death certificates and hospital records does not include poverty. These records continue to provide the basis for the compilation of national mortality and morbidity statistics by WHO Member States. See http://www.who.int/classifications/icd/en/ and http://www3.who.int/icd/vol1htm2003/fr-icd.htm

Conclusion

1. An information system that promotes single-loop learning focuses on improving programme efficiency according to pre-defined goals and on supporting greater control by higher authorities on lower authorities. This strategy for programme implementation involves less risk for both individuals within the organisation and for the agency itself but often results in modest, if any, gains in the living conditions of communities affected by the intervention.

Index